THE
Baseball Research
JOURNAL

Volume 44
Spring 2015
Number 1

Published by
the Society for American Baseball Research

THE BASEBALL RESEARCH JOURNAL, Volume 44, Number 1

Editor: Cecilia M. Tan
Design and Production: Lisa Hochstein
Cover Design: Lisa Hochstein
Fact Checker: Clifford Blau

Front cover: RASG ballot illustration: Lisa Hochstein
Photos provided by the National Baseball Hall of Fame Library, Cooperstown, New York.
(Left to right: Tris Speaker, Rabbit Maranville, Rogers Hornsby, Eddie Collins,
Harry Heilmann, Dazzy Vance, Earle Combs)

Published by:
The Society for American Baseball Research, Inc.
4455 E. Camelback Road, Ste. D-140
Phoenix, AZ 85018

Phone: (800) 969-7227 or (602) 343-6455
Web: www.sabr.org
Twitter: @sabr
Facebook: Society for American Baseball Research

Contents

Note from the Editor

Spring is here! I don't care if I still have six-foot high snow mounds in front of my house. If baseball season is here, it is officially spring, and winter can go stuff it. Migratory birds are onto something, leaving town and then coming back just in time for Opening Day and baseball season. I'm ready for a new season to unspool into history.

Every season has its twists and surprises. To be prepared for some of what's to come, I just peeked at MLB.com's "milestones" tracker. I see it predicts that if Alex Rodriguez returns to the field (as is currently expected) and stays healthy, he'll pass the 3,000 hit milestone by mid-June. In fact, he's poised to climb several of the all-time records lists; hits, runs scored, home runs, RBIs, games played, and a few other choice stats-ladders could see him moving up several rungs. But Rodriguez has demonstrated an uncanny knack for eliciting criticism in the face of success which will add intrigue to the numbers. If he passes Joe Morgan (34th) on the games-played list, or Stan Musial (8th) on the runs-scored list, comparisons beyond mere numbers will be inevitable. Can "character" be quantified?

I don't mean that as a rhetorical question. I believe in the future we will see "intangibles" made tangible, "team chemistry" formulas, and psychological "makeup" measured in a useful way. Any major league team that believes they'll find value and competitive advantage in it will be studying it. Scott Boras, when addressing the SABR convention in 2012, spoke at length about Harvey Dorfman, a pioneer in the mental aspect of baseball training. An article in this issue discusses Dorfman's life and works.

The difference between a team's Decision Sciences experts and many of us in SABR is this: their job is to look forward, our job is to look back. But ultimately the goal is the same: understand this game. We are still probing for ways to account for comparisons across eras, not only deadball/live ball but PED/non-PED. Our search for understanding requires cleaning the dataset, as Herm Krabbenhoft is doing with pre-1920 RBI records, and imagining what might have happened if things had been different, as Chuck Hildebrandt (with the help of thousands of SABR voters) did with simulations of All-Star Games that never were. We look at the rules and how they've changed, from Richard Hershberg's discussion of the origin of the "dropped third strike" rule to Gil Imber's analysis of the oh-so-recent introduction of video instant replay to MLB.

Stats show us unlikely is not the same as impossible, and that our idea of "usual" may be unusual. A "typical" issue of the *Baseball Research Journal* contains 15–20 articles which are "usually" between 2,500 and 6,500 words long. That is like saying the typical big-league inning has five batters who see five pitches each. (I'm making those numbers up, by the way: I'm certain someone has determined the actual means and medians.) But what is memorable is often what is atypical or unusual. This issue of the *BRJ* is atypical in that it contains fewer articles than usual, but several are longer than usual, which balances out. Like we always say, you have to play the games.

Play ball!

— Cecilia M. Tan
Editor

The Retroactive All-Star Game Project

Chuck Hildebrandt, with Mike Lynch

I t's the top of the 10th inning, and there is one out in this hotly contested All-Star Game. A runner is on third by way of the triple, another on first via the intentional walk, but now the pitcher has this batter on the ropes with a 2–2 count. The crowd is evenly split between National League and American League partisans, and as the Senior Circuit pitcher stares in toward his catcher, the Junior Circuit batter waits tensely on the delivery, preparing to respond to whatever is offered.

As Midsummer Classics go, this one has been a doozy.

The runner dances off third as the pitcher gets his sign, goes into the set, waits a couple of beats…then quickly delivers a low outside fastball that the right-handed hitter pulls deep into the hole to the right of the shortstop, Rabbit Maranville, who backhands the ball and one-hops the throw to his first baseman, Hal Chase—alas, a step too late to get the out. And so Ray Chapman gets his single, moving Wally Pipp to second and scoring Tris Speaker from third, and ex-Buf-Fed hurler Fred Anderson is now on the hook for the loss for the Nationals, which finally does come to pass as Anderson himself strikes out in the bottom of the frame to end the contest and hand the Americans a 5–4 victory on this warm and rainy July Friday at the Polo Grounds.

At this point, you, the "knowing Fan," might have simultaneously snapped your neck, blinked hard, and stared into the preceding paragraph asking yourself, "Wait, what? Rabbit Maranville? Hal Chase? Ray Chapman, Wally Pipp, Tris Speaker? These guys were never in the All-Star Game, were they? And who the heck is Fred Anderson, anyway?"

And you'd be right: They never were in a real All-Star Game, because we all know that the first one wasn't played until 1933 at Chicago's Comiskey Park. But it was not for lack of the All-Star Game idea to ever come up in the first place, for it did as early as 1914, in a series of articles in the popular monthly *Baseball Magazine*. So it *might* have happened. And with the help of some modern-day innovations, we did make it "happen," using a combination of the most comprehensive baseball stats website on the planet, a simple-to-use

online survey website, and one of the very best game simulators on the market.

But the best thing you'll learn from this article is that, as much fun as it was to play the games out and to see those results unfold, it was uncovering an unexpected insight into the legacy of the stars from that era that surprised and delighted us the most.

INCEPTION

The idea for the Retroactive All-Star Game (RASG) project first occurred to Chuck Hildebrandt in February of 2013, when Baseball-Reference.com (B–R) added splits back to the 1916 season in their excellent Play Index.[1] Included within the new feature were the standard half-season splits, and the idea of putting together All-Star rosters based on first-half stats immediately leapt to Chuck's mind. He jotted down this project idea and set it aside.

About a year later, thumbing through an old *Baseball Research Journal*, Chuck came across an article written by Lyle Spatz about retroactive Cy Young Award winners, and later, an online article Lyle wrote about retroactive Rookie of the Year awards, both going back to 1901 and featuring winners chosen by SABR member vote.[2,3]

Reminded of his own idea, Chuck googled around online to see whether there was a record of anybody ever having undertaken anything like a retroactive All-Star game project, or having written an article about the idea. Outside of threads existing in various online forums, he didn't find anything like this specifically, but during his research he did find that between late 1914 and early 1916, *Baseball Magazine* had advocated for a midseason All-Star game (or more exactly, an All-Star series). The timing of the magazine articles lined up well with the availability of the splits data back to 1916 at B–R, and now there was a plausible historical context to support the idea. This all struck Chuck as kismet, and so the impetus to go forward with the RASG project was born.

The next several sections provide a great amount of detail about how the project was developed and managed. If you're not so interested in how the sausage was made, feel free to skip ahead to the section labeled

"Topline Results" on page 9. However, if you're a process nerd as the authors are, then here you go!

GROUNDWORK

The first thing Chuck wanted to find out was, just what had been said about the All-Star concept before the actual games were launched in 1933? He reasoned that if there were a way to tie in this project to what had actually been said or written about the topic, it would make the premise seem all the more historically plausible.

Baseball Magazine published four separate articles about the possibility of an All-Star Series. The articles' timing of 1914 through 1916 was a great coincidence, since the splits data featured went back to 1916, creating a credible natural starting point for the first games of the project.[4]

At the time the articles were written, the choosing of all-time All-Star teams (referred to by the magazine as the "All America Baseball Club") was considered a "universal fad," and one article cites efforts by Spalding's Record to assemble All-Star teams (which they termed "National All-America" teams) covering five-year periods from 1871 on, culminating in a final All-Star ("Grand National All-America") team for the whole of baseball history through then-present day 1913.[5]

But the idea of playing actual live contests between "All-Star" teams consisting of the greatest players of the current time first appeared in the magazine in 1915, which the authors presciently envisioned as occurring midseason to slake the fans' thirst for determining which league was the better one even before the "World's Series" in the fall pitted both leagues' top teams against each other. The article also argued that a midseason All-Star series would "stimulate [fan] interest [and] vary the monotony of a long stretch of 150 games," the latter of which they deemed to be "a serious handicap," and which would also "advance the reconstruction period" following "two years of wanton destruction" wrought by "the Federal League war." The magazine went on to claim that an All-Star series would even provide something a World Series between two great but still flawed teams could not: "the best baseball the game can offer," even going so far as to maintain that such a Midsummer Classic would "represent a perfect baseball series under as nearly ideal circumstances as possible."[6,7]

It's interesting that the articles that influenced the RASG project specifically called for an All-Star series, versus a single game. Originally, the proposal was for a seven game series, "a single week's work," and preferably to be played in New York, Boston, or Chicago

in order to best handle the large crowds they believed such a series would generate, believing it would spark so much interest that "a man might well journey from the Pacific Coast" to take it in.[8]

The magazine justified the idea of a weeklong series by maintaining that regular season schedules would still proceed uninterrupted, and that the stars would simply vacate their teams for the week to play in the All-Star series while their regular teams continued to toil.[9] This proposal was the main reason the decision was made that our Retroactive All-Star contests would at first start out as a series, and an educated guess was made as to how it might evolve from there. (It was imagined that several owners, especially those in the heat of a pennant race, would have objected to losing their stars for a whole week at a stretch, and that a compromise of a three-game series would have been reached to mollify their concerns and secure their support.)

Next, Chuck sought a partner to "sim" the games, someone who was already an expert at doing so. He put out the call for a sim partner on the SABR-L newsletter, and out of several responses agreed to work with Mike Lynch, proprietor of the website Seamheads.com. Mike is an expert at using the Out of the Park (OOTP) game simulator, generally considered the most advanced baseball management simulation game available at the time of this project. It is also great good luck that Mike happens to be the proprietor of a popular and terrific historical feature website, and he was willing to write up game accounts and publish them on the site as the project evolved.

PROJECT DEVELOPMENT

With the partnership in place, and having established that the RASG would start with a three-game series during the 1916 season, the project details started coming together. Voting for All-Star starters would be conducted using SurveyMonkey.com, a website that allows ordinary people to field online surveys and polls. SABR also uses SurveyMonkey to conduct its own polls, and again as luck would have it, SABR generously offered to share its account to allow us to conduct the voting for the RASG project. After the voting for a season's All-Stars was to be completed, the reserves would be manually selected to fill out the rosters, which would then be sent to Mike to sim the game using OOTP 14, the latest available version of that game at the time.

Mike had been using OOTP to simulate games for almost 15 years and, as a big fan of the game, understood how the plethora of features it offered made it the right choice for this project. The ability to import historical seasons with ease and pinpoint accuracy (for example, roster sizes, strategic tendencies, and league stat totals are realistically reflected for each year), and also to easily manipulate rosters, kept setup and implementation time to a minimum. Employing the game's unique set of features to best effect, Mike was able to easily customize the simulated games for the Retroactive All-Star Project with minimum effort but also maximum accuracy, all the way down to stadium configurations and their ballpark factors.

Because of the many options available in OOTP, Mike could set up each All-Star game to be managed by the game's artificial intelligence engine, which eliminated any bias he himself might have inadvertently brought to play-calling during the game, while maintaining control of substitutions, an important aspect given the requirement to pull pitchers after three innings (or sooner if necessary), as well as to make the frequent pinch-hitting and defensive substitutions needed to accurately represent the unique in-game dynamic that typifies an All-Star Game.

The process of selecting venues for the game posed an interesting riddle. To reflect a real-life likelihood, we wanted to ensure that the game would be spread among the parks of the major-league teams, but without occurring too close in time to when those same clubs hosted their actual first All-Star games. It was decided to host the inaugural RASG series in Chicago's Comiskey Park, where the first All-Star game had been hosted in real life, and to alternate home-team status between leagues, as is done today. To select locations for subsequent All-Star contests, we reviewed real-life actual All-Star Game venues for the first 20 or so years

in history, in order to obtain a fair spread between the years a team hosts the games in its venue and make it equitable among all the franchises in the majors. Since the RASG was conducted in 16 separate seasons (we imagined that Retroactive All-Star contest would have been canceled for war during the 1918 season in RASG, as it had been in 1945 in real life), that created a neat situation in which each of the 16 major-league teams could host a RASG once each, with the spread between their first (RASG) game and their next real-life game ranging between 10 and 27 years, the fairest spread we could manage. RASGs were also awarded to clubs who had recently expanded their ballparks in real life, including Chicago's Cubs Park (1924), the Athletics' Shibe Park (1925), the Cardinals' Sportsman's Park (1926), and the Reds' Redland Field (1928).

(Note: The 1932 RASG game was awarded to the Phillies, who we imagine would have arranged with the Athletics to host the game at spacious Shibe [33,000 capacity], as their own Baker Bowl [18,800 capacity] would have been deemed too tiny at the time.)

VOTING/SELECTION PROCESS

The first step in setting up the RASG voting structure was to download the first-half stats for each player, for each year 1916 through 1932, and export them into an Excel spreadsheet, from which we could then format and post the stats for each team's starters onto the RASG ballot. Batters were, of course, listed with one set of stats; pitchers with another set. (Interesting tidbit: Even as late as the 1930s, the RBI was still not a commonly reported stat, even though it had become an official stat in 1920.[10] For example, when the

The Out of the Park *game simulator in action.*

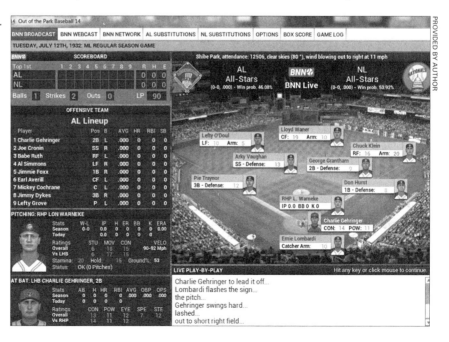

Chicago Tribune published major-league averages during the season, they did not start including RBIs in the table until 1931.[11,12] Given this historical reality, players' RBIs were not included on the RASG ballots.)

Next, we created a poll for each RASG on which we posted the candidates for each position in each league, with their first-half stats. The regular starters for each team were included on the ballot as long as they satisfied a minimum number of plate appearances (100) or innings pitched (77), which would have defined them as their teams' starters and thus tracks logically with how players are listed on All-Star ballots today. This created seemingly (and entertainingly) absurd situations in which players having terrible seasons ended up on ballots, such as A's right fielder Bill Johnson in 1917 (hitting .173 with only six runs scored); Indians catcher Steve O'Neill, also in 1917 (.179 average, no homers or steals); and Cubs shortstop Clyde Beck in 1930 (a .232 hitter during a year in which the entire *league* batted .303). But, as long as a player satisfied the aforementioned minimums and was his team's primary player at the position, he appeared on the ballot. Exceptions: pitchers with obviously terrible won-loss records were excluded, as long as there were teammates who had better records that could be listed. (Spoiler alert: None of the three players mentioned above was voted in as starters.)

Concurrently, we developed a "marketing plan" to stimulate voting interest, which called for promotional text written in the parlance of the times to be included in emails posted through SABR-L, posts in the *This Week in SABR* email newsletter, on the SABR website, and on each of the 30 MLB team blogs hosted by SBNation.com. We also benefited initially from a blog post and front page appearance on B–R, which led to over 1,000 votes cast in the very first RASG. By the third RASG, it finally dawned on us to maintain an email opt-in list so we could contact confirmed voters of previous RASGs, to remind them to both vote in the new RASG and to read the results and game accounts posted at Seamheads.com after the games were simmed and written up by Mike. This plan led to nearly nine thousand votes being cast throughout the life of the project.

The voting for each RASG began on a Friday and ran for two weeks, and included an initial announcement and two reminders to vote for that RASG. After the fourteenth and final day of voting, the ballot for that season's RASG ended and the ballot for a new season's RASG began, both as scheduled. Once a ballot ended, Chuck tabulated the votes to determine the eleven elected starters (one position starter plus three pitchers for each team) for each squad, and then each team's reserves were selected based on the most logical circumstance reflecting vote totals and/or first-half stats.

In a nod to real-life situations, before submitting rosters, Chuck would review the list of elected starters against B–R's terrific Defensive Lineup tool, which reports the starting lineup fielded by each team for each game played every season since 1914.[13] The goal was to make sure that the starter who was voted in for that game was not injured and out of his team's lineup in real life, thus rendering him unable to play even a simmed All-Star game that day. If a voted starter was indeed injured, he would be replaced by the next logical candidate, usually the player who received the second most votes. In one case, the Yankees' Bob Meusel was elected as the starting left fielder to the 1926 RASG, but in real life he had broken his left ankle sliding into a base in late June, putting him out for six weeks.[14] Since the RASG for that year was scheduled for July 13, Meusel could not have conceivably played the game, so the Senators' uninjured Goose Goslin was chosen to replace him. In another more colorful incident, AL starting catcher-elect Bill Dickey had to be replaced on the 1932 squad as, at the time of that year's RASG, he was in the process of serving a 30-day suspension arising from a Fourth of July donnybrook during which he slugged Senators runner Carl Reynolds, who'd bowled him over at the plate, breaking Reynolds's jaw in two places.[15] The comparatively saintly "Black Mike" Cochrane of the Athletics was selected to replace Dickey in that '32 affair.

As it so happened, in the majority of RASGs, there was at least one starter voted in who would not have been able to play that day because of injury or otherwise; the 1922 RASG saw four injured elected starters who needed to be replaced in this fashion.

Once this part of the process was completed and the entire roster was assembled, it was sent along to Mike so he could sim the game. At the same time, voting for the next RASG would have commenced and this voting/selection process would repeat itself.

SIMMING THE GAMES AND WRITING UP THE RESULTS

Once Mike received the roster for a year's RASG, he would begin the simming process by creating a new historical league in OOTP corresponding to the season in which that game was to take place. For the 1921 game, for example, he imported OOTP's 1921 season, including all 16 major-league teams and their actual rosters. He would then manually add a team to each league called "All-Stars," to be populated with players who'd been elected or selected to that league's All-Star team.

After selecting the OOTP options appropriate to the season being played—roster sizes, injuries, rules reflecting the era, etc.—Mike would transfer players from their regular teams to their league's All-Star team. Once the rosters were filled, Mike would create starting lineups and depth charts based on RASG voting by the "Knowing Fan." Batting orders would be constructed contingent upon where the players batted in their regular team's actual order, the handedness of the batter, and where his particular set of skills would be most useful during the game.

The top vote-getters among pitchers got their All-Star team's starting assignment, with the remainder being used as relievers. During the game itself, Mike would actively perform the role of manager for both teams only when it came to substitutions; otherwise, he allowed OOTP to manage in-game strategy itself: calling for steals, employing the hit-and-run, issuing intentional walks, etc. Substitutions would be made based on the inning, score, situation, and player's OOTP skill ratings. For example, a slugger with a poor glove would most likely pinch-hit early in the game, while a player with a good glove would typically be used later and stay in as a defensive replacement. Such decisions were emblematic of the level of realism we sought to inject into the project.

Once the games were played, Mike would carefully review the box scores and game logs so he could write the game accounts accordingly, simulating as closely as possible the writing style used by newspapermen of that era, and post the stories to the Seamheads website.

TOPLINE RESULTS

The first three-game Retroactive All-Star series was played during the weekend of July 14–16, 1916, with the American League hosting the Nationals at Comiskey Park at the corner of 35th Street and S. Shields on Chicago's South Side. The Junior Circuit took the first game, 4–0, as none other than Walter Johnson and Babe Ruth dominated the Nationals from the mound, but then the Seniors stormed back to take the next two games, 6–3 and 4–2, to win the set. In a series featuring 13 eventual Hall of Famers, including nine on the American side, the linchpin of the Nationals' series victory was Giants right fielder Dave Robertson, who went 7-for-12 and scored four of the NL's 10 total runs, including the game-winner in the pivotal Sunday rubber match.

The 1917 series was played in New York at the Giants' Polo Grounds, in which the American League returned the favor to the National League and took two games out of three, with the first-ever RASG home runs hit by Phillies slugger Gavvy Cravath and Cubs keystone sacker Larry Doyle. Notable in this series was the falling attendance throughout: from over 38,400 in Game One, to about 33,400 in Game Two and all the way down to well under 28,000 for the final tilt, it was becoming clear that All-Star fatigue was defeating the gate over time.

After the All-Star proceedings were canceled in 1918 due to World War I, the Retroactive Midsummer Classic was reduced to a single game in July 1919 and played at the Red Sox' Fenway Park in Boston, where the Seniors dumped the Juniors, 4–3, the former holding off a ninth-inning rally by the latter, stranding the tying run in the person of hometown shortstop Everett Scott on third base.

The Retroactive All-Star Games continued on through the Roaring Twenties and on into the early Depression years until the game returned once again to Comiskey Park for the 1933 "real" All-Star Game, featuring the real-life exploits we know so well today. But there were also several heroic moments that occurred during the simmed Retroactive games as well:

1. Guy Morton and Hippo Vaughn each threw six scoreless innings against their star-studded opposition in 1916 and 1917, respectively.
2. Ray Chapman went 5-for-5 in Game One of the 1917 series, a record that would have held up through at least 2015.
3. Ken Williams became the first player to homer twice in a game in 1923; Chuck Klein replicated this feat in 1930.
4. Eddie Collins set a record with four runs scored in 1925, and Earle Combs did the same with five RBIs in 1929, both of which would still be tied for the all-time record as of 2015.
5. Dazzy Vance "Carl-Hubbelled" the Americans in 1927, fanning five of the twelve batters he faced, all Yankees and three of them Hall of Famers (Gehrig, Lazzeri, and Ruth twice, adding Meusel for good measure).
6. Eddie Collins dominated his competition throughout his RASG career by going 15-for-35, plus six walks, in 13 games that included two doubles, a triple, a home run, and eleven runs scored, resulting in a scorching slash line of .429/.512/.629, the best for any All-Star with over 40 plate appearances, real or retro. (Closest: Ted Williams, .304/.439/.652 in 46 at-bats.)

For a complete listing of retroactive All-Star Game results, please see Appendix A at the end of this article.

THE UNEXPECTED INSIGHT

As interesting as the results of the simulated games and players' performances might be—or might not be, more likely, even for most serious baseball fans—the more interesting, and initially unexpected, insight we took from this project might very well be the idea of how players may have been viewed very differently than they are today, if they could have included any number of All-Star Games on their playing résumés, but simply never had the opportunity.

For instance, what if a very good player who finished his career before the first actual All-Star Game in 1933 had played several All-Star Games before that, if such games had been played as far back as 1916? Would we rate him significantly higher than he really is today? Or, what if a player who played in the first few real All-Star Games toward the end of his stellar career had instead played in a whole slew of them, had they existed during the prior seventeen seasons? What would be the effect on his legacy? And perhaps most interestingly, who are some of the players we practically never give a first thought to, let alone a second thought, that we would regard much more highly had they played or even started several All-Star Games between 1916 through 1932, since they were among the best players at their position in their league at the time?

In considering the effect that playing many All-Star Games has on a player's legacy, we believe that the best proxy for determining how good or great his career is involves the Hall of Fame: if he's already in, how the player has been inducted and how quickly; or if he's not in, whether he received votes, how many, and for how many ballots. We believe this idea lines up closely with how fans regard players, as well. And as far as we can tell, playing in All-Star Games really does matter: Through 2014, of the 128 Hall of Famers who played much or all of their careers in the real-life All-Star era, 53 of them—a full 41 percent—have their All-Star Game participation mentioned right on their plaques.[16] Additionally, Bill James, in his seminal book *Whatever Happened to the Hall Of Fame?*, cites participation in All-Star Games as a criterion within his "Keltner List" of Hall qualifications, and also awards points to a player for each All-Star

Game he participated in as part of the Hall of Fame Monitor evaluation method that he proposed in the book.[17]

It's possible that baseball writers or veterans don't always explicitly consider a player's participation in All-Star Games as a key criterion to guide their voting, but it also seems implausible to suggest that they give the idea less than short shrift by disregarding it entirely.

With that in mind, let's explore how participation in All-Star Games during the 1916–32 period might have affected the candidacy of certain players.

INNER CIRCLE HALL OF FAMERS

The first idea to address is whether any current inner circle Hall of Famer would have significantly benefited from playing in any of the All-Star Games that might have taken place between 1916 and 1932, or whether doing so would merely have afforded at least a minor boost by dint of its establishing his place in that particular section of baseball history.

Babe Ruth is probably the best example to contemplate here. In real life, the Babe played in two Midsummer Classics, the first two ever played actually, and started both. But had the Classic been launched in 1916, the Babe would have made, and started, the Games from the very beginning, and, of course, as a pitcher for the first two years. Whether as a starter or as a reserve, Ruth would have made the squad in 16 seasons, tying him with Mickey Mantle, and behind

Ballot for the All-Star Series, to be played July 14–16, 1916 at Comiskey Park, Chicago, Ill.

American League Player Candidates

AL 1st Basemen (Please vote for one [1] candidate)
- Chick Gandil, Cleve. | 302 AB / 25 R / 81 H / 109 TB / 0 HR / 9 SB / .268 PCT.
- Jack Fournier, Chi. | 226 AB / 28 R / 59 H / 96 TB / 3 HR / 11 SB / .261 PCT.
- Wally Pipp, N.Y. | 281 AB / 36 R / 70 H / 112 TB / 4 HR / 6 SB / .249 PCT.
- George Burns, Det. | 266 AB / 31 R / 81 H / 109 TB / 2 HR / 8 SB / .305 PCT.
- Joe Judge, Wash. | 218 AB / 31 R / 51 H / 71 TB / 0 HR / 14 SB / .234 PCT.
- George Sisler, St. L. | 295 AB / 43 R / 84 H / 112 TB / 3 HR / 18 SB / .285 PCT.
- Stuffy McInnis, Ath. | 230 AB / 20 R / 49 H / 59 TB / 1 HR / 2 SB / .213 PCT.
- Dick Hoblitzell, Bos. | 234 AB / 32 R / 62 H / 73 TB / 0 HR / 5 SB / .265 PCT.

AL 2nd Basemen (Please vote for one [1] candidate)
- Ivan Howard, Cleve. | 201 AB / 17 R / 42 H / 58 TB / 0 HR / 8 SB / .209 PCT.
- Joe Gedeon, N.Y. | 273 AB / 37 R / 60 H / 73 TB / 0 HR / 10 SB / .220 PCT.
- Del Pratt, St. L. | 309 AB / 30 R / 77 H / 120 TB / 3 HR / 15 SB / .249 PCT.
- Eddie Collins, Chi. | 278 AB / 29 R / 69 H / 87 TB / 0 HR / 8 SB / .248 PCT.
- Ralph Young, Det. | 265 AB / 33 R / 66 H / 82 TB / 0 HR / 11 SB / .249 PCT.
- Jack Barry, Bos. | 182 AB / 12 R / 37 H / 43 TB / 0 HR / 4 SB / .203 PCT.
- Ray Morgan, Wash. | 191 AB / 31 R / 48 H / 63 TB / 1 HR / 8 SB / .251 PCT.
- Nap Lajoie, Ath. | 257 AB / 19 R / 63 H / 80 TB / 2 HR / 8 SB / .245 PCT.

Online voting ballot for the 1916 RASG.

only fellow inner circle Hall of Famers Hank Aaron, Willie Mays, Stan Musial, Cal Ripken, Rod Carew, Ted Williams, and Carl Yastrzemski, as well as Pete Rose. Ruth would have started Games in 15 of those years, as well (he lost the 1922 vote to the Browns' Ken Williams—more on him later), the same as Carew, and behind only Mays, Ripken, and Aaron. (Note: Appearances and starts for every All-Star in history, including appearances of All-Stars who did not enter the game, as well as pitchers who did not bat, can be found in the All-Star Game Player Career Batting Register at Baseball-Reference.com.[18])

Making 16 All-Star teams would have been a great accomplishment, of course, and something we would absolutely expect of the greatest baseball player in history. Which is the point: Babe Ruth is *already* considered the greatest baseball player in history even without all the All-Star Game appearances he surely would have made. The idea that he might have played in 16 of them, rather than just the two in reality, does nothing to further elevate his status, but only because he is already at the pinnacle of the game's pantheon, and by definition, no one can be elevated above a pinnacle.

This same idea could be applied to a handful of other all-time greats, such as **Lou Gehrig**, who would have made 13 All-Star teams and started 10 games instead of the actual seven teams and five starts he made; **Walter Johnson** making six years of All-Star Games and starting three; **Grover Cleveland ("Pete") Alexander** with three starts in nine years of making the team; **Ty Cobb** starting seven games in seven years; or **Honus Wagner** starting every game of the first two (Retroactive) All-Star series during the last two years of his career. Making the All-Star rosters, and even being voted All-Star starters, would have been nice incremental honors for these players and may have even provided a handy data point to further argue for their supremacy, but even so, this probably would not have burnished their legacies to any substantive degree, simply because the legacy of each of these players is so nearly perfect to start with.

MIDDLE- AND OUTER-CIRCLE HALL OF FAMERS

On the other hand, there are some Hall of Famers outside the Inner Circle playing during the RASG period who may have, in a practical sense, benefited from numerous appearances in All-Star Games had they been played between 1916 and 1932.

Harry Heilmann is a good example. Author of a .342/.410/.520 slash line affixed by his 2,660 base hits; winner of four batting titles, including a .403 effort in 1923; and owner of a 148 career OPS+ (which is on-base-plus-slugging indexed to an average of 100, and adjusted for league and park factors); it nevertheless took Heilmann *12 ballots* to finally make the Hall of Fame. Alas, Heilmann played his final full season in 1930, three years before the real Midsummer Classic began. Had the All-Star Game begun in 1916, though, our voting would have had him starting nine All-Star Games.

Would this have been enough of a boost by itself to help get him elected to the Hall sooner than he was? Let's look at a list of the 26 players who started at least nine All-Star Games in real life:

Player	HoF?	Ballot	GP	GS
Willie Mays	Yes	1st	24	18
Hank Aaron	Yes	1st	25	17
Cal Ripken	Yes	1st	19	17
Rod Carew	Yes	1st	18	15
Stan Musial	Yes	1st	24	14
Mickey Mantle	Yes	1st	20	13
Ted Williams	Yes	1st	19	12
Barry Bonds	Not Yet	–	14	12
Ivan Rodriguez	n/e	n/e	14	12
Yogi Berra	Yes	2nd	18	11
Brooks Robinson	Yes	1st	18	11
Ozzie Smith	Yes	1st	15	11
Wade Boggs	Yes	1st	12	11
Tony Gwynn	Yes	1st	15	10
Reggie Jackson	Yes	1st	14	10
Johnny Bench	Yes	1st	14	10
Alex Rodriguez	n/e	n/e	14	10
Mike Piazza	Not Yet	–	12	10
Derek Jeter	n/e	n/e	14	9
Ken Griffey Jr.	n/e	n/e	13	9
Joe DiMaggio	Yes	3rd	13	9
George Brett	Yes	1st	13	9
Roberto Alomar	Yes	2nd	12	9
Steve Garvey	No	–	10	9
Ryne Sandberg	Yes	3rd	10	9
Ichiro Suzuki	n/e	n/e	10	9

n/e: not yet eligible as of 2015.

Of the players on this list of 26 elites, 18 are Hall of Famers voted in by the Baseball Writers' Association of America (BBWAA). Of the eight who are not, five are either active players as of early 2015, or are recently retired and not yet Hall-eligible. Of the three retired players who have achieved eligibility status, one is practically certain to be voted in: Mike Piazza, who has received 57.8 percent, 62.2 percent and 69.9 percent of total votes on his first three ballots, respectively. The candidacy of Barry Bonds, undeniably one of the

Had the All-Star Game begun in 1916, Harry Heilman might have started in nine Midsummer Classics.

greatest hitters in history, has been stuck in neutral in his first three ballots due to broad (and controversial) allegations of steroid usage. Steve Garvey is the only player on this list of nine-time (or more) All-Star Game starters who failed to make the Hall after 15 years on the ballot, although in fairness, no one would confuse Garvey's .294/.329/.446 slash line and 117 OPS+ with Heilmann's gaudy numbers.

But just as important a point to consider is how *quickly* the eligible players were voted into the Hall. Fourteen of the 18 Hall of Famers above were first-ballot inductees, two went in on the second ballot, and the other two on the third ballot. That is to say, none of these 18 eligible players had to wait even as long as four ballots. Bonds (who has his own peculiar set of problems) and Garvey (who simply did not have a Hall-worthy career) notwithstanding, Piazza is the first of this list to have to wait at least that long, but only because of the glut of slam-dunk first ballot inner circle Hall of Famers that arrived in 2014 (Greg Maddux, Tom Glavine, Frank Thomas) and 2015 (Randy Johnson, Pedro Martinez, John Smoltz). Given his strong showing on his third ballot in 2015, and with the addition of only one surefire first ballot Hall of Famer in Ken Griffey, Jr. the following year, it seems likely that Piazza will go into the Hall in 2016, his fourth ballot. However, that is still a far sight ahead of the 12 ballots it took to elect Heilmann. But then, Heilmann had no All-Star starts or appearances to boast. If Heilmann had had nine All-Star starts listed on his legacy baseball card, though—perhaps he would have gone in much sooner? Probably? Certainly? Our opinion is that

the answer might lie closer to the right side of the perhaps-to-certainly continuum than to the left.

Bill Terry was, in reality, a three-time All-Star starter, but had the Game existed before 1933, he is likely to have been an eight-time All-Star, as well as a starter in six seasons. He is well-known as the most recent National Leaguer to have hit over .400 in a season (.401 in 1930), but he is also the current owner of the fifteenth-highest career batting average in history, at .341, higher than such first-ballot elects as Lou Gehrig, Tony Gwynn, and Stan Musial. Terry was a dangerous spray hitter who could hit doubles, triples, and home runs each in great numbers, and he ended his career with a gaudy 136 OPS+ after 14 years.

Terry also had to wait 14 ballots before finally getting his Hall nod. How does that compare to Hall-eligible All-Star Game starters for six seasons in real life?

Player	HoF?	Ballot	GP	GS
Frank Robinson	1st	1974	14	6
Harmon Killebrew	4th	1971	13	6
Mark McGwire	Not Yet	On Ballot	12	6
Billy Herman	Yes	Vet	10	6
George Kell	Yes	Vet	10	6
Kirby Puckett	1st	1995	10	6
Fred Lynn	No	--	9	6
Arky Vaughan	Yes	Vet	9	6
Joe Torre	Yes	Mgr	8	6
Walker Cooper	No	--	8	6
Bill Dickey	9th	1946	8	6
Charlie Gehringer	6th	1938	6	6

Mgr: Elected as Manager; Vet: Veterans Committee selection.

As with Heilmann, Bill Terry's selection to the Hall seems to have been unusually delayed when compared to others who actually did achieve what might have been Terry's level of All-Star Game renown. The key exception appears to be Joe Torre, who in his maximum 15 ballots could not obtain any more than 22 percent of the vote. Granted, Torre had a fine 129 OPS+, which is within shouting distance of Terry's, but he also had a .297 lifetime batting average, which falls short of the minimum benchmark of .300 typically required of those who would be considered great hitters. Dickey's (.313 lifetime BA) OPS+ was 127; Gehringer's (.320) was 124; and Puckett's (.318) was 124. As hitters, they were clearly not as good as Terry on either a batting average or OPS+ basis, yet they all got inducted far sooner than Terry. As for non-Hall of Famers Fred Lynn (.283/.360/.484, 129 OPS+, off after two ballots) and Walker Cooper (.285/.332/.464, 116 OPS+, three wartime AS selections, off after 10 ballots), the combination of low batting average and the absence of other key HoF markers worked to prevent serious consideration for their induction.

There are a few others to note here: **Frankie Frisch** (.316/.369/.432, 110 OPS+) was on three All-Star teams and started twice in reality, but would have been on 11 teams and started five times; he went in on the sixth ballot. **Gabby Hartnett** (.297/.370/.489, 126 OPS+) was on six teams and started thrice, but would have been on 11 teams with seven starts; he did not go in until the twelfth ballot. **Jimmie Foxx** (.325/.428/.609, 163 OPS+) was on nine All-Star teams already along with four starts, but he would have been on 13 and started seven; he for some reason was made to wait until his seventh ballot for the call. **Al Simmons** (.334/.380/.535, 133 OPS+) was a starter on all three of his All-Star teams, but would have been on nine teams with eight starts; he was held out from the Hall until the ninth ballot. **Dazzy Vance** would have been in rare company among pitchers: Already well into his forties with the advent of the All-Star Game, he would have been only one of seven pitchers to start four or more All-Star Games, which, combined with his NL record seven straight league-leading strikeout totals, three ERA titles, and MVP award, may very well have gotten him a writers' nod to the Hall well before his sixteenth ballot.

All this is not to say that lack of, or even paucity of, All-Star Games was the sole reason the elections of these players to the Hall were delayed by several years beyond what would seem reasonable, given their accomplishments. But it is fair to ask: If most similarly accomplished, or even less accomplished, players with long real-life All-Star records were able to skate into the Hall far, far sooner, would the existence of the All-Star Game before 1933—giving a great player like Heilmann the opportunity to be referred to as a nine-time All-Star starter, versus being unable to mention it altogether—have shortened the path to their election by any number of ballots?

Rogers Hornsby is a bit of a special case. Falling sharply off the performance cliff like Wile E. Coyote just before the real-life All-Star Games started, Hornsby would have placed on the RASG roster in 14 seasons, and started every one of them. He is arguably the greatest right-handed hitter in baseball history, owner among starboard-siders of the all-time highest career batting average that anchors a slash line of .358/.434/.577, while clubbing 301 home runs at a time when that was a truly remarkable total. (It was, in fact, the fifth-highest career total at the time of his retirement). Hornsby was a seven-time batting champion, a two-time MVP, and boasts a career OPS+ of

175 that still ranks fifth-highest all-time. Even so, he still did not enter the Hall until his fifth ballot, even ignominiously placing sixteenth on his third ballot behind Johnny Evers and Rabbit Maranville, and barely ahead of Ray Schalk. Would eighteen All-Star starts have helped Hornsby's case for an earlier election, even as his gaudy stats did not? Considering that Hornsby was universally regarded as a jerk, not least of all by the beat writers of the time, our guess is probably not.

VETERANS COMMITTEE HALL OF FAMERS

Contrary to the opinions of some, the Veterans Committee serves as a good and necessary counterbalance to the neglect of certain qualified players by the voting baseball writers. It's true that the Veterans Committee sometimes takes a lot of heat, and deservedly so at those times their selections appear to be little more than a sop to certain players of slight talent and accomplishment because they happened to be dandy fellas and/or gritty guys, players such as Ray Schalk, Lloyd Waner, Rick Ferrell, and perhaps a dozen or so others you could name. But sometimes, there is a real injustice that the Veterans Committee addresses with the selection of some players who clearly deserve inclusion on the merits of their records, but for whatever reason were not voted in within their allotted number of ballots by the sportswriters.

Rogers Hornsby would have likely started in 14 All-Star Games.

Consider the case of **Joe Sewell**. Seen through the prism of the Hall of Fame, he appears to have possessed borderline talents. He finished his fourteen-year career with a slash line of .312/.391/.413, which translates to an OPS+ of 108, and had a reputation for two things: (1) defense ranging from average to decent; and (2) practically never striking out. He was not elected to the Hall of Fame by the writers, instead falling off the ballot after seven tries. But the Veterans Committee did see fit to elect him in 1977, maybe in part because he was a good guy from the old days, but probably also realizing that even though his numbers may have been only slightly above average for the time, he was still one of the three best shortstops in the game between the world wars. And the RASG voting bears that out: Sewell got eight straight starting nods from RASG voters between 1921 and 1928, and earned a ninth appearance as a reserve in 1929. How might an eight-time All-Star starter have fared with the voting baseball writers of the 1940s and 1950s? Probably better than falling off the ballot after only seven tries.

Another example is **Zack Wheat**, a fine left fielder and a worthy Hall of Famer, at least as far as the Veterans Committee was concerned. Despite his line of .317/.367/.450, his 129 OPS+ and 2,884 base hits in his exactly 10,000 plate appearances between 1909 and 1927, Wheat was shut out on 16 Hall of Fame ballots, never earning more than 23 percent of the writer vote. On six of those ballots, his vote tally totaled in the single digits. Yet in our RASG, Wheat earned starting nods for seven games in five years between 1916 and 1925, and possibly would have been named to three more had the Games been played before 1916. With that kind of pedigree on his CV, it's easier to envision Zack Wheat earning a sportswriters' nod for the Hall.

Then there's **Chuck Klein**, who at age 23 entered the National League like gangbusters. During his first six seasons and 3,710 plate appearances, he hit .359 overall and led the NL in home runs an astounding four times; runs scored three times; hits, doubles, and RBIs twice, and even led the loop in stolen bases once. Oh, and he won a Triple Crown, as well. The problem is, he accomplished most of this prior to 1933, when there was no actual All-Star Game. He was named to the real All-Star team twice, in '33 and '34, with a starting nod that first year, but he certainly would have been voted starter a total of five times, and to the team six times, in his first seven seasons. Given the likely positive bias people naturally have for players who accomplish great things early in their careers, many more All-Star Games would almost certainly have made a substantial impact on Hall of Fame voters. As it turns out, with only two actual Games and a single start on his baseball card, Klein fell off the ballot after 12 tries and was granted a posthumous entry from the Veterans Committee in 1980. If he'd had five All-Star starts in his first seven seasons, though, how might that have affected his chances with the baseball writers voting on his bid for Cooperstown glory?

Other BBWAA vote results for real-life Veterans Committee Hall of Famers include **Travis Jackson**, a 1982 inductee, a career .291 hitting shortstop with enough muscle to power out 135 home runs, and who started one actual All-Star Game, but made six more Retro All-Star teams including four more starts—he fell off the ballot after 12 tries; **Earl Averill**, a center fielder who slashed .318/.395/.534 and was rostered on six actual All-Star teams and a starter on three, but who would have been on nine All-Star squads and started five—gone from the ballot after seven years; **Jim Bottomley**, the 1928 National League MVP who at various times in his career led his loop in hits, doubles, triples, homers, and RBIs, did not make a single real-life All-Star squad, but would have made six RASG squads with a starting bid in three of them—adios after 12 ballots; **Ross Youngs**, the Giant right fielder who during his ten-year career, which ended after the 1926 season at age 29, slashed .322/.399/.441, had an OPS+ of 130, and would have earned four All-Star starts in the Retroactive era and been named as a reserve on a fifth squad, somehow still made it through 17 ballots before falling off; and perhaps most surprisingly, **Frank "Home Run" Baker**, who you'd be forgiven for believing easily earned a BBWAA election to the Hall given his three home run crowns, his .307 career batting average, his 135 OPS+, and his evocative sobriquet, but who in fact fell off the ballot after his eleventh bid in 1951 and then easily picked up a Veterans Committee nod four years later.

Perhaps not all of these Veterans Committee selections would have made the grade with the writers during that phase of Hall of Fame qualification, but it does seem likely that with the ability to claim multiple All-Star Game starting bids and overall team selections, they would have done much better in the balloting than they actually did.

NON-HALL OF FAMERS: "DO YOU KNOW ME?"

Not every player who was good enough for a long enough stretch of time to earn multiple All-Star nods during the RASG era would have been, or even should have been, voted into the Hall of Fame (although with the notorious version of the Veterans Committee operating in the 1970s, they still might have made it in—who knows?). But even so, many of the players who made multiple appearances in our Retroactive All-Star Games are not at all well-known, or are downright anonymous even to savvy fans of baseball history.

Marty McManus fills this bill. After a teenaged stint working for Uncle Sam during and immediately after World War I, McManus saw a season in the Western League at Tulsa in 1920 before finishing out the year for the Browns in St. Louis, and he never went back down to the minors before completing his long major-league career. McManus averaged over 130 games per year spread out among every spot in the infield over the next 14 seasons with the Browns, Tigers, and Red Sox before moving to the Braves for his last season in 1934, finishing with a slash line of .289/.357/.430 for an OPS+ of 102, very respectable for a middle infielder. He fell just 74 hits short of 2,000, and smacked 120 homers (third all-time among second basemen at retirement) and 401 doubles while stealing 126 bases (leading his league with 23 thefts in 1930), receiving MVP votes four of his seasons. A man characterized by his own wife as having an "ungovernable temper," he was nevertheless acknowledged in an AP report when traded as being "one of the best second basemen in the game."[19] The fans participating in RASG recognized as much from his stats, too, voting him a three-time starter, and he made the roster as a reserve for three more teams. During the period 1922 to 1930, only Joe Sewell was a better American League infielder (outside of first basemen) in terms of lifetime Wins Above Replacement (WAR), and McManus's own WAR was the equal of that of Pie Traynor, an elected Hall of Famer who was roughly the same age, and higher than that of Rabbit Maranville, both in their prime at the same time and both fairly well-known today. Yet, judging by his puny total of four Hall votes in 1958 and 1960, it's fair to say that McManus himself is largely unknown today. If Marty McManus could claim six actual All-Star appearances, might he be at least as well-known as Traynor and Maranville?

Cy Williams is probably better known than McManus because of his power exploits at the plate. A lifelong National Leaguer who plied his trade first with the Cubs and then with the Phillies, Williams was one of the first players in the live-ball era to start clouting home runs at a prodigious rate, although he also led the league in home runs during the dead-ball year of 1916, one of four times he eventually led his loop in circuit clouts. Like McManus, he, too, stopped just short of 2,000 hits (finishing with 1,981), but he also retired in 1930 with 251 career home runs, which at

that time was the third-highest career homers in history behind only Ruth and Hornsby. Williams slashed .292/.365/.470 for an OPS+ of 125 and eventually earned himself placement on 13 Hall of Fame ballots between 1938 and 1960, even though he never achieved even as much as 6 percent of the baseball writers' votes in any given year. There seems little doubt his home-run power gave him some staying power on Hall of Fame ballots, even if he could not break through to the other side, but despite this circumstance and his on-field achievements, it seems odd he did not get a Veterans Committee nod for his body of work. Perhaps, though, had he been voted an All-Star starter five years while starting seven All-Star games, as he did in RASG, he might have gotten the boost he needed to be considered a better bet for the Hall of Fame, at least by the Old-Timers.

We mentioned earlier the other power-hitting Williams of this era, **Ken Williams**. He's not very well-known today and that might be due in part to his name: "Ken Williams" is a fine name, sure, but it's also a fairly generic-sounding name; it's a name that's similar to the guy in the paragraph above who started belting lots of homers at about the same time; and theirs is a last name that in later years became more or less the sole property of one of the greatest pure hitters in the history of the game. Even more starkly than his not-brother Cy, Ken started belting home runs quite suddenly with the advent of the live ball, going from 10 in 1920 to 24 the next year to an American League-leading 39 the year after that. When Ken hung up his spikes at the age of 39 after the 1929 season, he, too, was quite far up the list of career home run leaders—fourth to be exact, with 196. But he was also a more accomplished hitter overall than Cy. In over two thousand fewer plate appearances, he hit more triples and almost as many doubles as Cy; his lifetime batting average of .319 exceeded Cy's by nearly 30 points; and his slugging exceeded Cy's by 60. Ken's career slash stats after 14 years, mostly with the Browns but also during stints with the Red Sox and Reds, crossed the finish line at .319/.393/.530 accompanied by an OPS+ of 138, roughly equivalent to those of Reggie Jackson, Duke Snider, Chuck Klein, and Bill Terry, Hall of Famers all. Ken Williams probably could not expect to make the Hall with only 5,600 or so plate appearances (although having fewer than that didn't seem to hurt Hack Wilson or Frank Chance), but had Ken Williams actually made the six All-Star appearances with four voted starts that he earned in the RASG project, it's a good bet that we would have a better idea today of who he is and what he did.

Here's a question that, if you offered it up to the knowledgeable baseball fan of today, you might very well get a blank stare in return: "What can you tell me about **Larry Doyle**?"

Yet, the baseball fans of a hundred years ago probably could have told you a lot about Larry Doyle. After all, Doyle was voted the MVP of the National League while playing second base for the league-champion Giants in 1912—and this after having finished third in the voting for MVP for the league-champion Giants the year before. In fact, so well-known and highly regarded at the time was Doyle that *Baseball Magazine*, in one of its articles advocating an All-Star Series, specifically mentioned Doyle, along with Ty Cobb, Tris Speaker, Eddie Collins, and Gavvy Cravath, as being among "the greatest aggregation of batters in the world."[20]

Doyle was a career .290/.357/.408-hitting second baseman, and if that sounds just so-so at first blush, consider that his lifetime 126 OPS+ is the eighth-highest among keystone sackers in baseball history—just six points behind Joe Morgan and Jackie Robinson, the same as Robinson Cano (as of mid-2014), and ahead of 13 second basemen currently enshrined at Cooperstown, including BBWAA-elected Charlie Gehringer, Roberto Alomar, Ryne Sandberg, and Frankie Frisch. Doyle led the NL in hits twice; doubles, triples, and batting average once each; and he slugged 74 homers at a time when that really meant something. Sadly, even though he was considered the equal of many inner-circle Hall members at the time, he is barely known today, perhaps in part because he fell off the Hall ballot after three years and only seven votes. But had he been voted an All-Star starter four straight years as he was in RASG—and at the end of his career to boot—how would that have helped his chances for both the Hall and posterity?

As illuminating as these examples are, there are two that stand out as particular favorites of ours:

Larry Gardner was, by election and selection, a three-time RASG All-Star and two-time starter. Certainly not bad, considering his career tracked along that of Larry Doyle's, so he would have been at the end of his career when RASG started, as well. He is also a largely anonymous player from the period, even though he was second-best third baseman, after Home Run Baker, in all of baseball from 1910 to 1921 in terms of WAR. Much of that high ranking results from his fielding, as he had the best dWAR (a player-comparison metric of defensive value that incorporates offensive productivity weighted by position) during the period, but he was no slouch with the bat, either. He led all third sackers of the period in hits and triples, and was second in doubles.

When Ken Williams hung up his spikes at the age of 39 after the 1929 season, he was fourth on the list of career home run leaders, yet he is largely unknown to fans today. Would his likely six All-Star Game selections with four starts have changed that?

Gardner ended with a .289/.355/.384 slash line, and a 109 OPS+. This is quite a nice line, but seemingly not Hall-worthy…until you consider that George Kell, another third sacker, finished his career with a 112 OPS+, the rough equivalent of Gardner's. Yet George Kell ended up in the Hall of Fame, while Larry Gardner *did not earn even a single vote* from the writers! (By the way: Kell was named to 10 All-Star teams and a starter on six of them. Think that might have had something to do with his selection?)

Lastly, let's consider the case of **Jack Fournier**. A veteran of 13 full seasons in the majors, with a three-year Pacific Coast League-sized hole in the middle, Fournier swung a mean bat. He clubbed the horsehide at a .313/.392/.483 clip in his career, and once the live ball made its debut, added the home run to his skill set, even leading the NL as a Dodger with 27 in 1924. Fournier, of course, never played in a real All-Star Game, although the sweet-swinging first baseman placed on the RASG roster four times, and was voted a starter three times, during the 1920s. But of course, there was no actual All-Star Game in the 1920s, and possibly as a result Fournier, like Gardner, did not receive a single Hall of Fame vote from the writers. Yet Fournier ended his career with an OPS+ of 142 and a lifetime oWAR of 44.9. This is the rough equivalent to the output of a star who played a decade later: Hack Wilson, possessor of a lifetime OPS+ of 144 but an oWAR of only 42.5. (oWAR is a player comparison metric that includes a player's offensive production and a positional adjustment.) Yet Hack is a Hall of Famer who, although selected by the Veterans rather than being voted in by the BBWAA, nevertheless was a mainstay on 15 ballots before his eventual old-timers selection. Some people would point out that Hack Wilson was never an All-Star himself, as his decline coincided with the beginning of the Midsummer Classic, and that he led the league in home runs four times while setting a league season record in that stat, as well as a major-league season record of 191 RBIs, a level of accomplishment that Fournier could not match on any front. And all that would be correct. But the point here is not to advocate that Jack Fournier should be a Hall of Famer as Hack Wilson is, or that Wilson should not be if Fournier isn't. The point is that without the kind of credentials that help a player's Hall chances, such as league leadership in key stats or season records—or All-Star appearances—we get a situation in which a player who had essentially the same career as a well-known Hall of Famer ends up being, for all practical purposes, an anonymous footnote in the annals of baseball history. Even casual baseball fans know who Hack Wilson is. But only hard-core baseball nerds would have any idea who Jack Fournier is, let alone what he accomplished, and for all that he did accomplish, it seems very unjust that he should not have received even a single vote for the Hall of Fame. Several All-Star appearances, and starts, might have helped Fournier's legacy.

As sim-gaming baseball geeks, when we first started the RASG project, we were most interested in how the games might come out, perhaps showing us who the better league might have been, or at least which one had the better stars, and how All-Star Game records might have been rewritten. But as we got further into the project, we realized that the true insights arising from this exercise lay in how players who never had the opportunity to play in All-Star Games during the peaks of their careers may have suffered in their legacies and their chances at the Hall of Fame, when compared to players of similar or even lesser accomplishments in later generations.

That is ultimately what made this an eye-opening experience for us, and we hope it was for you, as well. ∎

Acknowledgments

The authors would like to thank Jacob Pomrenke of SABR for providing access to the Society's SurveyMonkey.com account, from which we conducted public voting for the starters of the Retroactive All-Star Games; Sean Forman of Baseball-Reference.com, who provided a blog post and tweets, which increased visibility of the project; and the proprietors of the 30 MLB team websites at SBNation, who allowed us to publicize the project and publish game results as FanPosts on their sites.

Notes

1. "Baseball-Reference.com Play Index," accessed August 12, 2014, www.baseball-reference.com/play-index/. Paid subscription required as of February 2015 to access the Play Index.
2. Lyle Spatz, "Retroactive Cy Young Awards," *The Baseball Research Journal* 17 (1988): 2–5.
3. Lyle Spatz, "SABR Picks 1900-1948 Rookies of the Year," SABR Research Journals Archives, accessed August 12, 2014, http://research.sabr.org/journals/sabr-picks-1900-1948-rookies-of-the-year.
4. A few months after RASG started, B-R added splits data for 1914 and 1915, but the project had advanced too far by that time to practically go back and include those seasons.
5. F. C. Lane, "The All-America Baseball Club," *Baseball Magazine*, 1913 December Vol. XII No. 2: 33–44; F. C. Lane, "The Greatest Baseball Team of All History," *Baseball Magazine*, 1914 May Vol. XIII No. 1: 33–42, 96.
6. F. C. Lane, "An All-Star Baseball Contest for a Greater Championship," *Baseball Magazine*, 1915 November Vol. XVI No. 1: 57–64.
7. F. C. Lane, "Why Baseball Should Have an All-Star Series," *Baseball Magazine*, 1916 March Vol. XVI No. 5: 48–52.
8. Lane, "An All-Star Baseball Contest for a Greater Championship," 64.
9. "Why Baseball Should Have an All-Star Series," 52.
10. Mike Lynch, "The Complicated History of RBI," August 6, 2014, http://www.sports-reference.com/blog/2014/08/the-complicated-history-of-rbi.
11. "Major League Averages," *Chicago Daily Tribune*, August 24, 1930.
12. "Major League Averages," *Chicago Daily Tribune*, August 16, 1931.
13. Neil Paine, "Feature Watch: Team Batting Orders & Lineups," August 24, 2009, www.baseball-reference.com/blog/archives/2286.
14. Bill Deane, *Baseball Myths: Debating, Debunking, and Disproving Tales from the Diamond*, (Lanham, MD: Scarecrow Press, 2012), 121.
15. "Baseball Brawls: Bill Dickey Broke Carl Reynolds' Jaw With One Punch," Reading Eagle, August 14, 1960.
16. "National Baseball Hall of Fame and Museum: Plaque Gallery", accessed August 12, 2014, http://baseballhall.org/museum/experience/plaque-gallery.
17. Bill James, *Whatever Happened to the Hall of Fame?: Baseball, Cooperstown, and the Politics of Glory* (New York: Simon & Schuster Inc., 1994, 1995), 284, 360.
18. "All-Star Game Player Career Batting Register", accessed August 12, 2014, www.baseball-reference.com/allstar/bat-register.shtml.
19. Bill Nowlin, "Marty McManus," SABR Baseball Biography Project, accessed September 17, 2014, http://sabr.org/bioproj/person/3567429b.
20. "Why Baseball Should Have an All-Star Series," 51.

APPENDIX A. Retroactive All-Star Game Results

Year	Site	Result	Top Performances	Game Account/Box Score
1916	Comiskey Park, Chicago	NL 0-6-4, AL 4-3-2	Dave Roberston, (NL) 7 for 12, 4 R, 2 2B; Guy Morton (AL), 6 IP, 0 R, 6 SO, 0.83 WHIP	goo.gl/pvd48q
1917	Polo Grounds, New York	AL 5-1-6, NL 4-7-3	Ray Chapman (AL), 7 for 14, 1 2B, 5 RBI; Hippo Vaughn (NL), 6 IP, 0 R, 3 H, 6 SO	goo.gl/TcfXzD
1918	Canceled because of World War I			
1919	Fenway Park, Boston	NL 4, AL 3	Eddie Collins (AL), 3 for 3, 1 R; Rabbit Maranville (NL), 1 for 1, GWRBI	goo.gl/ecTK8X
1920	Braves Field, Boston	AL 6, NL 0	Buck Weaver (AL), 3 for 3, 1 R, 1 3B; Babe Ruth (AL), 2 for 4, 1 3B, 1 R, 2 RBI	goo.gl/orDfoa
1921	Dunn Field, Cleveland	AL 10, NL 8	George Sisler (AL), 3 for 3, 2 BB, 2 R, 2 2B, 1 RBI; Carl Mays (AL), 3 IP, 3 H, 1 UER, W	goo.gl/BxakKd
1922	Forbes Field, Pittsburgh	AL 11, NL 2	Ty Cobb (AL), 3 for 4, 1 3B, 2 R, 2 RBI; Walter Johnson (AL), 3 IP, 0 R, 0.67 WHIP, W	goo.gl/zDs4Fg
1923	Yankee Stadium, New York	NL 10, AL 8	Ken Williams (AL), 2 for 5, 2 HR, 4 RBI; Charlie Hollocher (NL), 4 for 5, 1 R, 3 RBI	goo.gl/uhqaOL
1924	Cubs Park, Chicago	NL 6, AL 1	Zack Wheat (NL). 2 for 4, 2 R, 1 HR, 2 RBI; Dazzy Vance (NL), 3 IP, 0 R, 1 H, 1 BB, 1 SO	goo.gl/HRYAy6
1925	Shibe Park, Philadelphia	AL 19, NL 5	Harry Heilmann (AL), 4 for 4, 1 HR, 4 RBI; Eddie Collins (AL), 3 for 4, 4 R, 1 2B, 2 RBI	goo.gl/2YaR7b
1926	Sportsman's Park, St. Louis	NL 11, AL 5	Babe Herman (NL), 2 for 3, 2 BB, 1 R, 1 2B, 4 RBI; Goose Goslin (AL), 1 for 3, 1 HR, 3 RBI	goo.gl/tcrpGK
1927	Griffith Stadium, Washington	NL 4, AL 2	Dazzy Vance (NL), 3 IP, 0 R, 1.00 WHIP, 5 SO; Travis Jackson (NL), 2 for 2, 1 R, 1 RBI	goo.gl/OQxxoo
1928	Redland Field, Cincinnati	AL 13, NL 0	Heinie Manush (AL), 4 for 6, 2 R, 1 3B, 2 RBI; George Pipgras (AL), 3 IP, 1 H, 0 R, 1 SO	goo.gl/DrLYq6
1929	Sportsman's Park, St. Louis	AL 10, NL 7	Earle Combs (AL), 4 for 5, 2 R, 1 HR, 5 RBI; Jimmie Foxx (AL), 4 for 4, 1 R, 1 RBI	goo.gl/R5FLIi
1930	Ebbets Field, Brooklyn	NL 8, AL 6	Dazzy Vance (NL), 3 IP, 9 up, 9 down; Bill Walker (NL), 3 IP, 1 BB, 10 up, 9 down; Chuck Klein (NL), 2 for 3, 1 BB, 2 HR, 4 RBI	goo.gl/pOeNYz
1931	Navin Field, Detroit	AL 5, NL 3	Red Kress (AL), 2 for 4, 2 R, 1 2B, 1 HR; Lefty Grove (AL), 3 IP, 9 up, 9 down	goo.gl/kUsmla
1932	Shibe Park, Philadelphia	AL 6, NL 2	Al Simmons (AL), 1 for 4, 1 HR, 3 RBI; Lefty Grove (AL), 3 IP, 2 H, 0 R, 0.67 WHIP	goo.gl/e7JcNl

Note: All goo.gl shortened URLs pointing to game accounts published on Seamheads.com were correct and operational as of February 21, 2015.

APPENDIX B. Real-Life All-Star Appearances vs. Combined Appearances

REAL LIFE TOP 20						COMBINED TOP 20					
Player	From	To	Years	G	GS	Player	From	To	Years	G	GS
Stan Musial	1943	1963	20	24	14	Stan Musial	1943	1963	20	24	14
Willie Mays	1954	1973	20	24	18	Willie Mays	1954	1973	20	24	18
Hank Aaron	1955	1975	21	24	17	Hank Aaron	1955	1975	21	24	17
Ted Williams	1940	1960	17	18	12	**Babe Ruth**	**1916**	**1934**	**16**	**19**	**15**
Cal Ripken	1983	2001	18	18	17	Ted Williams	1940	1960	17	18	12
Brooks Robinson	1960	1974	15	18	11	**Rogers Hornsby**	**1916**	**1931**	**14**	**18**	**18**
Pete Rose	1965	1985	16	16	8	Cal Ripken	1983	2001	18	18	17
Mickey Mantle	1953	1968	16	16	13	Brooks Robinson	1960	1974	15	18	11
Al Kaline	1955	1974	15	16	7	Pete Rose	1965	1985	16	16	8
Yogi Berra	1949	1962	15	15	11	Mickey Mantle	1953	1968	16	16	13
Rod Carew	1967	1984	15	15	15	Al Kaline	1955	1974	15	16	7
Roberto Clemente	1960	1971	12	14	7	Yogi Berra	1949	1962	15	15	11
Ozzie Smith	1981	1996	14	14	11	Rod Carew	1967	1984	15	15	15
Ivan Rodriguez	1992	2007	14	14	12	Roberto Clemente	1960	1971	12	14	7
Carl Yastrzemski	1963	1983	14	14	7	Ozzie Smith	1981	1996	14	14	11
Tony Gwynn	1984	1998	13	13	10	**Harry Heilmann**	**1916**	**1926**	**10**	**14**	**9**
Nellie Fox	1951	1963	12	13	8	Ivan Rodriguez	1992	2007	14	14	12
Ernie Banks	1955	1969	11	13	7	Carl Yastrzemski	1963	1983	14	14	7
Barry Bonds	1990	2007	13	13	12	Tony Gwynn	1984	1998	13	13	10
Wade Boggs	1985	1996	12	12	11	**Lou Gehrig**	**1926**	**1938**	**13**	**13**	**10**
Reggie Jackson	1969	1984	12	12	10	Nellie Fox	1951	1963	12	13	8
Roberto Alomar	1990	2001	12	12	9	**George Sisler**	**1916**	**1927**	**9**	**13**	**12**
Johnny Bench	1968	1983	12	12	10	**Eddie Collins**	**1916**	**1926**	**9**	**13**	**9**
Derek Jeter	1998	2012	12	12	8	Ernie Banks	1955	1969	11	13	7
Dave Winfield	1977	1988	12	12	8	Barry Bonds	1990	2007	13	13	12

Bold: Record includes Retroactive All-Star games.

APPENDIX C. Combined RASG/Real-Life All-Star Top Performances

Top Batters by OPS (min. 40 PA)

Player	From	To	G	GS	PA	AB	R	H	2B	3B	HR	RBI	SB	CS	BB	SO	BA	OBP	SLG	OPS
Eddie Collins	1916	1926	13	9	41	35	11	15	2	1	1	4	0	1	6	2	.429	.512	.629	1.141
Charlie Gehringer	1927	1938	12	9	46	36	4	15	3	1	0	3	2	0	10	0	.417	.543	.556	1.099
Ted Williams	1940	1960	18	12	57	46	10	14	2	1	4	12	0	0	11	10	.304	.439	.652	1.091
Stan Musial	1943	1963	24	14	72	63	11	20	2	0	6	10	0	2	7	7	.317	.389	.635	1.024
Al Simmons	1926	1935	10	9	41	41	8	14	7	0	2	9	0	0	0	9	.341	.341	.659	1.000
Joe Cronin	1930	1941	10	10	40	35	5	12	6	0	0	6	0	1	5	5	.343	.425	.514	.939
Willie Mays	1954	1973	24	18	82	75	20	23	2	3	3	9	6	1	7	14	.307	.366	.533	.899
Al Kaline	1955	1974	16	7	40	37	7	12	1	0	2	6	1	0	2	6	.324	.375	.514	.889
George Sisler	1916	1927	13	12	49	47	9	16	7	0	0	10	1	2	2	0	.340	.367	.489	.857
Lou Gehrig	1926	1938	13	10	45	37	8	9	1	0	2	6	0	0	8	10	.243	.378	.432	.810
Brooks Robinson	1960	1974	18	11	47	45	5	13	0	3	1	5	0	0	1	4	.289	.319	.489	.808
Nellie Fox	1951	1963	13	8	41	38	7	14	0	0	0	5	0	0	2	3	.368	.390	.368	.759
Cal Ripken	1983	2001	18	17	52	49	4	13	3	0	2	8	0	0	2	5	.265	.308	.449	.757
Babe Ruth	1916	1934	19	15	63	53	9	13	2	1	1	7	0	0	9	18	.245	.365	.377	.742
Mickey Mantle	1953	1968	16	13	52	43	5	10	0	0	2	4	0	1	9	17	.233	.365	.372	.737

Bold: Record includes Retroactive All-Star games.

Top Pitchers by ERA (min. 10 IP)

Player	From	To	G	GS	W	L	SV	WPCT.	ERA	IP	H	R	ER	HR	BB	SO
Mel Harder	1934	1937	4	0	1	0	2	1.000	0.00	13.00	9	0	0	0	1	5
Juan Marichal	1962	1971	8	2	2	0	0	1.000	0.50	18.00	7	2	1	0	2	12
Bob Feller	1939	1950	5	2	1	0	1	1.000	0.73	12.33	5	1	1	0	4	13
Randy Johnson	1993	2004	8	4	0	0	0		0.75	12.00	7	1	1	1	2	12
Dave Stieb	1980	1990	7	2	1	1	0	.500	0.77	11.67	6	4	1	1	6	10
Jim Bunning	1957	1966	8	3	1	1	0	.500	1.00	18.00	7	3	2	0	1	13
Ewell Blackwell	1946	1951	6	1	0	0	1		1.32	13.67	8	2	2	0	5	12
Don Drysdale	1959	1968	8	5	2	1	1	.667	1.40	19.33	10	4	3	2	4	19
Hal Newhouser	1943	1947	4	1	0	0	0		1.69	10.67	8	3	2	0	3	8
Babe Ruth	1916	1917	5	2	1	2	1	.333	2.25	16.00	9	4	4	0	5	10
Stan Coveleski	1917	1925	4	2	0	0	0		2.25	12.00	13	4	3	0	1	8
Lefty Grove	1926	1938	9	6	0	1	1	.000	2.35	23.00	24	8	6	1	4	15
Vic Raschi	1948	1952	4	2	1	0	1	1.000	2.45	11.00	7	3	3	1	4	8
Jack Morris	1981	1991	5	3	0	1	0	.000	2.53	10.67	14	3	3	0	4	8
Lefty Gomez	1932	1938	6	5	3	1	0	.750	2.70	20.00	12	7	6	3	3	11

Bold: Record includes Retroactive All-Star games.

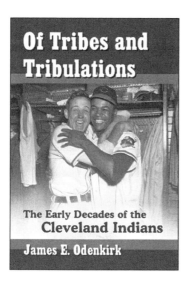
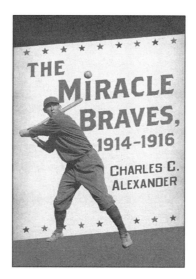
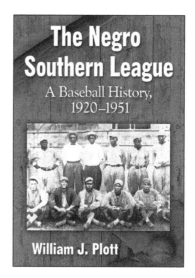
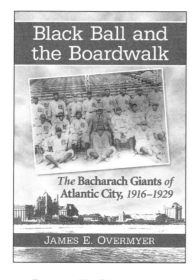
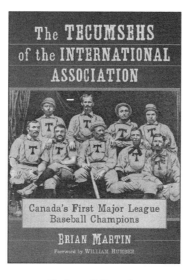
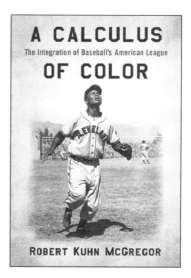

The Dropped Third Strike

The Life and Times of a Rule

Richard Hershberger

> 6.05 A batter is out when— ... (b) A third strike is legally caught by the catcher...
> 6.09 The batter becomes a runner when— ... (b) The third strike called by the umpire is not caught, providing (1) first base is unoccupied, or (2) first base is occupied with two out...
>
> — *Official Baseball Rules,* 2014 Edition

The dropped third strike is a peculiar rule.[1] Three strikes and you are out seems a fundamental element of baseball, yet there is this odd exception. If the catcher fails to catch the ball on a third strike, and first base is open, or there are two outs, then the batter becomes a runner. Most of the time this makes no difference: The catcher blocks the ball, and as the batter begins to stroll back to the dugout the catcher picks it up and tags him, if only for form's sake. Occasionally the ball gets a few feet past the catcher, and the batter takes this more seriously and makes a run for first base, only to be called out as the ball beats him there. But on rare, magical occasions, the rule matters. The pitcher throws a breaking ball in the dirt: the batter and the catcher lunge after it, neither successfully; it skitters to the backstop; and the batter ends up at first base with the gift of a new life. This doesn't happen often, but when it does it can be costly, as the Dodgers found in the 1941 World Series, when with two outs in the ninth inning the Yankees' Tommy Henrich missed the the third strike, followed immediately by catcher Mickey Owen missing it as well, extending the inning and allowing the Yankees to score four runs to take the lead and win the game.

Why is this? What purpose does it serve? If it is a penalty for wild pitching or poor catching, why only on the third strike? The rule seems inexplicably random.

The answers to these questions lie in the very early days of baseball. The strikeout and the dropped third strike turn out to be sibling rules, and the strikeout not quite so fundamental to the game as it would seem. The strikeout would grow into a centerpiece of the struggle between the pitcher and the batter, while the dropped third strike would move to the margins, surviving as a vestige of the early game.

The story begins in an unexpected source: a German book of children's games published in 1796 titled *Spiele zur Uebung und Erholung des Körpers und Geistes für die Jugend, ihre Erzieher und alle Freunde Unschuldiger Jugendfreuden* ("Games for the exercise and recreation and body and spirit for the youth and his educator and all friends in innocent joys of youth") by Johann Christoph Friedrich Gutsmuths.[2] Gutsmuths was an early advocate of physical education. He is best known today, outside the rarified field of baseball origins, for his promotion of gymnastics. In 1793 he published the first gymnastics textbook, *Gymnastik für die Jugend* ("Gymnastics for Youth"). His 1796 work extended the scope to additional games. These include a chapter *Ball mit Freystäten—oder das Englische Base-ball* ("Ball with Free Station—or English Base-ball").

The game he describes, in quite some detail, is clearly an early form of baseball. There are two teams of equal size. The game is divided into innings, with the two sides alternating between batting and fielding. A member of the fielding side delivers a ball to a batter, who attempts to hit it. Once he hits the ball, he attempts to run around a circuit of bases, which serve as safe

Johann Christoph Friedrich Gutsmuths in 1796 published the first detailed description of baseball we know of.

havens, and to score by completing the circuit. The fielding side, in the meantime, attempts to put him out.

There are, of course, many differences from the modern game. Prominent among them is that there are only swinging strikes. Called strikes are as yet far in the future (enacted in 1858, and not even remotely consistently enforced before 1866). Less obvious is that there was no strikeout in the modern sense. The feature that would evolve into the strikeout was, in Gutsmuths' time, a special case of being thrown out.

The pitcher in Gutsmuths stands close to the batter, five or six steps (fünf bis sechs Schrit) away. He tosses the ball to the batter in a high arc (in einem gestrecken Bogen: literally "in a stretched bow"). There are no called strikes or balls. The pitcher is not required to deliver the ball to any particular spot, nor the batter to swing at any given pitch, but neither is there any incentive for the pitcher to toss a purposely ill-placed ball, or the batter to refuse to swing at a well-placed ball.

This presents a problem. If the pitcher proves so inept that he cannot make a good toss, he can be replaced by a more capable teammate. But what about an inept batter? The game can be brought to a halt by a sufficiently incompetent batter, unable to hit even these soft tosses. The solution is to add a special rule. The batter is given three tries to hit the ball (Der Schläger hat im Mal drei Schläge.) On his third try, the ball is in play whether he manages to hit it or not. He has to run toward the first base once he hits the ball, or he has missed three times (oder hat er dreimal durchgeschlagen). Either way, any fielder, including the pitcher, can retrieve the ball and attempt to put the batter out by throwing it at him. Thus a missed third swing is equivalent to hitting the ball.

This solution is very inclusive. It allows even the hapless batter to join in the fun of running the bases and having the ball thrown at him, which a harsher penalty of an automatic out would deny him. Gutsmuths points out that the batter is at a disadvantage with a missed third swing, since the pitcher is close at hand to pick up the ball and throw it at him (und da der Aufwerfer den Ball gleich bei der Hand hat, so wirft er gewöhnlich nach ihm), so the batter's ineptitude is penalized, but the fielding side still has to work for the out.

We see in the likelihood of the batter being put out the ancestor of the modern strikeout. We see in the possibility of his reaching the first base the ancestor of the dropped third strike rule. Both would come to fruition a half century later.

By 1845, when the Knickerbocker Base Ball Club put their rules in writing, some structural changes had been introduced that would change the effect of the three-strike rule. The pitcher had moved away from the batter, toward the center of the infield. This meant that the pitch was no longer a soft lob in a high arc but was swifter, with a more horizontal path. This in turn required that one of the fielding side be positioned to block balls that went past the batter. Another difference was that in the Knickerbocker game, unlike the version described by Gutsmuths, a batted ball could be caught for an out either on the fly or on the first bound.

The three-strike rule in 1845 takes this form: "Three balls being struck at and missed and the last one caught, is a hand out; if not caught is considered fair, and the striker bound to run." This retains the logic of the rule in Gutsmuths, but with the possibility of the third strike being caught by the catcher: Should the batter swing at and miss three pitches, the ball is in play, just as if he had struck it. If the catcher catches the ball, either on the fly or on the first bound, then the batter is out. This is no different from if any fielder had caught a batted ball. If the catcher fails to catch the ball, the batter runs for first base, just as if a batted ball had gone uncaught.

Is this a strike-out rule, or a missed third strike rule? The Knickerbocker rules make no distinction. They are the same rule. Over the ensuing years the strike-out aspect would move to the center and the missed third strike aspect move to the margins, surviving as an oddball vestige of an earlier age.

This unity was more theoretical than practical. Although balls got past the catcher far more commonly than they do today, through a combination of pitchers wildly overthrowing and the catcher having no mitt or protective equipment, even then the normal expectation was that the catcher would take the ball, sometimes on the fly but more often on the bound. A third strike usually meant an out, and this became the status quo to be maintained.

This became an issue in December of 1864, when the rules were amended to adopt the "fly game." Fair balls caught on the bound were no longer outs. They had to be caught on the fly. This change applied only to fair balls. Foul balls caught on the bound were still outs. This allowed catchers a chance to take foul balls hit into the dirt: a difficult and much admired play. This play gradually disappeared as catchers adopted protective equipment and moved up closer to the batter, leaving the less attractive play of a first or third baseman fielding a foul ball on the bound. The foul bound was eventually abandoned when the modern rule was adopted, briefly in 1879 and permanently in 1883 (by the NL, 1885 by the AA).

NATIONAL BASEBALL HALL OF FAME LIBRARY, COOPERSTOWN, NY

Mickey Owen and the Dodgers were the victims of the dropped third strike rule in the 1941 World Series.

The Knickerbocker rules stated that a third strike "if not caught is considered fair"—language which was retained through 1867. With the adoption of the fly game, it would seem to logically follow that a missed third strike, being considered fair, would only be an out if caught on the fly, like any other fair ball. The rules did not explicitly address this, and when the question was raised it was perfunctorily dismissed based on obscure and inconsistent logic:

Every ball caught on the bound—unless the strike be a fair ball caught in the field—puts a player out just the same in the fly game as in the bound. Thus a player is put out on three strikes by a bound catch in the fly game; for although the ball is not called foul, it is equivalent to being so from the fact of its first touching the ground behind the line of the bases, like a foul ball.[3]

[Enterprise vs. Gotham 6/6/1865] In this innings the Enterprise were put out in one, two, three order, the last man being put out on three strikes by the usual bound catch. By many present this was regarded as an illegitimate style of play in the fly game, but the rules admit of the bound catch in this instance, it being regarded in light of a foul ball from striking the ground back of the home base, the sentence in rule 11, which reads, "It shall be considered fair," referring to the character of the strike and not the ball.[4]

Not until 1868 was the text of the rule brought in line with the practice: "If three balls are struck at and missed, and the last one is not caught, either flying or upon the first bound, the striker must attempt to make

his run, and he can be put out on the bases in the same manner as if he had struck a fair ball." This revision, while not euphonious, removes any mysterious distinction between the strike and the ball being fair.

The missed third strike had been divorced from its original logic. No longer was a third strike regarded as a fair ball, which might or might not be caught. A third strike was expected to be an out. The catcher failing to catch the pitch, much less the batter taking first on a missed third strike, was the exception to this expectation. The fly rule was not understood to have anything to do with this. The fly game rule had been a topic of lively debate since it was first proposed in 1857. There is no record of third strikes entering into this discussion. When the fly game was finally enacted, the rules makers had no intention of it affecting third strikes. They seem not to have realized the logic of the matter before the fly game was adopted. By the time this was brought to their attention it was too late to rewrite the dropped third strike rule to accommodate the fly game. At that point they really had no choice but to bluff.

Had they succumbed to the argument that a third strike caught on the bound was not an out, this would have resulted in an important unintended consequence. A missed third strike, while usually to the benefit of the batter, could instead result in a double— or even triple—play. Catchers tried to take advantage of this by dropping the ball deliberately:

[Mutual vs. Union of Lansingburgh 9/17/1868] [bases loaded] Galvin…struck twice ineffectually; as he struck at the ball for the third time and failed to hit it, Craver, who, as usual, was playing close behind the bat, dropped the ball and deliberately picking it up stepped on the home base and threw it to third; Abrams passed it to second, but not before Hunt, who ran from first, reached the base. This sharp feat of Craver's was much applauded…[5]

This was not an easy or common play. Fielders did not yet wear gloves. There was no such thing as a routine play:

[Baltimore vs. Philadelphia 8/7/1873] The umpire gave [Charlie] Fulmer his base on called balls, and a singular series of misplays followed. Treacy made three strikes, and McVey [the catcher] missed the last in order to effect a double-play. He threw the ball splendidly to Carey [the second baseman], who missed it, and, instead of catching Fulmer, Charlie was soon trotting to

Thurman Munson is said to have intentionally dropped the third strike three times in one game.

third, where he would have been caught had not Radcliffe [the third baseman] missed the ball sent to him by Carey. Fulmer got home, and Treacy to second.[6]

Intentionally dropping the third strike to get a double play was an acceptable tactic precisely because it was difficult, requiring skillful execution. Had the dropped third strike rule applied to pitches taken on the bound, this play would have become more common, and much easier. The catcher would no longer have to consciously drop the ball while taking care not genuinely to lose control of it. Rather, a catcher playing back from the batter would automatically activate the rule, with the catcher well positioned to make his throw. The dropped third strike would move in from the margins, which the rules makers neither intended nor desired.

The logical discrepancy was removed in 1879, when the bound catch was removed both for foul balls and third strikes. The 1878 rules state that "The batsman shall be declared out by the umpire...if after three strikes have been called, the ball be caught before touching the ground or after touching the ground but once." The 1879 version removes the clause "or after touching the ground but once." The elimination of the foul bound out had been discussed for several years.

The discussion of abolishing third strike bound catch went along with it, if only for the sake of consistency.[7] This turned out to be premature for the foul bound out. It was restored the following year, and not permanently abolished until some years later.

With this change the logic of the rule was restored. Through the 1880s one section of the rules stated when the batter became a runner, including (quoting the 1880 version) "when three strikes have been declared by the Umpire." This is much as Gutsmuths had described it over eighty years before. But then in a subsequent section, the rules stated how the base runner could be put out, including "if, when the Umpire has declared three strikes on him while Batsman, the third strike be momentarily held by a Fielder before it touch the ground..." The modern rules organize these possibilities differently, but with the same result.

Such elegance was short lived. The final change was to remove the incentive for the catcher to intentionally drop the third strike. The logic of the intentionally dropped third strike is familiar: it is the same as that of the intentionally dropped infield fly—a play also well understood in the 1860s. In both, the fielder responds to a perverse incentive. Fielders usually are admired for their skill at catching the ball, but in these plays he instead purposely muffs it. In both, the base runner cannot know whether to stay at his base or to run. The result, if the play is well executed, is a double play where normally there would be but one out.

The intentionally dropped third strike and the intentionally dropped infield fly were considered skillful plays so long as they were difficult to execute. Both plays became easier as fielding equipment improved, and a sense of injustice developed. The infield fly rule was enacted in 1895, making an infield fly (with first and second bases occupied and fewer than two outs) an automatic out. The dropped third strike rule similarly was amended in 1887, to substantially its modern form. A runner on first base now removes the dropped third strike rule, thereby removing the potential for a cheap double play on a force, unless there are two outs, neutralizing the concern. This is confusing, but largely goes unnoticed. The infield fly rule invites controversy. A memorable example was on October 5, 2012, in a wild card playoff between Atlanta and St. Louis, when Atlanta's Andrelton Simmons hit a soft fly ball to shallow left field with runners on first and second. The ball dropped between the St. Louis shortstop and left fielder, as umpire Sam Holbrook called it an infield fly. Controversy followed about whether the infield fly rule should have been invoked, or if the rule should even exist. The dropped third strike rule avoids similar controversy, benefitting from unambiguous implementation. A casual observer might not understand when it does or does not apply or why, but there are no questions raised by its being invoked or not.

While the tactical purpose of intentionally dropping the third strike is long gone, at least one catcher of the twentieth century is said to have done it three times in one game though that story may be apocryphal. Marty Appel tells of the day in the early 1970s when he, in his capacity as Yankees public relations director, included in his daily press notes that Carlton Fisk had two more assists than did Thurman Munson. Munson took this poorly, and proceeded in that day's game to set the record straight with three dropped third strikes, each followed by a throw to first for an assist. His point made, whether about Fisk or the meaningfulness of the statistic, he completed the game in the normal manner.[8]

What is the place of the rule today? It could be abolished and few would notice. Neither, on the other hand, is there any movement to abolish it. It flies under the radar. Absent a reform movement to completely rewrite the rules, it will remain indefinitely. It is a quirky rule, seemingly without purpose, a vestige of baseball's earliest days. It is part of the charm of the game. ■

Notes

1. The rule is variously called the dropped, missed, or uncaught third strike rule. "Uncaught" is the most accurate of the three, but the least euphonious and by far the rarest. Google n-grams shows that "dropped third strike" is by far the most common, and so is used throughout this article.
2. This discussion is based on the translation by Mary Akitiff, published in David Block, Baseball Before We Knew It, University of Nebraska Press, Lincoln, 2005, 275–79.
3. *New York Clipper*, March 25, 1865. Henry Chadwick was at this time both the baseball editor of the *Clipper* and a member of the National Association's rules committee, and so his opinions, if not quite authoritative, were at the least those of an informed insider.
4. *New York Clipper*, June 17, 1865.
5. *New York Clipper*, September 26, 1868.
6. *Philadelphia Sunday Dispatch*, August 10, 1873
7. See for example *New York Sunday Mercury*, November 12, 1876, with a discussion of proposed rules changes to abolish fair-foul hits, i.e. hits that initially land fair then go foul. At that time such hits were considered fair. The proposal was to adopt the modern rule, and to abolish the foul bound out in compensation to maintain the balance between offense and defense.
8. Marty Appel, "Day Munson Taught Yankees' P.R. a Lesson," *Baseball Research Journal*, 1984.

The Work of Harvey Dorfman

A Professional Baseball Mental Training Consultant

Andrew D. Knapp and Alan S. Kornspan

Many years ago, Albert Spalding recognized the importance of psychology in the development of baseball players.[1] Specifically, he acknowledged that considerable information could be gained from studying athletes within the psychology laboratory. Subsequently, Babe Ruth entered the Psychology Laboratory at Columbia University where psychologists analyzed characteristics and qualities which allowed Ruth to reach a high level of performance.[2] Thus, throughout the early part of the twentieth century individuals recognized that information learned in the psychology laboratory could benefit baseball players.

By the late 1930s, professional baseball front office personnel began to value the importance of psychological training for successful athletic performance.[3] Specifically, Coleman Griffith and Jack Sterrett were hired by Philip Wrigley to provide psychological expertise to the Chicago Cubs organization for the 1938 baseball season.[4] Griffith believed that his experience consulting with the Chicago Cubs clearly showed the value of having a psychologist provide services to professional athletes. In fact, Griffith stated: "The experience gained during the summer of 1938 shows clearly that the method of having a trained man travel with the team can produce results of great value."[5]

Approximately a decade later, the St. Louis Browns hired David Tracy to provide hypnosis and psychological consulting to the St. Louis Browns.[6] Tracy chronicled his work in a book titled, *Psychologist at Bat*.[7] After Tracy's work with the St. Louis Browns others in professional baseball took note of how psychology could influence performance both on and off the field of play. Not surprisingly, hypnosis began to be an intervention used with baseball players. Accounts of hypnotists aiding professional baseball players began to become more common in the 1950s, 1960s and 1970s.[8] For instance, an example of psychological consulting in baseball was the Kansas City Royals utilization of psychologists as part of the training and scouting of baseball players.[9] In fact, during the 1970s additional reports of psychologists consulting with professional baseball teams began to be chronicled.[10]

In general before the 1960s there was little application of sport psychology to aid athletes and coaches in using mental skills to help athletes enhance performance. However, in the 1970s leaders in the field of sport psychology began to work with athletes on the mental side of sport. In fact, the United States Olympic Committee formed a sport psychology committee to help to advance sport psychology work with athletes. By the 1980s, the use of sport psychology became increasingly popular with Olympic and professional athletes.[11]

Although psychologists have a long history of involvement within professional baseball, a dearth of literature has explained how professional baseball organizations began to utilize the services of full-time mental training consultants during the 1980s. An individual who began consulting full-time as a mental training consultant in professional baseball during this time period was Harvey Dorfman. For over twenty-seven years, Dorfman worked with three professional baseball organizations and the Scott Boras Corporation. Additionally, to advance the field of mental training applied to baseball, Dorfman produced four baseball specific mental training books.[12] Moreover, Dorfman explained his employment in professional baseball in a three part autobiographical memoir documenting his life's work.[13]

Thus, the purpose of the present manuscript is to pay tribute to the life and work of Harvey Dorfman (1935–2011). In order to document Dorfman's work, primary source material was utilized from three autobiographical texts: *Persuasion of My Days, Copying It Down*, and *Each Branch, Each Needle*.[14] Also, newspaper and magazine articles written about Dorfman were used as well as additional books that Dorfman composed.

Therefore, the manuscript begins by providing a discussion of Dorfman's life prior to consulting. This is then followed by a description of how Dorfman began working in professional baseball. His approach to consulting with athletes is overviewed next. A description of his work with the Oakland Athletics, the Florida Marlins, Tampa Bay Rays and the Scott Boras Corporation follows. Finally, the paper concludes with feedback from those who consulted with Dorfman and the status of mental training in professional baseball today.

WHO WAS HARVEY DORFMAN?

Harvey Allen Dorfman was born on the northeast side of New York City in the Bronx in 1935. Throughout Dorfman's early childhood, although not able to participate in much physical activity, baseball had a profound influence on his early years. For instance, Dorfman recounted a memory of his first baseball game at the Polo Grounds. In this contest the New York Giants competed against the Chicago Cubs. Dorfman recalled that his father encouraged him to pay attention to the game. Throughout the game, he sat silently observing the competition and was fascinated by the athletes' movements rather than what was occurring within the contest. Dorfman believed that his attendance at that game led him to develop a desire to actively participate in baseball.[15]

Initially, Dorfman became involved in baseball during the eighth grade. While playing for the Sharks who were a community league team, Dorfman became more confident in his baseball ability. Subsequently, he left the Sharks and joined a team closer to his home. Dorfman reminisced that the highlight of his baseball career was pitching a two-hit shutout during high school.[16]

After completing high school, Dorfman entered Brockport College in September 1953. Dorfman majored in general education and was the goalie for the soccer team.[17] In fact, Dorfman's soccer team at Brockport College won a co-national championship.[18] After graduation, Dorfman entered into employment as a teacher and coach. Throughout these early years of teaching and coaching, Dorfman coached football and basketball and also served as an athletic director.[19] Later in his career, Dorfman served as an academic dean. In 1980, his final season as a basketball coach, Dorfman's team won the Vermont State Girls Basketball Championship.[20]

In 1960, Dorfman married Anita Wiklund and they had two children, Melissa and Danny. Dorfman earned a master's degree in educational psychology from Brockport College in 1961.[21] Throughout his career Dorfman became an influential mental training consultant in professional baseball working with three organizations and the Scott Boras Corporation. Dorfman also consulted with National Hockey League (NHL) teams including the Vancouver Canucks and the New York Islanders.[22] His many influential publications related to the mental game of baseball included

the following books: *The Mental Game of Baseball*, *The Mental Keys to Hitting*, *The Mental ABC's of Pitching*, and *Coaching the Mental Game*.[23]

HOW DORFMAN BEGAN CONSULTING IN PROFESSIONAL BASEBALL

After Dorfman completed his coaching tenure, he continued to instruct at the high school level and also taught evening and summer graduate level courses at the University of Vermont, St. Joseph the Provider, and Castleton State College.[24] Additionally, he was a freelance writer for the *Rutland Herald*. Many of the articles he authored have been published in a recent book.[25] These articles related to people and places in Vermont and appeared in a column titled "Miscellany." In addition, Dorfman began writing baseball columns for the *Berkshire Sampler*. A main purpose of these articles was to gain interest and attention for the Pittsfield (Massachusetts) Rangers, a Double-A minor league team of the Texas Rangers organization.[26]

The baseball columns written for the *Berkshire Sampler* led to an interview with Roy Smalley who was the number one draft pick for the Texas Rangers organization. According to Dorfman, their conversation was quite extensive and they subsequently developed a friendship. Specifically, whenever Smalley traveled to Boston with the Texas Rangers, they would meet for lunch. These meetings were sustained even after Smalley joined the Minnesota Twins.[27]

After Smalley was traded to Minnesota he became acquainted with Karl Kuehl who was a coach for the organization. Smalley then introduced Dorfman to Kuehl prior to a game because he believed that they would have a lot in common. This initial meeting led to various breakfast gatherings between Dorfman and Kuehl. Dorfman recalled a meeting in which Kuehl brought 3" x 5" cards with notes all over. These cards contained details about the thought patterns of baseball players during competition. Kuehl's hope was to use this information to author a text on the mental game of baseball.[28]

Dorfman had the background that Kuehl surmised could help him complete a book related to the mental component of baseball. Specifically, Dorfman had an adequate comprehension of the game, academic training in psychology, and was an author. Hence, Kuehl asked Dorfman to co-author a book on the mental game of baseball. Initially, Dorfman declined Kuehl's offer; however, he eventually agreed to co-author the text. In order to prepare the manuscript for publication, Dorfman began to interview athletes during the 1983 baseball season.[29] During this process Dorfman was provided with positive feedback about the mental game of baseball. Additionally, these interviews resulted in players asking Dorfman for assistance with the mental game of baseball.[30]

While Dorfman continued gathering research data for the manuscript, Kuehl left Minnesota and served as a consultant to the Oakland and Philadelphia organizations.[31] In August 1983, Kuehl joined the Oakland Athletics organization as the team's director of the minor leagues.[32] With a strong belief in the importance of the mental game and the knowledge that other teams had previously hired performance enhancement consultants, Kuehl hired Dorfman.[33]

In a consulting role, Dorfman was a counselor/ instructor during the summer of 1984 with the Oakland A's Double-A affiliate in Albany, New York. He provided mental game consultation to players and staff. As Dorfman experienced success, he was offered full-time employment with the Oakland Athletics. Initially, Dorfman was unsure about accepting the position, however with Kuehl's encouragement, Dorfman agreed to join the Athletics organization as a full-time instructor.[34]

When Dorfman was hired by the Oakland Athletics in 1984, he became one of the few full-time mental training consultants employed by a professional baseball club. However, other organizations were utilizing the services of mental training consultants. For instance, the Houston Astros, in 1986, initiated a mental skills training program enlisting Jim Johnson and Ronald Smith to work with the Astros organization.[35] Similarly, Ken Ravizza began consulting with the California Angels organization during the mid-1980s and implemented mental training programs both at the major and minor league levels.[36] The Baltimore Orioles, Chicago White Sox, St. Louis Cardinals, and Texas Rangers were also reported to have consultants as part of their staff.[37]

In addition to providing services to major league baseball organizations, Dorfman was an active contributor in helping to advance the field of sport psychology. For instance, Dorfman was part of a panel who described their work in professional baseball at the inaugural Association for the Advancement of Applied Sport Psychology (AAASP) conference in 1986. The panel, Sport Psychology Consultation for Professional Baseball, was organized by Ken Ravizza and included Ron Smith and Karl Kuehl.[38] Additionally, Dorfman, while still with the Oakland A's organization, was part of 1993 AAASP panel titled, Issues and Implications in Professional Sport Consulting.[39] Ronald Smith noted Dorfman's contributions to baseball and the sport psychology discipline when he stated, "Since 1989, the baseball specific sport psychology market

has been dominated by Harvey Dorfman and Karl Kuehl's seminal work, The Mental Game of Baseball"[40]

DORFMAN'S TEACHING OF MENTAL SKILLS AND CONSULTATION PHILOSOPHY

Dorfman's main responsibility with the Oakland Athletics organization was to provide performance enhancement consulting. Within the provision of mental training services to the organization, Dorfman explained the mental skills he taught to baseball players in his book, The Mental Game of Baseball and also published an article in The Sport Psychologist which detailed his approach.[41] The consulting services provided were primarily focused on mental skills training for the purpose of enhancing performance. His philosophical belief was that on-field distractions were the cause of an athlete's anxiety. Hence, this nervousness could usually be alleviated by educating and teaching athletes specific mental skills to relieve tension.[42] Specifically, Dorfman stated, "I work on performance first and foremost…But mental skills are a tremendous part of the game. Just like a hitting coach, or a pitching coach, I am a mental skills coach."[43]

Dorfman preferred to provide mental training to athletes during individual sessions rather than group sessions. He believed that even the most successful athletes tend to be self-conscious in group meetings. Thus, generally, the only time group meetings were held was during spring training and instructional league camp. These meetings consisted of baseball related themes such as courage, responsibility, preparation for at-bats, playing with pain, and winning attitudes.[44]

Although Dorfman generally focused on providing mental training services he noted that other consulting services were available through the organization.[45] One such service that Dorfman provided while employed with the Oakland Athletics was academic services which were provided to all players in the minor and major leagues. Dorfman's job was to act as the liaison between the player and the college or university he was attending or wished to attend. The Oakland Athletics organization encouraged athletes to obtain a college degree and wanted to accommodate their academic needs in order to not affect their baseball careers.[46] The team also encouraged community service as players were involved in the community in order to establish a connection between the professional athlete and the fans. Despite the wide range of services provided, Dorfman's main responsibility was to serve as a performance enhancement instructor.[47]

In 1997 Dorfman explained the type of knowledge that one needs to provide mental skills training to

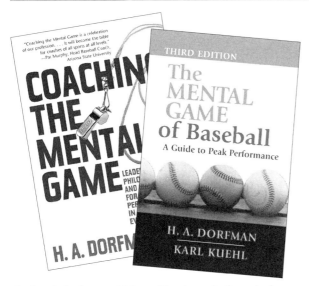

Dorfman's books are widely read by players in the major leagues.

athletes. Dorfman stated, "There are three things you need to know in order to do what I do...Obviously you have to know psychology, what's inside people's heads. Two you have to be a communicator. You have to be able to talk to players in their language. The third thing is, you have to know the game."[48] Dorfman also stated, "If I'm just talking about relaxation techniques or feeling or thinking blue, the players are not going to relate to that. But I can talk to them in the context of their at-bats, of their deliveries, of the game."[49]

Throughout the years since Dorfman began consulting with major league baseball players, sport psychology research has demonstrated the importance of the mental aspects in successful baseball performance. Specifically, Ronald Smith and Donald Christensen found that a minor league baseball player's mental skills were predictive of whether or not they persisted in their pursuit of playing in the MLB. Thus, they found that those with lower levels of coping ability were more likely to not be playing professional baseball two to three years after their mental and physical skills were assessed.[50]

One approach that Dorfman focused on with his athletes was helping them to develop a routine before each pitch or each at bat. Recent research has been supportive of the use of routines in helping athletes improve their pitching performance.[51] In general, the sport psychology research conducted by sport psychology researchers since the 1980s has shown that mental skills training (such as the type of techniques taught by Dorfman) has been effective in enhancing performance .[52]

THE FLORIDA MARLINS

At the start of the 1993 Major League Baseball (MLB) season, the Florida Marlins joined the National League as an expansion team. As a new organization, Dave Dombrowski, the General Manager of the Marlins, sought the assistance of Dorfman. The Oakland Athletics allowed Dorfman to provide consultation to the Marlins while also consulting with the Oakland Athletics.[53] Dorfman's work with the Florida Marlins was reported in April 1993.[54] Initially, Dorfman was a temporary mental training consultant for the organization and also provided presentations to the Marlins major and minor league staffs.[55] In addition, Dorfman also provided consultation to Dombrowski about hiring a full-time mental skills consultant.[56] Ultimately, Dorfman would be hired in November 1993 as the full-time instructor and performance enhancement consultant for the Florida Marlins.[57]

As Dorfman began working for the Marlins, Renee Lachemann, the manager, was very accepting of Dorfman's work. This was demonstrated as Lachemann distributed copies of *The Mental Game of Baseball* to every player during spring training. Also, during Dorfman's first visit to Miami, Lachemann stated, "He told me he was coming ... I said, Yeah I can use you."[58] Lachemann also believed that it was helpful to have Dorfman on staff because of the helpful information he provided.[59]

Dorfman was very busy while serving as a consultant for the Marlins. Specifically, a newspaper report stated, "team counselor Harvey Dorfman has a full appointment book."[60] During the many appointments, consultation was provided during both practice and in uniform while sitting in the dugout during games. Initially, most of Dorfman's work with the Florida Marlins was with the major league staff, while very little time was spent providing consultation to the minor league teams. Also, approximately seventy-five percent of his time was spent working directly with the pitching staff.[61]

The Marlins had great success while Dorfman was employed by the organization. In fact, in 1997 they made the World Series. During the games Dorfman was able sit in the dugout where he assisted players by helping them stay focused on what they needed to do to be successful and also support them in staying positive about their effort.[62] Dorfman helped the Florida Marlins have success as they won the 1997 World Series. As a result, Dorfman received a Florida Marlins World Series ring.[63]

THE TAMPA BAY DEVIL RAYS

After the Florida Marlins won the World Series, Dorfman made the decision to take a new position with the Tampa Bay Devil Rays.[64] As this transition occurred, the Rays' general manager Chuck Lamar stated, "It's a tremendous plus for any organization, especially one just starting out that has to maximize players' abilities."[65] Dorfman was influenced to join the Devil Rays by his friend and Marlins pitching coach Larry Rothschild, who was the Devil Rays' first manager.[66] In recounting Dorfman's work, Larry Rothschild stated, "He's irreplaceable. He just had an unbelievable way of describing in one sentence something that it took other people paragraphs to describe." Rothschild also stated, "He had a way of getting right to the point and analyzing things quickly."[67] Due to a family illness Dorfman decided to end his association with the Rays at the end of the 1998 baseball season.[68]

SCOTT BORAS CORPORATION

After leaving the Tampa Bay Rays, Dorfman joined the Scott Boras Corporation. Working for this organization was ideal for Dorfman since he was able to provide consultation while not having to travel as much. Initially, Dorfman began working with Scott Boras clients in 1999. His work with the Scott Boras Corporation remained consistent with the past services he provided for the A's, Marlins, and Devil Rays organizations. Specifically, Dorfman worked with those who approached him for assistance and thus did not initiate mental training sessions with athletes.[69]

When Dorfman joined the organization, clients represented by Boras were made aware of the services that Dorfman provided. To initiate consulting, Dorfman met with players during the 1999 spring training in Florida and Arizona. During the season, Dorfman traveled to meet with players when they needed assistance and subsequently he would follow up with phone calls. During the off-season, players would visit Dorfman's home for consultation. Dorfman continued to travel to provide consultation to athletes until approximately 2006 when he stopped traveling and only met with clients in North Carolina.[70]

INFLUENCING FUTURE MENTAL TRAINING CONSULTANTS AND PROFESSIONAL ATHLETES

Dorfman was certainly interested in advancing the profession of sport psychology. Specifically, he was a member of the Association for the Advancement of Applied Sport Psychology (AAASP) and participated on various panels at professional sport psychology conferences. He also contributed to the development of the profession through taking part in think tanks with other mental training consultants.[71] Additionally, in his last published memoir he discussed those individuals he mentored as they prepared for a career in sport psychology. In particular, Dorfman provided his thoughts about obtaining employment in the sport psychology profession. He explained that over the years he was contacted by many individuals interested in obtaining a career in sport psychology.[72]

In addition to influencing individuals to become mental training consultants and providing insight to those with an interest in sport psychology, Dorfman consulted with many athletes and coaches who had great success in the game of baseball. Several have credited Dorfman with being influential in their attainment of success. However, Dorfman did not believe that mental training consultants should take credit for the success of those that they have worked with.[73] Although, Dorfman did not take credit for an athlete's performance success, many of the athletes he worked with were very complimentary toward Dorfman's work. See Table 1 for professional baseball players' thoughts about Dorfman's work.

CURRENT STATE OF MENTAL TRAINING CONSULTATION IN MLB

When Dorfman began consulting with major league baseball players, few professional teams had full-time mental training consultants. However, not long after Dorfman began to work full-time with the Oakland Athletics organization, other teams began employing sport psychologists and mental training consultants to work with their organizations. Presently, almost 30 years later, most MLB teams employ a mental training consultant or sport psychologist. Teams that have been reported to have consultants through media reports or have listed professionals on their websites include:

Arizona Diamondbacks[74]	Milwaukee Brewers[85]
Atlanta Braves[75]	Miami Marlins[86]
Baltimore Orioles[76]	Minnesota Twins[87]
Boston Red Sox[77]	Pittsburgh Pirates[88]
Chicago Cubs[78]	New York Mets[89]
Chicago White Sox[79]	New York Yankees[90]
Cleveland Indians[80]	Texas Rangers[91]
Colorado Rockies[81]	San Francisco Giants[92]
Detroit Tigers[82]	Seattle Mariners[93]
Kansas City Royals[83]	Tampa Bay Rays[94]
Los Angeles Angels of Anaheim[84]	Washington Nationals[95]

In total, at least 22 of the league's 30 teams have been reported to have a sport psychologist or mental training consultant on staff. Clearly, Dorfman's work has had an influence on changing the culture and acceptance of mental training and sport psychology as an integral part of professional baseball today.

SUMMARY

Harvey Dorfman had a very accomplished life which is documented in Table 2. He spent 21 years (1962–83) as an educator, academic dean, athletic director, and coach. As an athlete, Dorfman's 1955 collegiate soccer team won the National Championship. While coaching, Dorfman's basketball team won the Vermont state championship. In addition, he was an author and taught at the college level.

An article that Dorfman wrote led him to Roy Smalley who then introduced Dorfman to Karl Kuehl. In 1983, Kuehl and Dorfman began research on a joint project that would result in a book, *The Mental Game of Baseball*. Before the text was published, Kuehl influenced Dorfman to become a full-time professional baseball instructor. Dorfman officially joined the Oakland Athletics in 1984 as a mental training instructor, making him one of the few full-time mental training consultants in professional baseball. During his tenure with the organization, the A's won the 1989 World Series.

Dorfman provided services to the Florida Marlins beginning in 1993. Following the end of the season, Dorfman opted to join the Florida Marlins full-time and began working with the team for the 1994 season. In Oakland, Dorfman split his time between the major league team and all of the minor league affiliates; however, in Florida, he initially spent most of his time in Miami with the major league team and was in the dugout for almost every game. With the help of Dorfman, the Marlins won the 1997 World Series. Following the Marlins World Series victory, Dorfman joined the Tampa Bay Devil Rays. Dorfman spent one season with the expansion team and then began consulting with the Scott Boras Corporation in 1999.

Harvey Allen Dorfman passed away on February 28, 2011. Perhaps one of the greatest things that can be taken away from his work is the influence he had on the individuals that he worked and what he has done for the game of baseball. He helped numerous clients through mental training consultation and some went on to be the greatest players in the game. For those interested in becoming consultants his work is a great example of how mental training can help baseball players enhance performance. Students studying sport psychology who plan to work as mental training consultants can learn about the success that Dorfman achieved. Dorfman was one of the first full-time mental training consultants to have a tremendous amount of success over a long period of time in professional baseball. ■

Table 1. Athletes Thoughts about Harvey Dorfman's Work

Baseball Player	Thoughts about Dorfman's Work
Jim Abbott	When I was playing major league baseball, Harvey Dorfman's teaching would help guide my approach, on and off the field. Little did I know that years after I had retired, I would still find myself asking how Harvey would view a certain situation.[96]
Rick Ankiel	He's the best....I like the way he talks about baseball. He teaches you different keys on focusing.[97]
Jeff Conine	He breaks it down and brings common sense to the forefront....Things you already know he just reinforces. I don't know if you just forget them or what but he just says do this or why don't you think about this. Just common sense stuff that everybody knows but in the process of getting into a slump you forget about. He's really good at waking you up and making it simple.[98]
Roy Halladay	I'm certain I never would have had the success I've had if it weren't for the time I've spent with him and the things I've learned from him.[99]
Raul Ibanez	The stuff he taught us, for the players and the people whose lives he blessed, those teachings—and the caring, and the passion—we can pass that along to other people. And through them, he can live on longer than any of us will be alive, if we can make sure it just keeps getting passed down. And I hope that happens because I wouldn't have had the career I've had without him.[100]
Mark Kotsay	He's a good guy....He asked me what I was trying to do in those situations. And I said I was trying to drive the guy in. That I felt responsible for getting him in. He said that's not the thing. That all I could control was trying to have a quality at-bat. So that's what I am doing now, just trying to relax.[101]
Al Leiter	What helped me it was after years of a lot of understanding of what a pitcher's job was. Harvey Dorfman got my mind where it needed to be. That's the whole part of superior athletes that are able to separate what the emotions are and what the elevated anxiety will be to being able to focus at the task at hand.[102]
Jamie Moyer	The mental side of the game has gotten me to where I am today. Author and friend Harvey Dorfman really helped me in that area.[103]
Dustin Pedroia	He matched his message with the person who needed to hear it, which is exactly why he is the best sports psychologist in the world. He's the kind of guy who can figure out your personality in five seconds. Talk about being born to do a job. Harvey was born to do what he does.[104]

Table 2. A Timeline of Dorfman's Work

Date	Event
1953	Entered Brockport College
1955	Dorfman's soccer team shares national championship
1957	Graduated from Brockport College
1961	Earned Master's degree from Brockport College
1975	Dorfman begins writing a baseball column for the *Berkshire Sampler*
1984	Dorfman begins full-time consulting work with Oakland A's
1986	Dorfman presents work with the Oakland A's at the First Association for the Advancement of Applied Sport Psychology Conference
1989	Oakland A's win the World Series
1989	Dorfman and Kuehl publish *The Mental Game of Baseball*
1993	Dorfman begins full-time consulting work with the Florida Marlins
1997	Florida Marlins win the World Series
1998	Dorfman hired as full-time consultant for Tampa Bay Devil Rays
1999	Dorfman hired by the Scott Boras Corporation
2000	Dorfman publishes *The Mental ABC's of Pitching*
2001	Dorfman publishes *The Mental Keys to Hitting*
2003	Dorfman publishes *Coaching The Mental Game*
2010	Inducted into the College at Brockport: State University of New York Golden Eagles Athletic Hall of Fame
2010	Dorfman publishes two autobiographical memoirs about his life's work in professional baseball: *Copying It Down, An Anecdotal Memoir: Sport as Art* and *Each Branch, Each Needle; An Anecdotal Memoir: The Final Stories*
2013	Dorfman's book *Babbling Echoes: Soundings from Yesteryear* is published posthumously

Notes

1. Edward Marshall, "The Psychology of Base Ball Discussed by A. G. Spalding," *The New York Times*, November 13, 1910,
2. Albert H. Fuchs, "Psychology and the Babe," *Journal of the History of the Behavioral Sciences*, 4 (1998): 153–65.
3. Christopher D. Green, "Psychology Strikes Out: Coleman Griffith and the Chicago Cubs," *History of Psychology*, 6 (2003): 267–83.
4. Christopher D. Green (2011). "The Chicago Cubs and the Headshrinker: An Early Foray into Sports Psychology," *Baseball Research Journal*, 40(1) (2011): 42–5.
5. Coleman R. Griffith, "General Report Experimental Laboratories Chicago National League Ball Club January 1, 1938–January 1, 1939," In Coleman R. Griffith Papers RS 5/1/21, Box 13, Folder, Chicago National League Ball Club Experimental Laboratories General Report, 1938–1939, 9, Courtesy of the University of Illinois Archives.
6. Alan S. Kornspan and Mary J. MacCracken, "The Use of Psychology in Professional Baseball: The Pioneering Work of David F. Tracy," *Nine: A Journal of Baseball History and Culture*, 11(2003): 36–43.
7. David F. Tracy, *The Psychologist at Bat* (New York: Sterling, 1951).
8. Alan S. Kornspan and Mary J. MacCracken, "The Use of Psychology in Professional Baseball: The Pioneering Work of David F. Tracy," "State Psychologist Given Baseball Job," *The Progress*, May 27, 1957, 12; "Whitey Ford Quits Smoking, Finds That His Stamina Has Increased," *Post-Crescent*, D5, May 5, 1963, D5 ; "Perry Wins 5th," May 12, 1966, *The Lima News*, D1; Dennis Morabito, "Kirkpatrick Hit Sparks 2–1 edge," *Valley Independent*, May 31, 1975, 6.
9. Richard J. Puerzer, "The Chicago Cubs College of Coaches: A Management Innovation that Failed," *The National Pastime*, 26 (2006): 3–17; Bob Bender, "Royals Outline Plans for Baseball Academy." *The St. Petersburg Times*, February 18, 1970, 2C.
10. "Angels Mentally Sound According to Psychologist," *St. Joseph Gazette*, August 8, 1973, 10.
11. Alan S. Kornspan, "History of Sport and Performance Psychology" in *The Handbook of Sport and Performance Psychology* edited by Shane M. Murphy, 3–21. New York: Oxford Press.
12. Harvey A. Dorfman and Karl Kuehl, *The Mental Game of Baseball: A Guide to Peak Performance*. (2nd ed.) (South Bend, IN: Diamond Communications, Inc., 1995); Harvey A. Dorfman, *The Mental ABC's of Pitching: A Handbook of Performance Enhancement* (Lanham, MD: Diamond Communications, 2000); Harvey A. Dorfman, *The Mental Keys to Hitting: A Handbook of Strategies for Performance Enhancement* (South Bend, Indiana: Diamond Communications, 2001); Harvey A. Dorfman, *Coaching the Mental Game: Leadership Philosophies and Strategies for Peak Performance in Sports and Everyday Life* (Lanham, MD: Taylor Trade Publishing, 2003).
13. Harvey A. Dorfman, *Persuasion of My Day; An Anecdotal Memoir: The Early Years* (Lanham, MD: Hamilton Books, 2005); Harvey A. Dorfman, *Copying It Down; An Anecdotal Memoir: Sport as Art* (Lanham, MD: Hamilton Books, 2010); Harvey A. Dorfman, *Each Branch, Each Needle; An Anecdotal Memoir: The Final Stories* (Lanham, MD: Hamilton Books, 2010).
14. Dorfman, *Persuasion of My Day; An Anecdotal Memoir: The Early Years*; Dorfman, *Copying It Down; An Anecdotal Memoir: Sport as Art*; Dorfman, *Each Branch, Each Needle; An Anecdotal Memoir: The Final Stories*.
15. Dorfman, *Persuasion of My Day; An Anecdotal Memoir: The Early Years*, 11–2.
16. Dorfman, *Persuasion of My Day; An Anecdotal Memoir: The Early Years*, 73–7.
17. Dorfman, *Persuasion of My Day; An Anecdotal Memoir: The Early Years*, 93–8.
18. Dorfman, *Persuasion of My Day; An Anecdotal Memoir: The Early Years*, 121; Daniel Cody, "Golden Eagles of Brockport: National Collegiate Soccer Co-Champions of 1955" (2004) *Papers on the History of the College at Brockport*. Paper 19, accessed December 15, 2013, http://digitalcommons.brockport.edu/cgi/viewcontent.cgi?article=1018&context=student_archpapers
19. Dorfman, *Copying It Down; An Anecdotal Memoir: Sport as Art*, 14–24.
20. Dorfman, *Copying It Down; An Anecdotal Memoir: Sport as Art*, 38–41, 57–61; Burr and Burton's Academy's *The View*, "Harvey Dorfman Teacher and Coach," accessed December 15, 2013, www.burrburton.org/uploaded/Alumni/Documents/View/THE_VIEW_Winter_2011.pdf Dorfman's record as high school basketball coach at Burr and Burton academy was 60–24 and he won over 71 percent of the games he coached.
21. Dorfman, *Persuasion of My Day; An Anecdotal Memoir: The Early Years*, 157–60. Dorfman, *Copying It Down; An Anecdotal Memoir: Sport as Art*, 25.
22. Dorfman, *Copying ilt Down; An Anecdotal Memoir: Sport as Art*, 129–35.
23. Harvey A. Dorfman and Karl Kuehl, *The Mental Game of Baseball* (Lanham, MD: Taylor Trade Publishing, 1989); Harvey A. Dorfman, *The Mental Keys to Hitting: A Handbook of Strategies Peak Performance* (South Bend, IN: Diamond Communications, 2000); Harvey A. Dorfman, *The Mental ABC's of Pitching: A Handbook for Performance Enhancement* (South Bend, IN: Diamond Communications, 2001), Harvey A. Dorfman, *Coaching the Mental Game: Leadership Philosophies and Strategies for Peak Performance in Sports, and Everyday Life* (Lanham, MD: Taylor Trade Publishing, 2003).
24. Dorfman, *Copying It Down; An Anecdotal Memoir: Sport as Art*, 57.
25. Harvey A. Dorfman, *Babbling Echoes: Soundings from Yesteryear* (Lanham, MD: Hamilton Books, 2013).

26. Dorfman, *Persuasion of My Day; An Anecdotal Memoir: The Early Years*, 57–8.

27. Dorfman, *Copying It Down; An Anecdotal Memoir: Sport as Art*, 57–8.

28. Dorfman, *Copying It Down; An Anecdotal Memoir: Sport as Art*, 58–9.

29. Dorfman, *Copying It Down; An Anecdotal Memoir: Sport as Art*, 59.

30. Dorfman, *Copying It Down; An Anecdotal Memoir: Sport as Art*, 59.

31. Bob Chick, "Relaxing Comes Naturally for This Farm Director," *Evening Independent*, December 21, 1983, 1C.

32. Brian Kappler, "Expos Batters Feast on Giants in Runaway Win" *Montreal Gazette*, August 18, 1983, 57.

33. Chick, "Relaxing Comes Naturally for This Farm Director," 1C.

34. "A's Hire Counselor to Help Players," *Modesto Bee*, August 22, 1984, D8; Dorfman, *Copying It Down; An Anecdotal Memoir: Sport as Art*, 60–1.

35. Ronald E. Smith and Jim Johnson, "An Organizational Empowerment Approach to Consultation in Professional Baseball," T*he Sport Psychologist*, 4 (1990): 347–57.

36. Kenneth Ravizza, "Sportpsych Consultation Issues in Professional Baseball," *The Sport Psychologist*, 4 (1990): 330–40.

37. "What's Up Doc," *The South East Missourian*, June 14, 1982, 4; "Can Cards Win Without Counselor," *Palm Beach Post*, October 19, 1982, B12; "Relax, Relax..it's Only a Game," *Eugene Register Guard*, September 4, 1983, 7B; "Hiring Shrink a Capital Idea," *Spokane Chronicle*, August 3, 1988, 14; "Dr. Charlie Maher Retires from GSAAP," accessed December 15, 2013, http://gsappweb.rutgers.edu/about/spotlight/maher.php; Douglas Frank, "MVP: Most Valuable Psychologist," September 22, 2000 accessed December 15, 2013 from http://urwebsrv.rutgers.edu/focus/article/MVP%3A%20Most%20Valuable%20Psychologist/195; Joan M. Biskupic, "Baseball Team Hires Psychologist to Beef Up Batters," July 4, 1985 accessed December 15, 2013, http://newsok.com/ball-team-hires-psychologist-to-beef-up-batters/article/2113835.

38. Kenneth H. Ravizza, Ronald E. Smith, Karl Kuehl, and Harvey Dorfman, "Sport Psychology Consultation for Professional Baseball," Workshop presented at the National Association for the Advancement of Applied Sport Psychology, Jekyll Island, Georgia (1986).

39. Cal Botterill, Harvey Dorfman, James Loehr, Richard Coop, Kenneth Ravizza and Wayne Halliwell, "Issues and Implications in Professional Sport Consulting," Symposium Presented at the National Association for the Advancement of Applied Sport Psychology Conference, Montreal, Canada (1993).

40. Ronald E. Smith, "Heads up Baseball: Playing the Game One Pitch at a Time [Book Review]," *AASP Newsletter*, 12 (1) 1997: 16–7.

41. Harvey A. Dorfman, "Reflections on Providing Personal and Performance Enhancement Consulting Services in Professional Baseball," *The Sport Psychologist*, 4 (1990): 341–46.

42. Dorfman, "Reflections on Providing Personal and Performance Enhancement Consulting Services in Professional Baseball," 342.

43. Marc Topkin, "Spring is a Perfect Time to Practice Winning," *St. Petersburg Times*, March 15, 1998, 4C.

44. Dorfman, "Reflections on Providing Personal and Performance Enhancement Consulting Services in Professional Baseball," 342. For more detailed accounts of interventions and the methods Dorfman provided to professional baseball players please see, Jamie Moyer and Larry Platt, *Just Tell Me I Can't: How Jamie Moyer Defied the Radar Gun and Defeated Time* (New York: Grand Central Publishing, 2013) and Dorfman's books, *Persuasion of My Day* and *An Anecdotal Memoir: The Early Years*.

45. Dorfman, *Reflections on Providing Personal and Performance Enhancement Consulting Services in Professional Baseball*, 343.

46. Dorfman, *Reflections on Providing Personal and Performance Enhancement Consulting Services in Professional Baseball*, 343.

47. Dorfman, *Reflections on Providing Personal and Performance Enhancement Consulting Services in Professional Baseball*, 343.

48. "Dogs Working on Mental Skills Too," *Portland Press Herald*, May 4, 1997, 5D.

49. "Dogs Working on Mental Skills Too," *Portland Press Herald*, 5D.

50. Ronald E. Smith and Donald S. Christensen, "Psychological Skills as Predictors of Performance and Survival in Professional Baseball," *Journal of Sport and Exercise Psychology*, 17 (1995): 399–415.

51. Justin Otto, Noah Getner, Dan Czech, Trey Burdette, and David Biber, "Baseball Pitcher's Pre-Performance." *The Journal of Excellence,* 16 (2014): 84–97.

52. Robert S. Weinberg and Daniel Gould, *Foundations of Sport and Exercise Psychology.* (6th ed.) (Champaign, IL: Human Kinetics Publishers, 2015).

53. Dorfman, *Copying It Down; An Anecdotal Memoir: Sport as Art*, 136.

54. Dan Lebatard, "Psychologist Hired," *Miami Herald*, April 17, 1993, 5D.

55. Gordon Edes, "A Confidence Man Marlins Can Trust," *Sun Sentinel*, April 22, 1993, accessed November 7, 2013, http://articles.sun-sentinel.com/1993-04-22/news/9302070355_1_marlins-rene- ; Victor Lee, "Marlins hire psychologist to help set up team's counseling program," Palm Beach Post, January 20, 1993, 3C.

56. Victor Lee, "Marlins hire Psychologist to Help Set Up Team's Counseling Program," 3C.

57. "Transactions." *The New York Times*, November 19, 1993, accessed November, 7, 2013 from www.nytimes.com/1993/11/19/sports/transactions-408093.html; Specifically, this transaction stated, "Florida Marlins—Named Harvey Dorfman instructor-counselor in charge of performance enhancement and staff development at the major and minor league levels."

58. "Lachemann Welcomes Psychologist," *Miami Herald*, August 25, 1993, 6D.

59. Gordon Edes, "A Confidence Man Marlins Can Trust," *Sun-Sentinel*, April 22, 1993 from accessed December 16, 2013, http://articles.sun-sentinel.com/1993-04-22/sports/9302070355_1_marlins-rene-lachemann-harvey-dorfman.

60. Gordon Edes, "Bad on Average: Marlins Will Hit Won't They?," *Sun-Sentinel*, April 16, 1996 from accessed October 12, 2012, http://articles.sun-sentinel.com/1996-04-16/sports/9604150542_1_marlins-tom-glavine-base.

61. Dorfman, *Copying It Down; An Anecdotal Memoir: Sport as Art*, 150.

62. Dorfman, *Copying It Down; An Anecdotal Memoir: Sport as Art*, 158–62.

63. "Marlins Get World Series Rings," *Philadelphia Inquirer*, April 11, 1998, C5.

64. Marc Topkin, "Rays Hire Counselor to Perfect Mental Game," *St. Petersburg Times*, December 11, 1997, 2C.; "Transactions," *The New York Times*, December 11, 1997, accessed October 13, 2012, www.nytimes.com/1993/11/19/sports/transactions-408093.html.

65. Topkin, "Rays Hire Counselor to Perfect Mental Game," 2C.

66. Marc Craig, "Yankees Remember Late Baseball Author Harvey Dorfman" *Star-Ledger*, March 3, 2011 Retrieved from www.nj.com/yankees/index.ssf/2011/03/yankees_remember_late_baseball.html.

67. Craig, "Yankees Remember Late Baseball Author Harvey Dorfman."

68. Dorfman, *Copying It Down; An Anecdotal Memoir: Sport as Art*, 168–69.

69. Dorfman, *Each Branch, Each Needle; An Anecdotal Memoir: The Final Stories*, 1–12.

70. Dorfman, *Each Branch, Each Needle; An Anecdotal Memoir: The Final Stories*, 1–12.

71. Artur Poczwardowski and Larry Lauer, "The Process of the Redondo Beach Sport Psychology Consulting Think Tank" *The Sport Psychologist,* 20 (2006): 74–93.

72. Dorfman, *Each Branch, Each Needle; An Anecdotal Memoir: The Final Stories*, 43–50.

73. Dorfman, "Reflections on Providing Personal and Performance Enhancement Consulting Services in Professional Baseball," 344.

74. Steve Gilbert, "D-backs Take Mind-Over-Matter Approach," October 3, 2011, accessed November 7, 2013, http://mlb.mlb.com/news/article.jsp?ymd=20111003&content_id=25466718&c_id=ari&partnerId=rss_ari.

75. Carroll Rogers, "Braves host prospects for rookie development week—updated with roster," January 4, 2011, accessed November 7, 2013from http://blogs.ajc.com/atlanta-braves-blog/2011/01/14/braves-invite-top-prospects-to-turner-field-for-rookie-development-week.

76. Brittany Ghiroli, "Orioles add sports psychologist to staff," February 23, 2012 accessed November 7, 2013, http://baltimore.orioles.mlb.com/news/article.jsp?ymd=20120223&content_id=26829668.

77. Ian Browne, "Sox prospects gather for rookie program" January 11, 2010, accessed November 7, 2013,http://mlb.mlb.com/news/article.jsp?ymd=20100111&content_id=7900182&vkey=news_bos&fext=.jsp&

c_id=bos ; Ian Browne, "Red Sox Focusing More on Mental Skills This Spring," February 13, 2013, accessed November 7, 2013 from http://mlb.com/news/article.jsp?ymd=20130213&content_id=41595810&notebook_id=41605262&vkey=notebook_bos&c_id=bos.

78. Paul Sullivan, "Cubs' Prospects Get Advice from Mark Prior," *Chicago Tribune*, accessed November 7, 2013, http://articles.chicagotribune.com/2013-01-17/sports/chi-cubs-prior-20130117_1_cubs-prospects-cubs-convention-marc-strickland.

79. Daryl Van Schouwen, "Psychologist Helps White Sox With Approach," *Chicago Sun Times*, accessed November 7, 2013, http://blogs.suntimes.com/whitesox/2012/03/psychologist-helps-white-sox-w.html.

80. "Cleveland Indians—Front Office Directory," accessed November 7, 2013, www.mlb.com/team/front_office.jsp?c_id=cle.

81. "Rockies announce Minor League staff for 2013," Colorado Rockies, accessed November 7, 2013, http://mlb.mlb.com/news/article.jsp?ymd=20130204&content_id=41384370&vkey=pr_col&c_id=col.

82. "USD Grad Serving as Detroit Tigers' Performance Enhancement Instructor," accessed November 7, 2013, http://www.goyotes.com/genrel/080803aaa.html.

83. "Royals Announce Minor League Coaching Staff for 2014," accessed November 7, 2013, http://kansascity.royals.mlb.com/news/article.jsp?ymd=20131101&content_id=63611222&vkey=pr_kc&c_id=kc.

84. Mark Saxon, "Angels Psychologist Focuses on Attitude" March 8, 2011 assessed November 8, 2013, http://sports.espn.go.com/los-angeles/mlb/columns/story?id=6191479.

85. "Milwaukee Brewers Front Office," accessed November 7, 2013 from http://milwaukee.brewers.mlb.com/team/front_office.jsp?c_id=mil.

86. "Hurricanes, Marlins, Reap physical benefits from mental acuity, accessed January 24, 2015, www.foxsports.com/florida/story/ miami-hurricanes-miami-marlins-duke-johnson-dan-jennings-sports-pschologist-benefits-102514.

87. "Minnesota Twins—Front Office Directory," accessed November 7, 2013, http://minnesota.twins.mlb.com/team/front_office.jsp?c_id=min.

88. "Pittsburgh Pirates—Front Office Directory," accessed November 7, 2013 http://pittsburgh.pirates.mlb.com/team/front_office.jsp?c_id=pit.

89. Anthony DiComo, "Through hitting system, Mets aim to build a winner," accessed January 24, 2015, http://newyork.mets.mlb.com/news/print.jsp?ymd=20140417&content_id=72395802&c_id=nym.

90. "New York Yankees—Managers and Coaches," accessed November 8, 2013, http://newyork.yankees.mlb.com/team/coaches.jsp?c_id=nyy.

91. "Rangers Announce Changes to Pro, Amateur, and International Scouting Staffs", January 31, 2012 accessed December 16, 2013, http://texas.rangers.mlb.com/news/article.jsp?ymd=20120131&content_id=26529524&vkey=pr_tex&c_id=tex.

92. "Giants Announce Minor League Coaching Staff for 2014 Campaign," accessed January 24, 2015 http://m.giants.mlb.com/news/article/67408298/giants-announce-minor-league-coaching-staff-for-2014-campaign.

93. "Mariners announce Minor League Coaching Staff for 2013 Season," accessed November 7, 2013, http://seattle.mariners.mlb.com/news/article.jsp?ymd=20121206&content_id=40565324&c_id=sea.

94. "Minor League Operations", Tampa Bay Rays Media Guide, 2013, accessed November 8, 2013, http://mlb.mlb.com/tb/downloads/y2013/minors.pdf.

95. "Washington Nationals—Executive Offices", accessed November 8, 2013, http://washington.nationals.mlb.com/team/front_office.jsp?c_id=was&sv=1

96. Dorfman, *Each Branch, Each Needle: An Anecdotal Memoir*, back cover.

97. M. Berardino, "A Time to Forget," *Fort Lauderdale Sun Sentinel*, February 17, 2001, accessed October 10, 2012 from http://articles.sun-sentinel.com/2001-02-17/sports/0102170127_1_rick-ankiel-richard-ankiel words.

98. Juan C. Rodriguez. Lowell might need some mental exercise, *Sun-Sentinel*, July 6, 2005, accessed November, 7, 2013 http://articles.sun-sentinel.com/2005-07-06/sports/0507060055_1_scott-olsen-marlins-mike-lowell.

99. Todd Zolecki. "Halladay Dealing with the Loss of His Mentor," March 1, 2011, accessed November, 7, http://philadelphia.phillies.mlb.com/news/article.jsp?ymd=20110301&content_id=16779834&vkey=news_mlb&c_id=mlb.

100. Jayson Stark, "Big Leaguers Will Never Forget Dorfman," March 2, 2011, accessed November 7, 2013, http://espn.go.com/mlb/blog/_/name/stark_jayson/id/6175536/harvey-dorfman-%20words-touched-many-major-leaguers.

101. David O'Brien, "Marlin Win is Grand," *Fort Lauderdale Sun Sentinel*, June 22, 2000, accessed November 7, 2013, http://articles.sun-sentinel.com/2000-06 22/sports/0006220074_1_mark-kotsay-marlins-luis-castillo.

102. Carroll Rogers, "MLB Network's Al Leiter has advice for Kris Medlen," October 4, 2012, accessed November 7, 2013, http://blogs.ajc.com/atlanta-braves-blog/2012/10/04/mlb-networks-al-leiter-has-advice-for-kris-medlen.

103. Jamie Moyer. "Age is Only a Number," January 22, 1012, accessed November 7, 2013, http://thestoriesofsuccess.com/ 2012/01/22/age-is-only-a-number-mlb-pitcher.

104. Dustin Pedroia and E. J. Delaney, Born to Play: My Life in The Game (New York: Simon Spotlight Entertainment, 2009), 72–3.

First-Generation Player Contracts

An MLB Success Story?

Barry Krissoff

Like most businesses, major league baseball (MLB) owners strive for optimizing profits by expanding revenue and limiting costs. Clearly, recent revenues have significantly increased with larger attendance, pricier tickets, the sale of MLB merchandise, and most importantly the growing and sizable television contracts. With revenue rising, it has been easier to negotiate with the Major League Baseball Players Association and share the larger economic pie and avoid costly shutdowns. Player salaries account for the majority of costs, consequently owners continuously look for ways to minimize financial outlays but still maintain the quality of their individual teams.

A recent approach to accomplish this goal is for owners to sign multiyear contracts with players that have limited or no major league experience. The Atlanta Braves have been particularly aggressive in this approach. The Braves signed shortstop Andrelton Simmons, first baseman Freddie Freeman, outfielder Jason Heyward, and pitchers Julio Teheran and Craig Kimbrel, all under 26 years old, to multiyear contracts starting in 2014 and totaling a combined $280 million.[1] Simmons and Teheran have less than two years of major league experience. The Braves' objective is to have these players locked up under contract during their prime playing years.[2] Other teams have signed $100 million plus extensions with their star players for seven to ten years or longer to keep them under team control possibly for their entire careers (Andrus in Texas, Braun in Milwaukee, Cabrera in Detroit, Kershaw in Los Angeles, Longoria in Tampa Bay, Stanton in Florida, Tulowitzki in Colorado, Votto in Cincinnati, Zimmerman in Washington to name a few).

In making these contractual decisions, owners and players are explicitly recognizing the rules of the game—the reserve rule under the Basic Agreement which limits mobility of players with less than six years' experience—and their risk return trade-offs. For the owners, the objective is to retain players who have the potential to contribute significantly to their teams in future years and who would have otherwise become free agents, but limit their future salaries. The owner must weigh the probability of future success of the player. If the owner negotiates a multiyear contract

and the player's performance is stellar, then the owner succeeds. However, if the player does not make the grade and/or is cut from the major league team, then the owner loses.

The players are on the opposite side of that equation. By signing a multiyear contract, they are locking in a $30 or $40 million payout, for example, but giving up the uncertainty of a much higher contract in the future (if they become superstars) or not having a major league contract at all (if they become busts). For players, who are likely to be more risk-averse than the wealthy team owners, the trade-off of the certainty of the $30 to $40 million contract may often be preferred. After all, the first $30 to $40 million that a player can earn on an early multiyear contract provides more utility than a potential extra $30 to $40 million when the player is already earning $100 million or more.

In this article we scrutinize the extent that teams are adopting the early signing of players and assess whether this approach has been successful. We examine first-generation contracts for pre-arbitration and arbitration (reserve rule) players relative to the contracts of established free agent players. We test the hypotheses that the negotiated first-generation contracts have a salary trade-off "discount" relative to comparable quality free agent players and whether the salary discount is smaller or larger when the first-generation contract extends into free agency.

Baseball fans know that first-generation players get paid less than free agents. But is this still true when we control for similar performance levels and contract lengths? If it is, how much lower are salaries of first-generation players? What about the first-generation player who chooses to sign a multiyear contract into free agency? If he is compensated less than a comparably skilled free agent player, the signing of early contracts is a successful cost-savings approach by team owners.

We believe our paper extends the literature in several important ways. First, we systematically compare the multiyear contracts of first-generation and free agent players focusing on the average yearly constant dollar value of the contracts, the number of years of the contracts, the players' performance for both batters and pitchers, and player and team characteristics. Descriptive statistics based on these variables offer a first pass at understanding the growth of first-generation contracts as a new business strategy for team owners. Secondly, we analyze the factors that contribute to variation in salaries for first-generation and free agent players who have signed multiyear contracts. We estimate salary and length of contract equations dependent on the status of the player, performance metrics, and player and team characteristics.

In our estimation procedure, we evaluate the magnitude of the salary discount that first-generation pre-arbitration and arbitration players may receive relative to each other and to free agent players. Our approach is similar to previous studies.[3] Here, the discount is separated into two components: (1) estimates of the markdown generated by MLB monopsony power due to the reserve rule and to players' risk-return trade-offs for multiyear contracts and (2) estimates of any additional salary deviation reflecting an extension of contracts into free agency. A first-generation player agreeing to a contract spreading into free agency chooses to postpone possible future negotiations with any major league team for a potentially much higher salary.

In our model we use the total contribution a player makes towards winning, in both offense and defense, as a performance statistic, Wins Above Replacement (WAR).[4] Additionally, we consider the character of the negotiation process by including the role of sports agents in influencing the value of the contract. Popular press frequently makes reference to a sports agent or agency having a significant effect on salary determination. Our period of study is 2003–14, a time of relative harmony between ownership and players.

A LOOK AT THE DATA: FIRST-GENERATION VERSUS FREE AGENT MULTIYEAR CONTRACTS

MLB teams and first-generation players negotiated well over three hundred multiyear contracts worth around $7.4 billion over the 2003 to 2014 period.[5] There are almost as many first-generation as free agent contracts, although MLB teams have greater flexibility on whether to sign multiyear contracts under the reserve rule relative to the free agent players. The average annual salary for first-generation contracts is $5.1 million in constant 2010 dollars for batters and pitchers. There is a considerable range—see the box and whisker plot in Figure 1. Some of these players signed modest major league contracts directly out of school while others had major league experience and were close to free agency. Former Texas Rangers outfielder Julio Borbon

Andrelton Simmons signed a seven-year, $58 million contract with less than two years of major league experience.

averaged $400,000 for his four year 2007–10 contract, although he did not reach the major leagues until 2009. In contrast, perennial all-star Detroit Tiger Miguel Cabrera averages $18.1 million for his eight year 2008–15 contract. After attaining over five years of major league service, Cabrera agreed to the contract rather than waiting for his free agency eligibility.[6]

Pitchers generally received smaller contracts than batters, about 10 percent lower than the average batter's contract, nearly $4.9 million. On the low end, Brian Matusz was a highly rated draft selection by the Baltimore Orioles who penned a four-year major league contract, 2008–11, for an annual average remuneration of $870,000. Matusz did not join the major league club until 2009. On the high end, San Francisco Giant Tim Lincecum tallied $19 million in 2012 in a two-year contract. Lincecum initialed the agreement when he had slightly over four years of major league experience and has subsequently reached an agreement for a two-year extension for 2014 and 2015.

The second set of box and whisker plots in Figure 1 show the distribution of salaries for batters and pitchers that are eligible for free agency with multiyear contracts. Free agent players are able to negotiate with any team and this unrestricted capability allows them to compete for a market equilibrium salary. Comparing

Figure 1. MLB Salaries

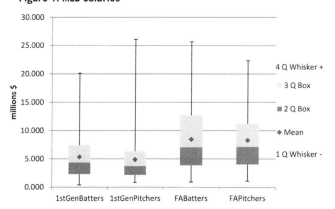

37

first-generation and free agent player contracts reveals some anticipated outcomes. First-generation players are paid about 60 percent of what free agent players are compensated on average. Hence, this implies the approximate value that first-generation players are willing to accept in order to gain the certainty of a multiyear contract and known salary, given that they are constrained by the reserve rule. Similarly, this is the approximate future savings to owners by locking in players to a multiyear contract early in their careers rather than facing an arbitration process or competing for them in the free agency market. Of course, this assumes that the players are of equal value in their achievements, which is the subject that we turn to now briefly and in more detail in the empirical section to follow.

Generally, better performing players receive higher compensation. To confirm this, we divide first-generation batters and pitchers into quartiles based on their annual salaries. For each quartile the average salary and performance metric Wins Above Replacement (WAR) are calculated (Table 1). Many consider WAR to be the most comprehensive measure of a player's contribution to winning.[7]

Obviously, actual performance is an uncertainty at the time of signing the contracts. Team owners and players base their contract negotiations and decisions on projections and/or prior performance. Our expected performance metric is calculated as the three year WAR average prior to the year of the contract.[8] If there was no prior experience, then the WAR achieved for the number of playing years under contract up to the 2014 season was used. For example, for Pedro Alvarez's 2009–12 contract, we used a WAR of 1.33 reflecting his performance over the 2010–12 seasons rather than a WAR of 0 since he had no playing time prior to the contract or in 2009. Thus, we made every effort to evaluate first-generation and free agents on an equal footing.[9]

As anticipated, performance tapers off as we move from the higher to the lower salary quartiles. First-generation batters in the 4th quartile achieved an average WAR of 4.41 and command a salary of $11.2 million; batters in the 3rd quartile did not perform quite as well, attaining a WAR of 2.60, and earning $5.5 million. Similarly, WAR declines as we move from the third to the second and first quartiles. For pitchers, we observe a parallel pattern except the quartile salaries and performance levels are lower. We repeat the procedure for free agent players and again find that better performing players are paid higher salaries, at least on average.

Now, let's turn our attention to comparing the quartiles across first-generation and free agent players. The first-generation salaries for batters are about 55 to 70 percent of free agent salaries and for pitchers about 45 to 70 percent of free agent salaries. Yet, when it comes to performance, we find that first-generation batters and pitchers have accomplished similar WAR levels to free agents. These descriptive statistics suggest the players signing a first-generation contract provide higher value on average to team owners, given their productivity levels compared to free agent players.

However, we need to take another step beyond the descriptive statistics to distinguish the variation of salaries attributable to a player's status and other contributing factors. In particular, in the regression model developed in the next section, we present five status classifications: pre-arbitration, pre-arbitration where contracts extend into free agency, arbitration, and arbitration extending into free agency, and free agents, and isolate the differences in players' salaries under multiyear contracts depending on their status for a given performance level, contract duration, and team and player characteristics.

THE MODEL FRAMEWORK

The basic model that we employ to explain the variation of major league baseball salaries is borrowed from the empirical analysis of Krautmann, Krautmann and Oppenheimer, Meltzer, and Link and Yosifov (KOMLY). We update and expand their estimated equation by concentrating on first-generation and free agent player multiyear contracts:

$$RSal_{ij} = \beta_1 + \beta_2 Status_{ij} + \beta_3 Perf_{ij} + \beta_4 Player_i + \beta_5 Team_j + \beta_6 Length_{ij} + \varepsilon_{ij}$$

where RSal is average annual salaries in constant 2010 dollars over the length of a player's multiyear contract, Status are the five fixed effects variables (designated as a 1 for each classification, 0 otherwise[10]), Perf is the player's performance, Player (i), and Team (j) are specific characteristics of the player and team, Length is the duration of the contract, and ε is an independently, normally distributed error term.

For performance, we focus on WAR and also plate appearances or innings pitched. We would expect that a player who has a stronger performance, plays more, and has a greater contribution to winning would be paid more than other players, the coefficients on $\beta 3 > 0$, other things being equal. We consider four Player and Team variables: the strength of the hitting or pitching position, the sports agency of the player, the strength of the team at the time of the signing of the contract, and the geographical location of the team. Different batting and pitching positions contribute differently to a team's success. First or third base, outfield or designated hitter for a batter and a starter for a pitcher are considered to be the stronger positions. We use dummy variables for the different batting and pitching positions with the strong position having an indicator that takes the value of 1, otherwise 0. We would anticipate batters and pitchers who play in the stronger relative to the weaker hitting positions of catcher, second base, and shortstop and weaker pitching role of relievers to receive relatively greater salary contracts.

Baumer and Zimbalist discuss the importance of team winning and the size of the local market in contributing to a team's revenue.[11] A team that is successful is more likely to achieve increased revenue and sign a potentially high-caliber player for a higher salary than a perennial losing team. For team winning, we use a three-year winning average prior to the player signing the multiyear contract. Teams in larger metropolitan areas such as New York, Los Angeles, Chicago, and Dallas/Fort Worth/Arlington have the potential to generate more revenue and therefore may be more willing to negotiate higher salary contracts than teams in smaller cities. For our second team variable, we examine the role of population in affecting players' salaries.

To our knowledge the role of sports agents in propagating higher salary multiyear contracts has not been examined. Do specific sports agencies influence the signing of these contracts, their length and salary structure? There are around 160 sports agencies representing over two thousand baseball players.[12] Some of these agencies are very large and not only represent baseball players and other athletes but also artistic entertainers. Some specialize in representing baseball players and have many clients. The Boras Corporation for instance has over a hundred baseball clients and represents some of the biggest names in the sport. Other agencies represent only a few clients. In interviews with baseball players conducted over several weeks prior to the 2013 season, players indicated the importance of interpersonal relationship, and business and legal acumen in selecting agents.[13]

Thus, some well-connected agencies may be better equipped to provide these attributes and have the prestige to negotiate higher salaries. Do Scott Boras's comments at the 2013 Baseball Winter Meetings criticizing the large-market teams New York Mets, Chicago Cubs, and Houston Astros lacking lofty payrolls translate into higher salaries for his corporation's clients, whereas this may not be the case for another sports

Prior to Evan Longoria's first major league season in 2008, he negotiated a six-year deal for $17.5 million plus three club option years worth another $30 million. In 2012 Longoria and Tampa Bay agreed to a six-year, $100 million extension plus a 2023 club option.

agency?[14] We test for whether four agencies (The Boras Corporation, Creative Arts Agency, Relativity Sports, and The Wasserman Media Group) with over 100 player contracts each affect salaries by again using fixed effects variables, 1 for each agency, 0 otherwise.

The length variable is problematic for both conceptual and statistical reasons. The expected sign on the coefficient is ambiguous. KOMLY observe that players who are expected to have stronger performances by team owners, are more likely to negotiate and receive more money and longer contracts implying coefficient $\beta 6 > 0$. However, as discussed earlier, players may be interested in buying assurance of a long-term contract in lieu of compensation since they are likely to be risk-averse. KOMLY argue that players in essence purchase insurance by agreeing to a lower return on their productivity in exchange for the security of a long-term contract, implying that $\beta 6 < 0$ (KO, page 8).

Secondly, contract negotiations simultaneously determine salary and length and hence, an ordinary least squares regression would yield a coefficient estimate that would be statistically inconsistent. To circumvent these issues, we estimate both salary and length equations using a two stage least square regression. In this procedure, the two independent variables, salary and length, are regressed on all of the independent variables. The estimated values for length are then used in the salary equation and the estimates for salary are used in the length equation.

The length equation is specified as:

$$Length_{ij} = \alpha_1 + \alpha_2 RSal_{ij} + \alpha_3 Perf_{ij} + \alpha_4 Player_i + \omega_{ij}$$

where we use WAR as the performance variable and the player's age at the time of signing the contract and the number of days on the disabled list as the player

Jordan Zimmermann agreed to only a two-year contract with Washington in January 2014 so that he can potentially test the free-agent market in 2016.

variables. As a player ages, we would anticipate that teams would be less interested in signing a longer term contract. Similarly, if in prior years the player exhibited a greater proclivity for injury, then we would expect shorter contract lengths. ω is an independently, normally distributed error term.

EMPIRICAL RESULTS

Two stage least square regression results for batters and pitchers are presented in Table 2. In the salary equation, the independent variables explain 60 percent of the variation for batter salaries and 66 percent for pitcher salaries. Our main interest is the β2 fixed effect coefficients for the first-generation players. These coefficients are all negative as anticipated implying that first-generation relative to free agent players, all of whom have agreed to multiyear contracts, receive lower salaries. For example, pre-arbitration batters who sign contracts into free agency earn $2.73 million less than free agents for a comparable performance level, contract duration, and player and team characteristics. This is even more the case for pitchers, who receive $4.4 million less than comparable free agents These players are trading off potential payoffs as future free agents for the certainty of a multiyear contract while they are under the reserve rule.

The pre-arbitration players who sign contracts into free agency also receive lower salaries than arbitration and pre-arbitration players who do not sign a contract into free agency. Here, we find that pre-arbitration pitchers and batters are receiving approximately $600,000 to $800,000 less in annual salary than their peers who do not sign contracts into free agency. The uncertainty of injury or not making the grade as a major leaguer prevails in their thinking and they are willing to make the trade-off of lower salary for the certainty of the multiyear contract. With the frequency of injuries to

pitchers and the often needed Tommy John surgery, the willingness to take on the certainty of a multiyear contract for less money is not surprising, particularly among pitchers.

Arbitration players experience lower salaries relative to free agents as well. However, in contrast to the pre-arbitration players who sign contracts into free agency, the arbitration players who sign a contract extending into free agency reach agreement for a relatively small salary discount, $1.2 and $1.5 million for batters and pitchers relative to free agents. The proximity to free agency explains their stronger negotiating position.

The other arbitration players who do not sign a contract into free agency are willing to accept less money, $2.4 and $3.2 million for batters and pitchers relative to free agents, and accept the uncertainty of a higher payout when they reach free agency. For example, with four plus years of experience, Washington Nationals star pitcher Jordan Zimmermann was willing to sign a two-year $24 million contract in current dollars ($7.5 million in 2014 and $16.5 million in 2015) but not a longer contract into free agency. In assessing his skill level at or above the average arbitration player, Zimmermann might expect to surpass a $20 million annual salary in a multiyear deal ($16.5 million + $3.2 million coefficient multiplied by 1.09 conversion from constant 2010 to current dollars).

As for the other variables in the salary and length equations, their coefficients are generally significant and of the expected sign. The productivity coefficients β3 for WAR and plate appearances or innings pitched are positive and significant for both batters and pitchers. Batters in stronger hitting positions and starting pitchers receive more compensation than players in weaker hitting positions and relief pitchers, β4 > 0. Clubs that are more competitive in the three years prior to signing a ballplayer's contract, show a positive correlation with salaries, β5 > 0.

We included fixed coefficients for four of the top sports agencies. The coefficients are mostly positive but none is significant. Batters who employ Scott Boras or Relativity as their agents may receive salaries that are approximately $700,000 more than other sports agencies. Scott Boras's pitchers may attain $610,000 more than other sports agencies. The value of these coefficients suggests that there may be merit to the notion that particular sports agencies affect salaries, but the results are inconclusive and preliminary at this juncture. One difficulty in assessing the role of sports agencies is a lack of consistent data matching players with specific player agents and with agency affiliation at the time of signing a contract that might be several years old. Players change agents, agents change agencies, and agencies reconfigure into bigger or smaller entities. This is an area that may be worth future research.

The $\beta 6$ coefficient on the estimated length variable is nearly zero and not significant. We expected this coefficient to be positive because players who sign lengthier contracts generally receive higher salaries. However, as discussed earlier, this may be somewhat offset since risk-averse players are willing to forego some of the higher salary for lengthier contracts.

As for the length equation, the α coefficients have the expected signs and are mostly significant. Salary and WAR are positively related to length; higher salaries and stronger performances are associated with longer contracts. In contrast, a player's age and a greater incidence of injury are negatively related to length; teams are reluctant to sign older and more often injured players to long-term contracts.

Table 3 presents the salaries for first-generation and free agent batters and pitchers using the estimated regression coefficients at the sample means. We observe from the table that the average first-generation players receive between 50 to 85 percent of free agent player salaries adjusted for performance level, contract length, players' position, and team. Thus, our findings suggest that first-generation players are receiving lower salaries than free agents and the variation in the discounted salary depends on a player's status at the time of signing the contract. An average free agent starting pitcher, who plays for a team in an average sized metro area and average winning percent receives an estimated annual average salary of $8.8 million in 2010 dollars relative to a comparably productive pre-arbitration pitcher who has a multiyear contract into free agency, $4.4 million, and a comparably productive arbitration pitcher who has a multiyear contract into free agency, $7.3 million.

In the fifth column of Table 3 we calculate the value of the multiyear contracts for first-generation and free agent players given the number of contracts in our sample and the number of years under contract for each player. This cumulative total of these multi-year contracts is approximately $18.1 billion. If the first-generation players are paid at the same scale as free agents, then their salaries would be $3.3 billion higher (Low Bar). If the pre-arbitration and arbitration players who signed contracts into their free agency received a commensurate salary to free agents for the years that the contracts extend into free agency, then their salaries would be nearly half a billion dollars higher (High Bar). For baseball's team owners, the

Max Scherzer negotiated a seven-year, $210 million free agent contract with Washington in January 2015.

strategy of signing first-generation players appears to be a successful proposition. They are bearing the additional risk of these first-generation players not succeeding, but on average, we are finding that there is a cost savings and positive payout to ownership.

CONCLUDING COMMENTS

Our analysis has examined the recent trend of baseball owners assertively seeking multiyear contracts with highly touted players and those with limited major league experience. Owners have the incentive to sign these contracts to reduce the uncertainty of having to pay sizeable or, in some cases, extraordinarily hefty salaries to players in later years or lose a player to free agency. Players have the incentive to agree to these contracts to ensure a major league level salary for multiple years. Our descriptive statistics and analytical examination of these first-generation contracts compared to the salary contracts of players competing in the free agency market strongly suggests that this is an efficient strategy for team owners. The owners benefit by signing players to multiyear contracts with lower salaries, thus avoiding the arbitration years and/or free agency. The first-generation players receive an average salary of approximately 60 percent (and a range of 50 to 85 percent) of their free agent counterparts when we account for equal performance levels, length of contract, and player and team characteristics. A signing of Ryan Braun for 8 years at $45 million, of Bryce Harper for 5 years at under $10 million, or Paul Goldschmidt for 5 years at $32 million exemplifies the success of this strategy for team owners. For the Milwaukee Brewers the 5-year $10 million 2012–16 plus an option year contract for Jonathan Lucroy, with a batting average of over .300 in the 2014 season, an all-star selection, and 4th place finisher for MVP, looks like a particularly attractive signing. Of

Table 1. Salaries ($millions) and Performance of Players with Multiyear Contracts, 2003–14

| | FIRST-GENERATION | | | | | FREE AGENTS | | | |
| | Batters | | Pitchers | | | Batters | | Pitchers | |
	Salaries	WAR	Salaries	WAR		Salaries	WAR	Salaries	WAR
Average	$5.36	2.32	$4.87	1.30		$8.45	2.48	$8.31	1.33
Lowest	$0.40	2.26	$0.87	-0.55		$0.96	0.46	$1.10	-1.16
Highest	$20.12	9.03	$26.13	5.08		$25.70	9.83	$22.34	5.41
First Quartile	$1.44	0.53	$1.33	0.08		$2.09	0.52	$3.03	0.24
Second Quartile	$3.16	1.68	$2.87	0.82		$5.44	1.73	$5.33	0.84
Third Quartile	$5.53	2.60	$4.81	1.44		$9.95	2.98	$9.56	1.38
Fourth Quartile	$11.17	4.41	$10.30	2.80		$16.10	4.61	$15.24	2.86

Note: First-Generation players are under the reserve rule at the time of signing a multiyear contract. Salaries are in 2010 millions of dollars and are annual averages over the contract for each player. WAR is calculated as three year averages prior to the contract or over the years available over the contract. See text for more details.

Source: Baseball Prospectus

Table 2. Regression Results

Dependent Variable: Salary

Independent Variable	BATTER		PITCHER	
	Coefficient	t statistic	Coefficient	t statistic
Intercept	-5.37	-3.02*	0.43	0.25
Pre-Arbitration Contract into Free Agency	-2.73	-2.87*	-4.40	-4.33*
Pre-Arbitration Contract	-1.93	-2.32**	-3.77	-6.25*
Arbitration Contract into Free Agency	-1.22	-1.45	-1.54	-1.94***
Arbitration Contract	-2.36	-5.36*	-3.16	-7.98*
Contract Length	-0.09	-0.29	-0.13	-0.35
WAR	1.64	7.74*	2.14	8.22*
Plate Appearances/Innings Pitched	0.01	4.82*	0.02	3.32*
Batter/Pitcher Position	0.73	2.03**	1.21	2.43**
Census Population	0.08	2.13**	0.06	1.74***
Winning Percent	10.21	3.08*	5.30	1.71***
Boras Corporation	0.70	1.15	0.61	0.98
CAA Sports	0.32	0.48	-0.03	-0.05
Relativity Sports	0.70	1.06	0.44	0.66
Wasserman Media Group	-0.09	-0.11	-0.23	-0.30

Dependent Variable: Length

Independent Variable	Coefficient	t statistic	Coefficient	t statistic
Intercept	8.82	16.56*	6.91	18.76*
Salary	0.16	4.06*	0.10	3.66*
WAR	0.20	2.13**	0.13	1.31
Contract Age	-0.22	-12.26*	-0.15	-11.75*
Disabled List	-0.01	-1.64***	0.00	-1.92***
Salary Equation: R Square Adjusted	0.60		0.66	
Length Equation: R Square Adjusted	0.53		0.47	
Number of observations	397		338	

*Significance at 1 percent level
**Significance at 5 percent level
***Significance at 10 percent level

Note: We use the R software programing language for our regressions and would like to acknowledge the many contributors to the development of R as an open source software.

Table 3. Salary and Cost-Saving Estimates

	Estimated Salary at Sample Means ($ millions)	Number of Contracts	Contract Duration (Years)	Total Contracted Salaries ($ millions)	Total Salary Savings Low Bar ($ millions)	Free Agency at Sample Mean (Years)	Total Salary Savings High Bar ($ millions)
Batter							
First-Generation							
Pre-Arbitration	6.28	25	4	627.81	192.57		
Pre-Arbitration Contract into Free Agency	5.48	28	5.8	889.24	443.05	1.8	139.03
Arbitration	5.84	95	2.8	1553.66	628.55		
Arbitration Contract into Free Agency	6.98	30	5.7	1194.19	208.65	4.5	163.63
Free Agent	8.20	219	3.5	6288.20	0.00		
Pitcher							
First-Generation							
Pre-Arbitration	5.02	54	3.7	1003.71	753.85		
Pre-Arbitration Contract into Free Agency	4.40	14	4.9	301.95	301.50	1.1	67.68
Arbitration	5.64	80	2.8	1262.82	707.62		
Arbitration Contract into Free Agency	7.25	17	4.4	542.64	115.34	3.9	102.23
Free Agent	8.80	173	2.9	4413.25	0.00		
Total Cost Savings					3351.13		472.57

Note: The salary savings low bar assumes team owners would have to compensate first-generation players at the same scale as comparably performing free agents over the length of the contract. The salary savings high bar assumes team owners would have to compensate first-generation players who have signed contracts into their free agency at the same scale as comparably performing free agents over the free agent years of the contract. Salary estimates are calculated based at the sample mean for WAR, plate appearances or innings pitched, contract length, winning percent, and team location for a player in a strong hitting position but not for a contract with one of the big four sports agencies. Salaries are in 2010 constant millions of dollars and are annual averages over the contract for each player.

Source: Baseball Prospectus

course, this is not to say that there are not exceptions. There are players who receive first-generation contracts who never make the major leagues or are very marginal at the top professional level. This is the risk trade-off the owners are taking. Nevertheless, we conclude that, based on the last several years of data, multiyear contracts for first-generation players seems to be well worth the risk for team owners.

Can the first-generation players work out a better deal? Max Scherzer may be at the vanguard of a new approach for the players. Over the 2013–14 winter, Scherzer turned down a $144 million extension offer from his team, the Detroit Tigers, a year before his free agency. Scherzer, like other first-generation players, is risk-averse and wanted to reduce the risk of injury or low quality performance but did not want to sign a Tiger contract that he felt was below market rate. Other

entertaining performers, like singers and dancers, have purchased insurance to protect themselves from losing their voices or injuring their legs. Why shouldn't baseball players search for insurance to protect themselves against injury or performance decline also? And this is exactly what Scherzer did—he negotiated with insurance providers' assurance of a minimum payout in return for his paying an insurance premium. Scherzer may have been able to insure a salary of $144 million at a cost of around $14 million, a net of $130 million for Scherzer.[15] In contrast, the 2014–15 off season open market may offer Scherzer $175 million or more given our estimate that first-generation contracts for pitchers signing contracts into free agency are 82 percent of free agent contracts ($175 = $144/.82). If we subtract $144 million from $175 million, Scherzer's loss of signing a contract before free agency is $31 million. Clearly, opting to purchase insurance at a cost of $14 million is a more efficient approach than agreeing to a first-generation contract and not waiting for free agency.

The postscript to this story is that the Washington Nationals negotiated with Scherzer and his agent Scott Boras a 7-year, $210 million contract in January 2015. The annual payout is deferred to $15 million over a 14-year period, implying that the present value of the contract is $185 million. By obtaining insurance and waiting until he reached free agency, Scherzer was able to achieve a monetary gain of $41 million ($185–$144) less the estimated cost of insurance ($14). ∎

Appendix – Data

Our main source of data is from *Baseball Prospectus' Cot's Contracts 2009–2014* (www.baseballprospectus.com/compensation/cots). It includes information on the player's total and yearly salary under contract, the length of contract, the team he plays for, his fielding position, the number of years of major league experience, and the sports agent who negotiated the contract on behalf of the player. The contracts, which are in effect for the year 2009, start anywhere between 2003 and 2009, thus we have contracts originating as early as 2003. We use the guaranteed compensation including any annual salary, bonuses, and options. We do not include bonus incentives or salary if a team exercises an option since this occurs ex post to the contract. Performance statistics are also obtained from Baseball Prospectus. Major League Baseball was generous in supplying the data on the number of days a player was on the disabled list. Additional sources were used when information was incomplete, notably from Baseball-Reference.com, Spotrac.com, and MLB-TradeRumors.com. MLB Trade Rumors, in particular, contained the most complete and up-to-date information on the various sports agencies working on behalf of the players.

Acknowledgments

The author appreciates the thoughtful review comments and suggestions from John Wainio and two anonymous peer reviewers, and the editorial assistance from Cecilia Tan, Clifford Blau, and Rod Nelson. We want to also acknowledge baseball websites, most notably Baseball Prospectus, for developing and making available large data sets. Of course, any errors that remain are the responsibility of the author.

Notes

1. Jason Heyward was traded to the St. Louis Cardinals November 2014 for a young promising pitcher, Shelby Miller, a relief pitcher Jordan Walden, and a minor leaguer.

2. Cameron, Dave. "Braves Lock-up Andrelton Simmons Keep Inflating Extensions." Fangraphs, February 20, 2014 www.fangraphs.com/blogs/braves-lock-up-andrelton-simmons-keep-inflating-extensions.

3. See Krautmann, Anthony (1999) "What's Wrong with Skully-Estimates of a Player's Marginal Revenue Product." *Economic Inquiry*, 37(2): 369–81; Krautmann, Anthony and Margaret Oppenheimer (2002). "Contract Length and the Return to Performance in Major League Baseball." *Journal of Sports Economics* 3(1) 6–17; Meltzer, Josh (2005). "Average Salary and Contract Length in Major League Baseball: When Do They Diverge?" Unpublished manuscript Stanford University; and Link, Charles and Martin Yosifov (2012). "Contract Length and Salaries Compensating Wage Differentials in Major League Baseball." *Journal of Sports Economics* 13(1): 3–19.

4. To our knowledge this has not be done with one exception. Cameron does a bivariate analysis of the total value of contract salaries and cumulative projected WAR over the contract for 2014 free agents, "A Basic Model of Free Agent Pricing" Fangraphs March 10, 2014, www.fangraphs.com/blogs/a-basic-model-of-2014-free-agent-pricing.

5. The estimate is derived from Cot's Contract data 2009–13. It includes players with contracts as early as 2003 that extend into 2009 or later and players that have signed contracts between 2009 and 2013 including extensions. To the database, we added contracts that were signed right at or before the beginning of the 2014 season, but not those that were negotiated during or after the season. The appendix indicates a complete list of our data sources. We deflated annual salaries by the Consumer Price Index using 2010 = 100. All salaries are reported in 2010 dollars, unless otherwise stated.

6. Prior to 2008, Cabrera had one year contracts with the Florida Marlins. More recently, Cabrera and Detroit Tigers have agreed to an extension to 2023.

7. Baumer and Zimbalist refer to WAR as measuring marginal physical product although they express concern about the lack of industry standardization of WAR estimates from the three major sources, Fangraphs, Baseball-Reference, and Baseball Prospectus. Benjamin Baumer and Andrew Zimbalist. *The Sabermetric Revolution*, University of Pennsylvania Press, 2014.

8. For players with less than three year's playing time, the average was calculated based on one or two years' of experience. For players who were disabled for any of the three years prior to the signing of the contract, we assigned a WAR of 0 for the disabled year. This may understate the potential contribution of the player but it also may reflect the potential for injury during the length of the multiyear contract.

9. For a player who had no major league experience, we assigned a WAR of 0 and are likely understating their potential contribution. Since first-generation players are more affected by this limitation than free agents, we may be understating the contribution of first-generation players.

10. We use the four first-generation status variables in the equation, which are compared to free agent status.

11. Baumer, Benjamin and Andrew Zimbalist. *The Sabermetric Revolution University of Pennsylvania Press*, 2014. Other authors, such as Gennaro Diamond Dollar$ 2007 Maple Street Press, have a more detailed discussion of the value of a win in different regional markets.

12. Major League Baseball Trade Rumors, MLBTR Agency Database, www.mlbtraderumors.com/agencydatabase.

13. See for example, B.J. Rains "Why I Chose My Agent: David Wright" (March 13, 2013), part of a series of interviews conducted by Major League Baseball Trade Rumors, www.mlbtraderumors.com/2013/03/why-i-chose-my-agency-david-wright.html.

14. Ronald Blum. "Boras Blasts Mets, Cubs, Astros," November 14, 2013 http://finance.yahoo.com/news/boras-bashes-mets-cubs-astros-122953166.html.

15. See Dave Cameron, "Max Scherzer and the Incentives to Self-Insure" Fangraphs June 9, 2014, www.fangraphs.com/blogs/max-scherzer-and-the-incentives-to-self-insure.

Reviewing Instant Replay

Observations and Implications from Replay's Inaugural Season

Gil Imber

The 2014 baseball season's adoption of expanded instant replay review not only introduced another wrinkle into our national pastime, it opened the door into a brand new arena of statistical analysis over 50 years in the making. Thanks to the adoption of a manager's challenge system—which MLB has confirmed will remain in place for the 2015 season[1]—the new technology also added a significant element of strategy to the sport. Televised replay made its debut during the December 7, 1963, Army-Navy football game when 29-year-old CBS director Tony Verna, who passed away January 18, 2015, at the age of 81, pressed "rewind" on his Ampex tape machine for the first time during a game broadcast.[2,3] Since that effort 51 years ago, the technology has spread to all televised and otherwise streamed sports, culminating with the National Football League's pioneering decision in 1986 to try using replay to review the officials' on-field calls wherein a brand new off-field replay official had the power to stop play to conduct such a review. After the system was taken out of commission in 1991 due to concerns of delays, interruptions to game flow and overall sluggishness, replay was tweaked in an effort to better engage fans and teams alike (meanwhile, the NHL adopted its own version of limited replay in 1991).[4] When the NFL's system resurfaced in 1999, it was accompanied by a cutting-edge, engaging, and exciting challenge system: for the first time, coaches could decide which plays to review. At first, the coach received two challenges before being rewarded for successful appeals: a coach would receive a third challenge if he got his first two right.

Baseball was long resistant to adopting replay in any form—it was the last of the four major sports to adopt the technology and boasted lively attitudes against its adoption, including throwbacks to the pace-of-game arguments that took the NFL's system temporarily offline in 1991.[5] Hall of Fame umpire Bill Klem once said, when confronted with a photograph of a purported blown call, "Gentlemen, he was out because I said he was out," reflecting the human element and umpire-as-final-say argument also used against replay in baseball.[6] FOX Sports' Reid Forgrave penned the sardonic slogan, "Better Baseball Through Technology"[7]—while others quickly connected the dots between replay adoption and a lengthier ballgame.[8]

Nonetheless, pro baseball's journey into instant replay review followed football's path in several ways. During an otherwise benign May 31, 1999, Cardinals-Marlins contest, Florida batter Cliff Floyd drove a Kent Bottenfield fastball to deep left-center field, where it bounced off or atop the left field scoreboard and was ruled a double by second base umpire Greg Gibson. After a Marlins complaint that the fly ball struck the panel behind the Pro Player Stadium scoreboard, and therefore should have been ruled a home run, the umpires changed the call to a four-base award, prompting an equal-yet-opposite argument from St. Louis. This time, crew chief Frank Pulli opted to consult a dugout-adjacent TV camera to review the play. After the first replay review in MLB history, Pulli changed the call back to a double—effectively confirming Gibson's initial call. The Marlins responded by filing a protest in their 5–2 loss, which was ultimately denied by National League President Len Coleman, who acknowledged and admonished Pulli for unauthorized use of video replay while denying the Marlins' protest for Pulli's judgment call.[9]

Baseball would not revisit replay until 2008, when the league became the last of the four major American sports to authorize replay reviews for select on-field calls—whether a potential home run was fair, foul, in or out of play, or subject to spectator (fan) interference. At the time of its midseason adoption, baseball required its umpires to initiate and adjudicate the entire replay process while some managers, led by Chicago's Lou Piniella, already were campaigning for a challenge system: "I'd love to throw a red hankie."[10] Though limited replay remained in force from 2008 through 2013—producing 392 total replays in five-plus seasons, 132 of which (33.7%) were overturned[11]—Piniella would get his wish in late 2013, when MLB experimented with the notion of expanded replay and NFL-esque challenges. Having selected five games in the 2013 Arizona Fall League in which to experiment with a modified "unlimited challenge" version of the modern replay review system, MLB watched umpiring crew chief Tripp Gibson don the now-familiar headset

15 times, affirming 12 calls while overturning three for a 20% overturn rate.[12]

In a related story, a 2010 ESPN study of nearly 10,000 calls found that umpires are 20% inaccurate when it comes to "close" calls, which, all else equal, would support a 20% overturned call rate for an unlimited replay system, as occurred in the 2013 Arizona Fall League.[13] On the other hand, since ESPN's analysis also found that just 1.3 calls per game, on average, were close enough to merit replay review, further extrapolation of the data found that umpires are inaccurate less than 0.5% of the time, or, alternately, are 99.5% accurate.[14]

GROUND RULES: PREPARING FOR EXPANDED INSTANT REPLAY'S INAUGURAL SEASON

As Opening Day 2014 approached, Commissioner Bud Selig's Special Committee for On-Field Matters pared down the fall's unlimited replay regimen, settling on just one challenge per manager with the reward system of a second possible challenge if the manager experienced success with challenge number one.[15] Further adding to the mystique of replay, MLB announced that, beginning in the 7th inning, the umpiring crew chief could initiate replay review if a manager was out of challenges. To make strategic matters even more delicious, limited replays circa-2008 were grandfathered and combined with matters concerning new home plate collision Rule 7.13 into a replay class that would be unchallengeable—only the crew chief could initiate home run boundary or plate-blocking replay reviews. In order to appease the umpires' union, MLB agreed to staff its league's new state-of-the-art Replay Operations Center with two crews of umpires, which accounted for baseball's hiring of seven new officials to the full-time MLB staff in advance of the 2014 season.[16] In order to appease its owners, MLB authorized its teams to staff replay coordinators in clubhouses to review multiple feeds and camera angles, with a direct phone line to the dugout in order to advise a team whether it should challenge a play.[17]

Based on expanded replay's framework, teams would have to become "replay smart" to make the most of baseball's new technology. In addition to choosing the right replay coordinator—some teams chose rules-smart umpires—managers themselves not only would have to hone their argument craft to 'turn' or delay the umpire, thus allowing the coordinator more time to review video, they would have to figure out, in a world with finite challenges, just when to use one.[18]

For instance, when Giants manager Bruce Bochy unsuccessfully challenged an early-inning close call at first base in Arizona less than a week into the 2014

Umpire Frank Pulli could be considered the first major league umpire to use replay, when he used the dugout camera to rule on a play on May 31, 1999, at Pro Player Stadium. Crew Chief Pulli upheld the ruling of umpire Greg Gibson that Cliff Floyd be awarded a double and did not hit a home run. He was admonished by National League president Len Coleman for unauthorized use of video replay.

NATIONAL BASEBALL HALL OF FAME LIBRARY, COOPERSTOWN, NY

season, he lost his challenge for the rest of the game and had to argue the old-fashioned way when the Diamondbacks scored on an ensuing passed ball—although replays indicate the plate umpire's call was incorrect, the challenge-less Bochy couldn't do a thing about it: Score one run for bad replay strategy, and potentially one win, too, as Arizona won the ballgame by one, 5–4.[19]

METHODS: CHOOSING THE VARIABLES TO TRACK

With a bevy of data set to head our way in 2014, choosing the proper variables to document proved a most important task. Reframing the task in a way that considered the potential effect of replay review on the course of a game, however, made such a chore much simpler. In the end, replay reviews were logged individually (even in the case of two replay reviews which occurred during the same play[20]) and included the following variables:

- Type: Manager's Challenge or Crew Chief Review
- Umpires:
  – Name
  – Position (HP/1B/2B/3B)
  – Status (Full-Time MLB or Triple-A Fill-in)
  – Crew Chief (e.g., the umpire who actually spoke with New York)
- Quality of Correctness/Outcome: Call Confirmed/Stands/Overturned
- Teams:
  – City Short-Code (e.g., CIN for Cincinnati, TB for Tampa Bay)
  – Active Manager Name (e.g., the person who spoke with the umpire)

- Reason:
  - Appeal Plays
  - Base Touches
  - Boundary or Ground Rules
  - Catch/No Catch (e.g., a ball dropped on the transfer)
  - Catch/Trap (e.g., a ball either caught or trapped by a diving outfielder)
  - Fair/Foul
  - HBP/Foul (e.g., questions concerning a pitched ball vs. the batter)
  - HR Boundary Calls (those that were reviewable dating back to 2008)
  - Non-HR Fan Interference
  - Passing Runners
  - Rule 7.13 (the home plate collision rule)
  - Safe/Out
  - Time Plays (did the run score prior to the third out being recorded?)
- Variable Game Situation:
  - Inning-of-Review (including Top/Bottom)
  - Offense/Defense (was the requesting team at bat or in the field?)
  - W/L Pre-Review (was the requesting team winning/losing/tied at the time of review?)
  - W/L Final (did the requesting team win or lose the ballgame?)
  - Runs Scored by the requesting team
  - Runs Scored by the opposing team
  - Day of Week

NEW MEASURES OF PERFORMANCE

The following sabermetric definitions were created specifically for replay review analysis: Review Affirmation Percentage (RAP) is also known as collective replay

The double heard 'round the world? Greg Gibson was the second-base umpire on May 31, 1999 at Pro Player Stadium. He ruled that a ball had bounced off the scoreboard for a ground-rule double, a decision that was eventually upheld by crew chief Frank Pulli after he viewed video footage.

quality of correctness and is a value representing the frequency with which an umpire's call is affirmed (confirmed or stands) by replay affected as the result of both managers' challenges and crew chief reviews. Team Success Percentage (TSP) frames the issue from the team's perspective and is thus the inverse of RAP, while Manager's Challenge Success Percentage (MCSP) is similar to TSP, except that it only accounts for managers' challenges, removing crew chief reviews from the equation. None of these measures includes reviews of the record-keeping variety. In short:

RAP = Calls Affirmed by Replay Review ÷ Total Calls Replayed

TSP = 1.000 − RAP (or, alternately,
   Calls Overturned ÷ Total Calls Replayed)

MCSP = Challenges Overturned by
   Replay Review ÷ Total Calls Challenged

Please note that for the purposes of the instant replay review analysis contained herein, the term "percentage" is used, akin to the colloquially used "winning percentage." This term accordingly has taken on a vernacular meaning such that a replay-based "percentage" is presented in the form of an average running from .000 to 1.000, similar to the commonly used statistic, "batting average." The mathematical conversion from RAP, TSP or MCSP average to conventional percent is RAP/TSP/MCSP * 100. To illustrate, a RAP of .500 corresponds to a review being affirmed 50.0% of the time.

For instance, Team A plays a game that features three reviews: Team A's manager challenges a safe call in the fifth inning and, after the manager's challenge, the original call stands. In the sixth, Team A's manager requests the umpires review a home plate collision (Rule 7.13) play in which Team A's runner was ruled out, and, after the crew chief review, the original call is confirmed. In the seventh, Team A's manager requests the umpires review a safe call at first base and, after the crew chief review, the call is overturned. RAP, TSP and MCSP for this game would be calculated as follows:

RAP = 2 ÷ 3 = .667 (reviews were affirmed at a rate
   of .667, or 66.7% percent of the time)

TSP = 1.000 - .667 = .333 (the team's success
   percentage for all reviews was .333)

MCSP = 0 ÷ 1 = .000 (the manager's challenge
   success percentage was .000)

As an aside, if this game featured a fourth review, filed by Team B, the above statistics for Team A would be unaffected.

DATA AND TRENDS: TEAMS AND MANAGERS

Data were collected from the first MLB games with expanded replay on March 31, 2014, through the final day of the regular season on September 28. With 1,274 total replay reviews across 2,428 regular season contests (the replay system was unavailable for the two Dodgers-Diamondbacks Opening Series games in Sydney, Australia)[21], MLB saw an average of just over one replay review for every two games played, which featured 601 overturned calls, while 353 stood and 310 were confirmed (10 additional reviews were of the record-keeping variety).[22,23] In other words, a call was overturned slightly less frequently than once every four games, which aligns quite well with the ESPN data showing that umpires miss 20% of all close calls.[24] Collaterally, the present analysis on replay's 2014 debut serves to affirm the veracity of ESPN's 2010 study.

Replay use by team varied from a low of 32 (Milwaukee Brewers, New York Yankees) to a high of 61 (Chicago Cubs)—the average team experienced 42 reviews with 20 overturns (which follows the overall 47% overturn rate described above)[25]—yet there was actually a negative correlation between frequency of replay use and percentage of calls overturned.[26] For instance, no team in the top 11 of replay users had more than 50% of their replayed calls reversed; seven of the bottom 12 replay users (three teams tied for the 10th-least-used position) had greater than 50% of their replayed calls reversed (see Table 1). The upper 53% of teams ranked by replay usage (two tied for 15th place) accounted for 753 (59.6%) of all reviews, with 341 calls overturned (rate of overturn = 45.3%). Meanwhile, the lower 47% of teams went to replay a combined 511 times (40.4%), with 260 of their reviewed calls being overturned (rate of overturn = 50.9%). Roughly, the more reviews experienced by a given team, the greater the chance that some of these reviews were unsuccessful and/or frivolous.

To further illustrate the point, consider that when decision-making factored into replay use, defined as a team voluntarily electing to file a finite manager's challenge as opposed to requesting a "free" umpire-initiated crew chief review, teams fared much better than when the review was a freebie: 1,053 replay reviews were managerially challenged to the tune of a .474 RAP, whereas 221 reviews were of the crew chief variety and, at a RAP of .769, the .295-point difference in RAP constituted a sizeable distinction. Furthermore, the two most successful managers in challenging calls were New York Yankees skipper Joe Girardi and Miami's Mike Redmond, whose .793 and .731 MCSPs, respectively, were also associated with the fewest

number of affirmed calls for any individual teams (nine and 14, respectively). At this point, it is important to note that the Yankees and Marlins ranked tied-for-29th and 27th, respectively, among individual team replay use (Manager Ron Roenicke of the tied-for-29th-place Brewers ranked 12th in MCSP), giving some credence to the notion of replay discretion. As if in perfect balance, the worst-performing manager was Toronto's John Gibbons, whose .340 MCSP also featured the most affirmed calls for any individual team (39); the Blue Jays went to replay a total of 57 times, third-most in the league (#1 Chicago's Rick Renteria's .455 MCSP appeared noticeably below the league-average MCSP of .526 while #2 Tampa Bay's Joe Maddon fared even worse, with a .438 MCSP). As a corollary to the previous paragraph's conclusion, it appears the reverse was true as well. The fewer reviews experienced by a given team, the less the chance that some of these reviews were unsuccessful and/or frivolous.

DATA AND TRENDS: UMPIRES

Replay review statistics also advertised individual umpire affinity, revealing several trends amongst the men in black and powder blue. For instance, umpire Chris Guccione fared supreme with a .941 RAP (16/17) while minor-league fill-in Tom Woodring's .167 (1/6) was the lowest RAP of all umpires with more than five replays to their name (MiLB colleagues Jon Byrne, Jeff Gosney and Ben May all scored a .000 RAP, but only had two reviews apiece). As a whole, less tenured full-time MLB umpires, such as Guccione (hired full-time in 2009), second-place Scott Barry (.875 RAP, hired in 2011), fourth-place Vic Carapazza (.833 RAP, hired in 2013) and fifth-place Mike Estabrook (.813 RAP, hired in 2014) performed much better than both veteran full-timers with significant experience—Crew chiefs Gerry Davis (hired in 1984), Jerry Layne (1989), Tim Welke (1984), Gary Cederstrom (1997) and Jim Joyce (1989) all scored below .385 (MLB's longest-tenured umpire, Joe West [1978], for those wondering, was the outlier and performed well above average with his 28th-best .600 RAP)—and rookie call-ups with fewer than 100 MLB games under their belt, such as below-.300'ers John Tumpane, Stu Scheurwater, Seth Buckminster, and Woodring. On the other hand, veteran minor league fill-ins such as Mark Ripperger and Will Little (.714 and .667 RAPs, respectively) performed quite well. For the umpires, a peak window of replay performance existed sometime after working 100 games as a minor-league call-up and, often, before spending many years as a full-time big-leaguer.

Umpires at the first-base position were apt to have

their calls overturned more often than at any other base (.448 RAP), while home plate umpires experienced affirmed rulings with more frequency than their field umpire counterparts (.742 RAP).[27] Umpires were most questioned about safe/out calls at first base (n = 954), followed by HR boundary calls that would also have been reviewable dating back to 2008 (n = 97), issues of home-plate collision Rule 7.13 (n = 92) and whether a pitch at the plate hit the batter, bat, or nothing (n = 46). Issues of catch/trap in the outfield and fair/foul tied for the fifth-most common reason for review, with 21 reviews apiece. The most common overturned call was the catch/trap call (overturned 76.2% of the time), while the least overturned call concerned Rule 7.13 (overturned just 14.1% of the time).[28]

Though replay is still in its infancy, the fact that Major League Baseball in January 2015 hired some of replay's top performers amongst fill-in umpires—Ripperger and Little—to the full-time big league staff may reveal a new method of evaluation at MLB headquarters, especially after Park Avenue admitted that its 2014 postseason umpires were selected, in part, due to instant replay performance.[29,30]

INSTANT REPLAY DYNAMICS AND IMPACT ON GAME OUTCOME

At the end of the day, replay review may be about getting the individual call right, but it also has, from time to time, had an impact on how a game plays out. For instance, of the 1264 non-recordkeeping replays in 2014, teams entered the call-to-be-reviewed play leading 444 times, trailing 488 times, and tied 332 times. As it turns out, this 444–488–332 record turned into 614 wins and 650 losses at game's end, which corresponds to a .486 winning average. The measured change in W–L record from pre-replay to game final was plus 170 wins and 162 losses, a winning average of .512. In an all-else-equal world where the expected league average change in winning average would be .500, one could say that a team's invocation of replay review had a somewhat positive correlation with game outcome.

Filtering the data uncovered an interesting and powerful effect: When replay review resulted in an overturned call in 2014—in other words, when the outcome of replay benefited the team that challenged (or prodded the umpires to initiate)—teams that entered the replay situation with a 203–228–170 record finished their games with a record of 319–282 (.531 winning average), a net gain of 116 wins and 54 losses, or a whopping .682 winning average (see Figure 1). When replay review resulted in a confirmed or upheld call that did not benefit the requesting team, on the other hand, this delta-winning average dropped dramatically to just

.329, a game-changing overturned vs. affirmed difference of .353 points (see Figure 2).[31] Thus, the data indicate a correlation between replay success and winning a ballgame while also indicating a correlation between lack of replay success and losing.

Breaking down the data specifically by the 484 individual games in which the pre- and final statuses were incongruent—the 332 games tied at the time of review as well as those in which losing situations turned into wins (81 times), and vice versa (71 wins-to-losses)—the following results emerged:

When Call was Affirmed: Teams stole 27 wins (L-to-W) and 39 losses (W-to-L). Ties turned into 66 wins and 96 losses (93–135 overall, .408).

When Call was Reversed: Teams stole 54 wins and 32 losses. Ties turned into 95 wins and 75 losses (149–107 overall, .582).

Accordingly, result stealing (defined as a win-to-loss or loss-to-win outcome) occurred in 66 of the 663 affirmed cases and 85 of the 601 reversed cases. Proportionally, this favored the supposition that reversed calls were more strongly associated with change-to-outcome than affirmed calls, while the 81 total stolen wins (53 + 27) still only accounted for 6.4% of the 1264 total replay reviews; meanwhile, the 71 stolen

Figure 1. Overturned Reply W-L Record at Time of Review (Pre) vs. Game Outcome (Final)

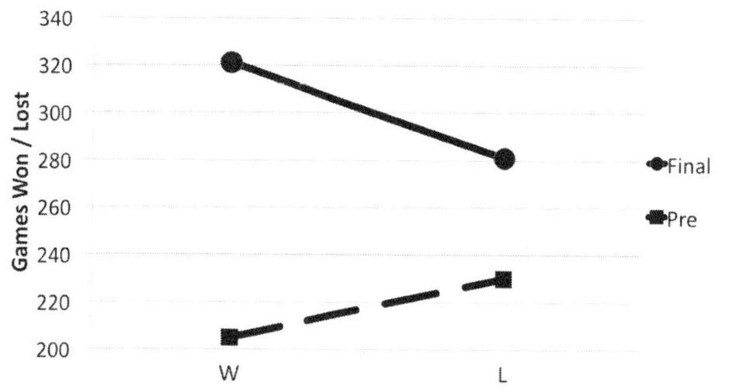

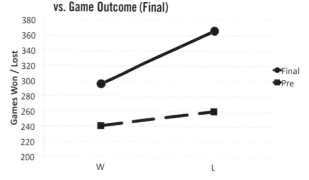

Figure 2. Affirmed Replay W-L Record at Time of Review (Pre) vs. Game Outcome (Final)

losses (39 + 32) accounted for 5.6% of the 1264 total reviews, suggesting that, all else equal, randomly choosing to replay a call has a slightly better shot of turning a loss into a win than a win into a loss. Of course, a loss remained a loss in a majority of those pre-loss cases (407 times), while a win remained a win 373 times—this "same pre-to-final" outcome manifested in 61.7% of all replay pairings, meaning that, all else equal, replay unequivocally had no bearing on win-loss game outcome a majority of the time.

As for our 332 ties, 161 became wins and 171 became losses (.485 WPCT), whose deviation from the zero-sum state of .500 pales in comparison to the distributions related to replay outcome: whether the call was affirmed or reversed (.408 and .582, respectively).

Replay review impact has also been measured by its tangible effect on runs scored or erased, broken into the categories of "mild," "medium," and "spicy" (see Figure 3).[32] Succinctly, these impact categories only apply to an overturned call pursuant to the following schedule:[33]

- A **mild** impact is one in which an overturned call did not lead to any incremental runs being scored or erased.

- A **medium** impact is one in which a reversed call led to a run(s) being scored or erased, but these runs did not determine the game outcome.

- A **spicy** impact is one in which a reversed call led to run(s) scored or erased that did determine which team won the game.

For instance, an overturned safe call in the bottom of the ninth inning of a 13–3 ballgame would both effectively end the game and be assigned an impact of "mild." Meanwhile, an overturned out call at home plate in the bottom of the ninth inning of this same 13–3 blowout would both make the score 13–4 and, barring a miraculous comeback, be assigned an impact rating of "medium." Finally, this same overturned out call at home plate in the bottom of the ninth inning of a tied ballgame would effectively end the game by scoring the winning run for the home team and, thus, merit the impact rating of "spicy."

Replay impact was mild a majority of the time (n = 432, 71.9%), followed by medium (137, 22.8%) and spicy (32, 5.3%). These 32 spicy plays account for 2.5% of the 1264 total non-recordkeeping replays. Sifting through these 32 spicy replay situations shows that all except one pair of replays were exclusive to one particular game—that is, only one game featured two spicy replay outcomes. That game was the August 19 Tigers-Rays contest, in which a fourth inning home run call was overturned to a foul ball and, in the fifth, a catch was overturned to a trap. The HR play took a run off the board for Tampa Bay while the trap gave Detroit an extra run. The Tigers ultimately won the game in extra innings.[34] As such, 31 of MLB's 2428 replay-capable games contained a "spicy" replay review, a percentage of 1.3%.

Thus, by this metric, replay rarely had a directly observable impact on game outcome and was correlated with a changed outcome of games a distinct minority of the time.

REPLAY BY TIME OF INVOCATION

By game phase, teams were more likely to have a successful replay outcome (an overturned call) early than late; league-wide TSP for the ballgame's first third (innings #1–3) was .585. This number steadily decreased throughout the contest, such that the mid-game (innings #4–6) TSP was .496 and the late game (seventh-inning onward) TSP was .388.[35] The most successful individual inning for review was the second, with 81 overturned calls out of 123 total replays (.659 TSP). When filtering out the freebie crew chief-initiated reviews, teams again fared better while actually amplifying the downward trend of success present in league-wide TSP: .680 MCSP for innings #1–3, .541 for innings #4–6 and .416 for innings #7 + .[36] Umpires either improved and/or replay initiators (managers for challenges and crew chiefs otherwise) regressed as games progressed into the later innings.

By day-of-week, most challenged calls were overturned during weekend series, specifically on Sundays and Saturdays (.570 and .563 MCSPs, respectively), followed by Fridays (.550), Thursdays (.518), Wednesdays (.506), Tuesdays (.489) and Mondays (.454), as if

Figure 3. Replay Outcomes

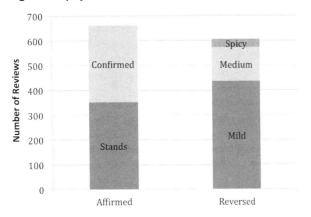

managers became better challengers as the week wore on, only to repeat the cycle the following week.[37]

As for time of year and the question of whether more calls were reversed later in the season, the data suggest no relationship between time-of-year and percentage of calls overturned.[38] The greatest percentage of overturned calls came in June 2014 (52.1% overturned) while the lowest followed in July (43.5% overturned). Meanwhile, number of replays requested peaked in August (229 replays, or 0.54 per game) after a valley in April (389 replays, or 0.47 per game). Due to the All-Star Break, July actually had the highest replays per game (.55) with the fewest number of games played. The month of September experienced the second-fewest number of total replays as well as replays per game (205 and 0.52, respectively). Thus, teams did not appear to consistently improve as the season wore on, though reviews occurred more frequently after the regular season's first month and prior to its final month.

IMPLICATIONS FOR FUTURE REPLAY STRATEGY

Insofar as team strategy is concerned, maximizing the benefit of the challenge is key. For instance, teams can "save" this crucial challenge by opting for the freebie crew-chief initiated review, if and when available, either as a preventative measure (e.g., against losing replay capability later on) or as a protective one (e.g., by keeping the challenge). As a preventative measure, replay challenge opportunity cost decreases throughout the contest, especially as inning number seven approaches, when the crew chief can initiate a review even if a team is out of challenges. With the probability of a missed call occurring during a game firmly lodged at less than 0.5%, the equal distribution of a missed call occurring during any particular half-inning of play is just .028%. With such odds, challenging any perceived missed call might seem like a no-brainer—except if you just happen to be the Giants playing the Diamondbacks in April 2014: then, a bad challenge can cost you a game. Even if the odds are squarely in a team's favor, it behooves every team to develop and invest in their video coordinators, replay technology and related education—especially early on in a weekend series game (perhaps in the second inning of a Sunday matinee as umpire eyes adjust to the bright skies and, more importantly, television cameras experience better frame rates to decipher close plays in the surplus of daylight[39]), when the chances of a call being overturned are highest. After all, replay review is an example of a scenario in which a clubhouse employee can have a direct impact on a team's winning percentage or probability.

MLB's longest-tenured umpire, Joe West, performed well above average with his 28th-best .600 RAP (Review Affirmation Percentage). West has been umpiring in the major leagues since 1978.

Early in 2014, MLB stated that the purpose of expanded instant replay was "for critical game situations and obvious misses, not the 'bang-bang' play."[40] It accordingly follows that a club's video replay coordinator should be very adept at not simply knowing whether Glove A actually tagged Jersey B, but should be able to decipher this caper with confidence. The chance that any single replay review was confirmed in 2014 was 24.5%, compared to 27.9% for 'stands' and 47.5% for 'overturned,' meaning that, pursuant to MLB's own framework, replay was used as intended just 47.5% of the time—and was flat out abused at least 24.5% of the time. The sure thing of overturning an "obvious miss" turned into somewhat of a coin flip because teams simply didn't use the new technology correctly, perhaps because video coordinators, bench coaches and/or managers—notably those in Toronto, Tampa Bay, and the other "lower half" teams—didn't know what to look for, didn't know the rules, or simply were unable to think like an umpire.

As a protective measure, rules regarding crew chief-initiated reviews prior to (and, to a lesser extent, after) the seventh inning suggest that sly managers would do well to request an umpire-initiated freebie review whenever possible, given that 47.5% of reviewed plays result in overturned calls.[41] On the other hand, crew chief reviewed plays were affirmed 76.9% of the time. Because the grandfathered home run boundary 7.13 call cannot be challenged and instead must be initiated by the crew chief—and because replay officials consider all aspects of a play during the review, which means the issue of fan interference is considered during a HR boundary call, for example—managers would be wise to request a crew chief review for any close play at the wall. Returning to the Bochy problem in Arizona, had the Giants requested a review pursuant to the Rule 7.13 framework, that, in 2014, mandated this type of review be initiated by the crew chief, perhaps the Giants would have been the beneficiaries of a crucial overturned call. After all, the Los Angeles Dodgers were granted a Rule 7.13 crew chief-initiated review in June on a tag play at home plate that didn't even involve the catcher![42]

As a matter of strategy, managers would be wise to challenge or request an-otherwise benign review when on defense, during stressful situations. Although replay regulations may prohibit actual mound visits during reviews, 2014's league-average 1:46 review—2:15 if the call stood—was precisely one minute and forty-six seconds of extra time for a reliever to prepare in the bullpen: over the course of the season, baseball spent 37 hours, 32 minutes, and 30 seconds watching umpires wear headsets, which should prove ample time for all manner of stall tactics.[43] Since reviews are freebies after the sixth inning anyway, and most bullpen management occurs during these later innings, exploitation of replay for warm-up time gain seems self-fulfilling.

Finally, while losing a replay review dropped a team's W–L average to .342, compounding this effort with an ejection for arguing the review's outcome was a nearly sure-fire way to lose the ballgame. There were 24 ejections for arguing a replay review in 2014, with the ejected party's team entering the ejection situation winning five times, losing 13 times and tied six times. Those ejected teams went on to win the game six times while experiencing a loss 18 times, for a net change of 1–5 (16.7 WPCT). Though the sample size is small, the trend is clear and has been occurring with ejections for years: Getting thrown out of a ballgame, especially for arguing a replay review, decreases win probability even in the relatively unusual circumstance in which the manager was right, which was the case in less than 30% of the 199 total ejections during the 2014 season.[44]

CONCLUSION

Baseball's foray into expanded instant replay review uncovered an entirely new arena for statistical analysis and opened a Pandora's box for adopting and applying strategy to a part of the game that didn't even exist prior to 2014. When baseball's replay committee first considered expanded instant replay, the committee discussed its implementation for "the game-changing play," with committee member Tony La Russa noting that, "it doesn't come around all that often."[45] As the 2010 "close call" study and 2014 replay review statistics both confirm, replay will not overturn a call all that often—just once every four

games—yet when it does, the positive effect this produces for the benefitting team can be notable, on the order of being associated with 116 additional wins, to 54 losses (WPCT 68.2), as opposed to the additional 53 wins and 108 losses (WPCT 32.9) associated with an unsuccessful replay. With a sample size of 1264 replays, however, significance was diminished by the simple fact that most games in which a team was winning ended up as a win, while most games that a team was already losing ended up as a loss. Replay had an impact on game outcome a minority of the time, and a direct "spicy" impact at a much lower rate.

Whether via manager's challenge or crew chief initiated review, game outcome correlated with replay result is worse for the replay-loser (affirmed call) and better for the replay-winner (reversed call). The key will continue to be discretion, and reserving challenge usage for situations in which an overturned call is the most likely outcome, which most often occurs during the third inning of a Sunday game on a catch/trap call by the first base umpire. ∎

Notes

1. Ken Davidoff, "MLB to tweak replay system, but managers' challenges will stay," *New York Post*, http://nypost.com/2014/11/21/mlb-to-tweak-replay-system-but-managers-challenges-will-stay/, November 21, 2014 (accessed November 25, 2014).
2. Jack Dickey, "Let's Review 50 Years of Instant Replay," *TIME*, http://ideas.time.com/2013/12/07/lets-review-50-years-of-instant-replay/, December 7, 2013 (accessed November 2, 2014).
3. Chris Erskine, "Tony Verna, TV director who introduced instant replay, dies at 81," *Los Angeles Times*, www.latimes.com/local/obituaries/la-me-tony-verna-20150119-story.html, January 18, 2015 (accessed February 6, 2015).
4. Gary Miles, "The NHL Gives OK to Replays, Reviews to Begin in 1991–92 Season," Philly.com, http://articles.philly.com/1991-06-25/sports/25787282_1_instant-replay-video-replays-nhl-officials, June 25, 1991 (accessed November 6, 2014).
5. Jack Curry, "Baseball to Use Replay Review on Homers," *The New York Times*, www.nytimes.com/2008/08/27/sports/baseball/27replay.html?_r=0, August 26, 2008 (accessed November 8, 2014).
6. "Bill Klem Quotes," *Baseball Almanac*, www.baseball-almanac.com/quotes/quoklem.shtml (accessed November 25, 2014).
7. Reid Forgrave, "Human element the heart of baseball," FOX Sports, www.foxsports.com/mlb/story/Baseball-replay-expansion-winter-meetings-heart-of-the-game-120111, May 28, 2014 (accessed January 7, 2015).
8. Cork Gaines, "MLB Games Are Taking Longer Than Ever And The New Replay System Is Making It Worse," *Business Insider*, www.businessinsider.com/mlb-games-length-instant-replay-system-2014-4, April 4, 2014 (accessed January 7, 2015).
9. "Marlins' 'Replay' Protest Denied," *Los Angeles Times*, June 4, 1999.
10. Associated Press, "MLB approves replay in series that start Thursday," ESPN, http://articles.philly.com/1991-06-25/sports/25787282_1_instant-replay-video-replays-nhl-officials, August 27, 2008 (accessed November 8, 2014).
11. Major League Baseball, *2014 Umpire Media Guide*, Ed. Michael Teevan and Donald Muller, 90.
12. "AFL Instant Replay: 20% of Challenged Calls Overturned," Close Call Sports/Umpire Ejection Fantasy League, www.closecallsports.com/

2013/11/afl-instant-replay-20-of-challenged.html, November 10, 2013 (accessed November 10, 2014).

13. T.J. Quinn and Willie Weinbaum, "Study shows 1 in 5 close calls wrong," ESPN, http://sports.espn.go.com/espn/otl/news/story?id=5464015, August 16, 2010 (accessed November 10, 2014).

14. Gil Imber, "Stats Prove MLB Umpires Call 99.5 Percent of Plays Correctly," *Bleacher Report*, http://bleacherreport.com/articles/911552-defining-the-human-element-mlb-umpires-call-995-of-plays-correctly, October 26, 2011 (accessed November 10, 2014).

15. Paul Hagen, "Expanded replay approved, to begin this season," MLB.com, http://m.mlb.com/news/article/66737912/mlb-approves-expanded-instant-replay-beginning-with-2014-season, January 16, 2014 (accessed November 15, 2014).

16. "Confirmed: MLB Hires 7 New Umpires to Full-Time Staff," Close Call Sports/Umpire Ejection Fantasy League, www.closecallsports.com/2014/01/mlb-hires-umpires-baker-blaser-rackley.html, January 14, 2014 (accessed November 15, 2014).

17. Ben Walker, "Replay wizards becoming key positions on MLB teams," Yahoo! Sports, www.closecallsports.com/2014/01/mlb-hires-umpires-baker-blaser-rackley.html, March 21, 2014 (accessed November 15, 2014).

18. Ken Fidlin, "Blue Jays' intrasquad game a fine warmup," *Toronto Sun*, www.torontosun.com/2014/02/25/blue-jays-intrasquad-game-a-fine-warmup, February 25, 2014 (accessed January 8, 2015).

19. Chris Haft, "Bochy loses challenge, then key opportunity," MLB.com, http://m.mlb.com/news/article/70668478/the-d-backs-scored-a-run-after-a-call-at-first-was-upheld-after-a-giants-challenge, April 2, 2014 (accessed November 16, 2014).

20. David Brown, "Two replay reviews confirm Indians triple play against Dodgers," Yahoo! Sports, http://sports.yahoo.com/blogs/big-league-stew/two-replay-reviews-confirm-indians-triple-play-against-dodgers-144150176.html, July 2, 2014 (accessed November 18, 2014).

21. Steve Gilbert, "Australia series to skip new replay system," MLB.com, http://m.dbacks.mlb.com/news/article/69150110/australia-series-to-skip-new-replay-system, March 11, 2014 (accessed November 18, 2014).

22. Gil Imber, "Umpire Ejection Fantasy League Portal: Historical Data," *Close Call Sports*, http://portal.closecallsports.com/historical-data (accessed November 20, 2014).

23. Although some sources indicate 1275 total replays, one of these plays was not reviewable. On September 20, during the sixth inning of the Tigers-Royals game, the Royals had runners on second and third with one out. The batter hit a line drive that was caught on the fly by Detroit's second baseman, who threw wildly past second base and into left field. By the end of this play, the Royals baserunner from third base had scored and the runner from second stood at third. Detroit subsequently appealed that the runner from third base failed to timely tag up and, after umpires signaled the runner safe, Detroit attempted to challenge the play. The umpires donned the replay headsets to New York, but were told the play was not reviewable and reconvened on the infield to discuss the sequence amongst themselves, the old-fashioned way. Meanwhile, Kauffman Stadium's "Crown Vision" video board displayed its own replays of the contentious play, pursuant to MLB's replay protocol for in-Stadium video. At least one report states that one of the umpires saw the replays on Crown Vision and elected to reverse the call based on this unauthorized video review, which I have not considered an official review—thus the 1274 vs. 1275 discrepancy. For more information, please see "Appeals: The Legalese of Reviewable Base Touching," Close Call Sports/Umpire Ejection Fantasy League, www.closecallsports.com/2014/09/appeals-legalize-of-reviewable-base.html, September 20, 2014 (accessed February 8, 2015).

24. 2428 games / 601 overturned calls = 4.04 games per overturned call. This is very similar to ESPN's 2010 data referenced in endnotes #13 and 14: 20% of 1.3 calls per game were missed, or 0.26 missed calls per game, which is the equivalent of approximately one missed call for every four games played.

25. 601 overturned calls / 1264 reviews = 47.5% overturn rate; the team average 20 overturned calls / 42 average reviews = 47.6% overturned.

26. "MLB Ejection & Replay Stats: 2014 Season Sabermetrics," Close Call Sports/Umpire Ejection Fantasy League, www.closecallsports.com/2014/09/mlb-ejection-replay-stats-2014-season.html, September 30, 2014 (accessed November 20, 2014).

27. 1B Umpires: 249 affirmed calls/556 replays = .448. 2B Umpires: 173 affirmed calls/349 replays = .496. 3B: 80 affirmed calls/134 replays = .403. HP: 167 affirmed calls/225 replays = .742.

28. Safe/Out: 451 affirmed/954 replays = .473 RAP. HR/Not HR: 71/97 = .732. Rule 7.13: 79/92 = .859. HBP/Foul: 24/46 = .522. Catch/Trap: 5/21 = .238. Fair/Foul: 14/21 = .667. Catch/No-Catch: 3/9 = .333. Ground Rule/Not HR Boundary: 6/9 = .667. Base Touch: 4/5 = .800. Other Fan Interference: 1/4 = .225. Time Play: 2/3 = .667…

29. "MLB Hires Tripp Gibson, Mark Ripperger, Will Little," Close Call Sports/Umpire Ejection Fantasy League, www.closecallsports.com/2015/01/mlb-hires-hw-grads-tripp-gibson-and.html, January 11, 2015 (accessed January 12, 2015).

30. "Report: Four first-time Series umps," The Associated Press & ESPN, http://espn.go.com/mlb/playoffs/2014/story/_/id/11715511/four-umpires-get-first-world-series-call, October 17, 2014 (accessed January 12, 2015).

31. W/L pre- of 241-260-162 became a W/L final of 295-368, or .445 winning average. The added 53 wins and 108 losses produced a winning average of just .329.

32. "Replay Impacts," ReplayOMeter, www.replayometer.com/impacts (accessed January 12, 2015).

33. "FAQ," ReplayOMeter, www.replayometer.com/faq (accessed January 12, 2015).

34. "Tigers @ Rays," MLB Advanced Media, http://mlb.mlb.com/mlb/gameday/index.jsp?gid=2014_08_19_detmlb_tbamlb_1&mode=plays, August 19, 2014 (accessed January 14, 2015).

35. For innings #1-3, 200 overturned calls/342 replays = .585. For innings #4-6, 199 overturned calls/401 replays = .496. For innings #7+, 202 overturned calls/521 replays = .388.

36. For innings #1-3, 187 overturned calls/275 replays = .680. For innings #4-6, 184 overturned calls/340 replays = .541. For innings #7+, 185 overturned calls/445 replays = .416.

37. Sunday: 102/179 = .570. Monday: 54/119 = .454. Tuesday: 69/141 = .489. Wednesday: 83/164 = .506. Thursday: 59/114 = .518. Friday: 88/160 = .550. Saturday: 99/176 = .563.

38. "Replays by Month," ReplayOMeter, www.replayometer.com/months (accessed January 12, 2015).

39. "Lighting for High Speed," Love High Speed, www.lovehighspeed.com/lighting-for-high-speed/ (accessed November 25, 2014).

40. Rick Hummel, "La Russa says expanded replay is 'remarkably effective,'" *St. Louis Post-Dispatch*, www.stltoday.com/sports/baseball/professional/la-russa-says-expanded-replay-is-remarkably-effective/article_d4c4d76e-08c0-5188-aae1-e0a5affa51b8.html, April 27, 2014 (accessed November 20, 2014).

41. 601 overturned / 1264 total calls = .475 TSP.

42. Derrick Goold, "Dodgers drub Cards, Lynn," *St. Louis Post-Dispatch*, www.stltoday.com/sports/baseball/professional/cardinal-beat/dodgers-drub-cards-lynn/article_d3968561-e404-5f03-8de1-7efdcf241657.html, June 28, 2014 (accessed January 14, 2015).

43. Tom Gatto, "MLB says it wants faster games; here's what it can do," *The Sporting News*, www.sportingnews.com/mlb/story/2014-09-23/bud-selig-pace-of-game-baseball-mlb-long-games-3-hours-replay, September 23, 2014 (accessed November 20, 2014).

44. Gil Imber, "Umpire Ejection Fantasy League Portal: Historical Data," Close Call Sports, http://portal.closecallsports.com/historical-data (accessed November 20, 2014).

45. Tyler Kepner, "Baseball's Expanded Replay Adds to Managerial Strategy," *The New York Times*, www.nytimes.com/2014/01/17/sports/baseball/major-league-baseball-adopts-expanded-video-review.html?_r=0, January 16, 2014 (accessed November 20, 2014).

Seeking Resolution of the Discrepancy for the 1912 NL Triple Crown

Herm Krabbenhoft

According to the official averages reported in the November 28, 1912, issue of *The Sporting News*, Heinie Zimmerman won the 1912 National League batting championship with a .372 average and the home run title with 14.[1] Five weeks later, *The Sporting News* reported that—according to the research of baseball writer Ernie Lanigan—Zimmerman also had the most RBIs (98).[2,3] Having topped the league in all three categories, Zimmerman won the Triple Crown.[4,5]

Zimmerman's NL Triple Crown was accepted throughout baseball and were printed in several major baseball publications, including Turkin and Thompson's classic *The Official Encyclopedia of Baseball*, *One for the Book*—the record book published by *The Sporting News*, and Elias's baseball record book *The Little Red Book of Baseball*.[6,7,8]

However, when one checks the official website of Major League Baseball today, one does not find Zimmerman in its tabulation of "Triple Crown Winners: Batting"—see Table 1.[9] A discrepancy exists between MLB.com's information and the record books.

Since MLB.com shows that Zimmerman was the NL's batting champion and home run king in 1912, but doesn't list him as a Triple Crown winner, the discrepancy boils down to MLB.com's reckoning of Zimmerman's RBIs. MLB.com shows Zimmerman with 99 RBIs in 1912, third in the Senior Circuit behind Honus Wagner (102) and Bill Sweeney (100).

Since RBIs were not recorded officially until 1920, MLB.com employs the RBI numbers generated from the phenomenal research effort directed by David S. Neft during the mid-1960s which culminated in Macmillan's 1969 publication of *The Baseball Encyclopedia* (frequently referred to as "Big-Mac").[15,16,17]

The question then is this: who actually led the NL in RBIs in 1912? Was it Zimmerman (according to Lanigan) or Wagner (according to Neft) or someone else? Table 2 compares Lanigan and Neft's RBI totals.[18,19] (MLB.com displays the Neft numbers for the top-six RBI accumulators.)

Neft shows Honus Wagner topping Zimmerman by three RBIs. The only position that Lanigan and Neft agree on is fourth place: Chief Wilson, but they disagree on all the RBI totals for all six players. At least one of the two researchers must be wrong, possibly both. Regrettably, the criteria used by Lanigan and by Neft to credit a player with a run batted in are unknown. No game-by-game RBI data are extant to support the full-season RBI numbers claimed by Lanigan or Neft.[20]

In 2013 I initiated a baseball research program—"Accurate RBI Records for Players of the Deadball Era"—in order to determine the longest consecutive games streaks for batting in at least one run during the 1901–19 period.[21,22,23] As part of this ongoing program I have ascertained the RBI records for each player on the 1912 Boston Braves, Chicago Cubs, New York

Table 1. Triple Crown Winners: Batting, According to MLB.com (accessed January 12, 2015).

Year	Player	Team (League)	Batting Average	Home Runs	Runs Batted In
1878	Paul Hines	Providence (NL)	.358	4	50
1894	Hugh Duffy	Boston (NL)	.438	18	145
1901	Nap Lajoie	Philadelphia (AL)	.422	14	125
1909	Ty Cobb	Detroit (AL)	.377	9	115
1922	Rogers Hornsby	St. Louis (NL)	.401	42	152
1925	Rogers Hornsby	St. Louis (NL)	.403	39	143
1933	Chuck Klein	Philadelphia (NL)	.368	28	120
1933	Jimmie Foxx	Philadelphia (AL)	.356	48	163
1934	Lou Gehrig	New York (AL)	.363	49	165
1937	Joe Medwick	St. Louis (NL)	.374	31	154
1942	Ted Williams	Boston (AL)	.356	36	137
1947	Ted Williams	Boston (AL)	.343	32	114
1956	Mickey Mantle	New York (AL)	.353	52	130
1966	Frank Robinson	Baltimore (AL)	.316	49	122
1967	Carl Yastrzemski	Boston (AL)	.326	44	121
2012	Miguel Cabrera	Detroit (AL)	.330	44	139

Notes: (1) According to the Elias Sports Bureau—the official statistician of Major League Baseball—Ty Cobb's Batting Average was .376 in 1909 and Lou Gehrig had 166 Runs Batted In in 1934.[10] (2) According to several sources, Ty Cobb had 107 Runs Batted In in 1909.[11,12,13,14]

Giants, and Pittsburgh Pirates—the teams for whom the top-six RBI accumulators played.[24] My data should resolve the discrepancy.

RESEARCH PROCEDURE

As in my previous papers on the subject of RBI records, I employed the method of "obtaining complete details" for every run scored by the teams in question in 1912. The "complete details" include the following:

(1) The player who scored the run.

(2) The run-scoring event—e.g., a 2-RBI double, a 1-RBI groundout, a 1-RBI grounder (batter safe on a fielding error), a 0-RBI grounder (batter safe on a fielding error), a 1-RBI bases-loaded walk, a 0-RBI balk, etc.

(3) The player who completed his plate appearance during the run-scoring event—i.e., the player who may have earned credit for batting in the run. [Note that when the run scored on a steal of home, a passed ball, a wild pitch, etc., no batter completed his plate appearance during the run-scoring event.]

I relied upon the descriptions given in the game accounts from multiple independent newspapers as well as many unpublished play-by-play accounts from Retrosheet.

In order to properly assign credit to a player for batting in a run, I adhered strictly to appropriate official scoring rules. Because runs batted in were not officially recorded until 1920, there were no official scoring rules for RBIs in 1912. One would think it logical to utilize the 1920 rules for awarding RBIs to players in earlier seasons, but in fact the official scoring rules for RBIs for 1920 (indeed, through 1930) provide no guidance whatsoever for properly assigning credit for RBIs in prior seasons. The entirety of the rule reads: "The summary shall contain: The number of runs batted in by each batsman." [Rule 86, Section B]

So, to assign credit for RBIs for the 1912 season, I utilized the 1931 official scoring rules—which do provide appropriate instruction:

Runs Batted In are runs scored on safe hits (including home runs), sacrifice hits, outfield put-outs, infield put-outs, and when the run is forced over by reason of the batsman becoming a base runner. With less than two outs, if an error is made on a play on which a runner from third would ordinarily score, credit the batsman with a Run Batted In. [Rule 70; Section 13]

These are essentially the same rules that are in effect today. The only significant difference is the provision introduced in 1939 which does not credit a batter with an RBI when the batter hits into a force groundout double play.

RESULTS

Table 3 presents the full-season RBI numbers achieved by Zimmerman, Wagner, Sweeney, Wilson, Doyle, and Murray according to my research, compared with Lanigan and Neft.[25,26,27] My research indicates while Honus Wagner and Bill Sweeney collected 101 and 99 RBIs respectively, that Heinie Zimmerman amassed 104 RBIs in 1912, led the league, and therefore won the Triple Crown in 1912.

DISCUSSION

Each of the RBI numbers determined in my research is gleaned from multiple independent newspaper accounts. Thus, I believe that my RBI numbers are reliable and that both Lanigan's and Neft's unsupported RBI

Table 2. Top-Six RBI Accumulators in National League for 1912 According to Lanigan and to Neft

Lanigan Player (Team)	Lanigan RBIs	Neft Player (Team)	Neft RBIs
Heinie Zimmerman (Chicago)	98	Honus Wagner (Pittsburgh)	102
Larry Doyle (New York)	97	Bill Sweeney (Boston)	100
Honus Wagner (Pittsburgh)	94	Heinie Zimmerman (Chicago)	99
Chief Wilson (Pittsburgh)	93	Chief Wilson (Pittsburgh)	95
Bill Sweeney (Boston)	92	Red Murray (New York)	92
Red Murray (New York)	88	Larry Doyle (New York)	90

Table 3. Unofficial RBI Leaders in National League for 1912 According to the Present Research

Rank	Player (Team)	Krabbenhoft	Lanigan	Neft
1	Heinie Zimmerman (Chicago)	104	98	99
2	Honus Wagner (Pittsburgh)	101	94	102
3	Bill Sweeney (Boston)	99	92	100
4	Chief Wilson (Pittsburgh)	94	93	95
5	Larry Doyle (New York)	91	97	90
6	Red Murray (New York)	88	88	92

Table 4. NL Batting Leaders for 1912 as presented on Retrosheet (accessed January 12, 2015).

	Batting Average			Home Runs			Runs Batted In	
Rank	BAVG	Player (Team)	HR	Player (Team)		RBI	Player (Team)	
1	.372	Zimmerman CHI	14	Zimmerman CHI		104	Zimmerman CHI	
2	.344	Sweeney BOS	12	Schulte CHI		101	Wagner PIT	
3	.341	Evers CHI	11	Cravath PHI		99	Sweeney BOS	
4	.330	Doyle NY	11	Merkle NY		94	Wilson PIT	
5			11	Wilson PIT				

numbers are incorrect. I encourage others to review the evidence I assembled and which has been published in *The Inside Game*.[28]

All of Neft's Big-Mac RBI numbers for 1891–1919 were adopted by Pete Palmer for his database of baseball statistics and these "Neft-Palmer" statistics are currently utilized throughout baseball. They are employed in the most-recent editions of *Total Baseball* and *The ESPN Baseball Encyclopedia* and on numerous baseball websites including Baseball-Reference.com and MLB.com. My research has also shown that Neft's RBI numbers are not completely accurate for the 1919 Boston Red Sox, 1906 and 1914–19 Detroit Tigers, or 1895 Philadelphia Phillies, either.[29,30]

I provided the evidence I collected to Pete Palmer for his review and Palmer has since incorporated all of the corrections in his database.[31,32] Palmer's updated numbers have been incorporated on Retrosheet, as well and are expected to appear on Baseball-Reference.com sometime in 2015.[33,34] Hopefully, Heinie Zimmerman's 1912 NL Triple Crown will also be recognized at some point down the road by/on MLB.com.[35]

CONCLUSION

My research resolves the discrepancy for the 1912 NL Triple Crown. Based on the RBI numbers ascertained for all six relevant teams, I determine that Heinie Zimmerman did lead the National League in RBIs for 1912. Therefore, with his league-leading marks in batting average and home runs, Heinie Zimmerman did earn the prestigious Triple Crown—again.[36] ∎

Acknowledgments

With tremendous gratitude I gratefully thank the following people for the fantastic help and cooperation they have provided to me in this research endeavor: Steve Boren, Keith Carlson, Dave Newman, Pete Palmer, Gary Stone, Dixie Tourangeau, and Dave Smith and Tom Ruane and their fellow Retrosheet volunteers.

Notes

1. "National League Batting Averages For 1912 Season," *The Sporting News*, November 28, 1912, 2.
2. "Hitting in a Pinch," *The Sporting News*, January 2, 1913, 5.
3. Fred Lieb, "Ernie Lanigan, Patron Saint of SABR," *The Baseball Research Journal*, Volume 2 (1973), 29. See also: Fred Lieb, "Ernie Lanigan," SABR BioProject, sabr.org website. Lieb wrote, "[Lanigan's] big gift to the field of baseball statistics is the important Runs Batted In (RBI) column of today."
4. It is pointed out that the term "Triple Crown" had not yet been used in baseball when Zimmerman achieved the feat. According to *The Dickson Baseball Dictionary*, the first use of the term "Triple Crown" in baseball was on page five of the July 9, 1936, issue of *The Sporting News*: "Gehrig insists that he will win the Triple Crown again…—batting, homers, and runs driven in." See: Paul Dickson, *The Dickson Baseball Dictionary, Third Edition*, W.W. Norton & Company, Inc., New York (2009), 891.
5. "Runs Batted In" was not an officially-recorded statistic when Zimmerman accomplished his Triple Crown achievement. RBIs became an official stat in 1920. From 1907 through 1919, RBIs were tracked unofficially by Ernie Lanigan, his RBI numbers having been reported annually in various publications, such as *The Sporting News*, *Baseball Magazine*, and *Sporting Life*.
6. Hy Turkin and S.C. Thompson, *The Official Encyclopedia of Baseball*, A.S. Barnes and Company, New York (1951). While no specific list of Triple Crown winners is given, the "League Leaders" section shows that for 1912 Heinie Zimmerman led the National League in batting (.372), home runs (14), and runs batted in (106). Each of Zimmerman's league-leading Triple Crown numbers was repeated in each subsequent edition through the final edition in 1979. The "106" RBIs shown for Zimmerman does not agree with the "98" RBIs first reported in *The Sporting News* (note 2) and subsequently given in notes 7 and 8. I should add that I have not been able to find out the original source of the "106" RBIs; I have also not seen the "106" RBIs mentioned anywhere besides *The Official Encyclopedia of Baseball*.
7. Leonard Gettelson, *One For The Book*, The Sporting News (Charles C. Spink & Son), St. Louis (1956), 78. The title of the book was changed to *Baseball Record Book* in 1972, to *Official Baseball Record Book* in 1973, and to *The Complete Baseball Record Book* in 1990. Zimmerman is included in the list of Triple Crown winners in each edition through 2004; Zimmerman was not included in the list of Triple Crown winners in the final four editions, 2005–08.
8. Seymour Siwoff, *The Little Red Book of Major League Baseball*, Al Munro Elias Baseball Bureau, Inc., New York (1957), 19. The title of the book was changed to *The Book of Baseball Records* in 1972, in which the list of Triple Crown winners was discontinued and in which only official RBI stats (i.e., those from 1920 forward) were included.
9. The list of "Triple Crown Winners: Batting" given on MLB.com can be accessed as follows: (a) in the "Search" field, type "Triple Crown Winners" and click enter; (b) click on the second link—"Rare Feats | MLB.com: History…Triple Crown Winners: Batting."
10. Seymour Siwoff, *The Elias Book of Baseball Records*, Elias Sports Bureau, New York (2014), 378, 379, 382, 383, 394, 395.
11. David S. Neft (Director of Research, Information Concepts Incorporated), Lee Allen (Historian, National Baseball Hall of Fame and Museum), and Robert Markel (Executive Editor, Macmillan Company), *The Baseball Encyclopedia*, Macmillan, New York (1969).
12. John Thorn, Phil Birnbaum, Bill Deane, *Total Baseball*, Sport Media Publishing, New York, Eighth Edition (2004).
13. Gary Gillette, Pete Palmer, *The ESPN Baseball Encyclopedia*, Sterling Publishing, New York, Fifth Edition (2008).
14. Baseball-Reference.com—accessed on January 12, 2015.

15. Neft, *The Baseball Encyclopedia*.
16. Herm Krabbenhoft, "RBI records 1891–1919," email to Pete Palmer (March 18, 2014 at 1:48 pm) in which I wrote, "Subsequent to *Big-Mac*, you used Neft's RBI numbers—exclusively (i.e., none of Lanigan's RBI numbers)—in your baseball statistics data base. Subsequently, your baseball statistics data base has been used in your BB Encyclopedias (*Total Baseball* with John Thorn and *The ESPN BB Encyclopedia* with Gary Gillette) as well as some/all Internet sites presenting RBI stats—e.g., Baseball-Reference. So, all of the 1891–1919 RBI numbers out there now are from your baseball statistics database and ultimately from Neft's RBI numbers in the first *Big-Mac*." On March 18, 2014 at 5:42 pm, Palmer replied to me via email, "I have no argument with anything you said." In a subsequent email to me (January 9, 2015) Palmer wrote that MLB.com obtained his data base of baseball statistics "probably in 2001 or so" and that "MLB has not done much with the data besides adding in current years." Along that line, in an email (July 16, 2012) to me from John Thorn (the Official Historian of Major League Baseball) about Hank Greenberg's 1935 RBI stats, John wrote: "Herm I have no sway with the mlb.com data. It is Pete Palmer's old *Total Baseball* database, with some tinkering by unknown hands."
17. Herm Krabbenhoft, "RBIs before 1920," retrolist@yahoo.com, post submitted March 29, 2014 at 12:57ᴘᴍ, with courtesy copies to John Thorn and David S. Neft. Here is one of the key items I expressed: "David S. Neft was the third person to compile RBI stats for the seasons before 1920. According to the presentation given in *The Numbers Game* by Alan Schwarz, Neft recruited people (many of them being college students) to go through game accounts in microfilmed newspapers and generate DBD RBI numbers for those players who played from 1891 through 1919. The result of Neft's research project was the first edition of *Big-Mac*—which utilized Tattersall's RBI numbers for the 1876–1890 seasons, Neft's RBI numbers for the 1891–1919 seasons, and the official DBD RBI numbers for the 1920–68 seasons. Neft's RBI numbers for the 1891–1919 seasons—as well as Tattersall's RBI numbers for the 1876–90 seasons—were subsequently incorporated by Pete Palmer into his data base of baseball statistics. Palmer's data base of baseball statistics—including Neft's RBI numbers for the 1891–1919 seasons and Tattersall's RBI numbers for the 1876–1890 seasons—has been utilized extensively in both printed encyclopedias (e.g., *Total Baseball* and *The ESPN Baseball Encyclopedia*) and on Internet websites (e.g., Baseball-Reference.com and MLB.com). It is important to point out that Neft's RBI numbers for the players from the 1891–1904 seasons are supported by DBD records ('ICI sheets') which are available on microfilm at the Baseball Hall of Fame Library. Regrettably, Neft's DBD RBI records for the players from the 1905–1919 seasons are no longer available." On March 29, 2014 at 1:09ᴘᴍ, Thorn responded via an email to me, "Fine summation, Herm. I have no quibbles with any of it." On March 29, 2014 at 4:37ᴘᴍ, Neft replied via an email to me, "Thanks for sending this to me. As far as I know this is an accurate statement of the history of this research."
18. "Hitting in a Pinch," *The Sporting News*, January 2, 1913, 5.
19. Neft, *The Baseball Encyclopedia*.
20. In a telephone conversation with Mr. Neft on June 25, 1913, I asked him about there not being any game-by-game RBI data for the 1905–1919 seasons. Mr. Neft told me that the intention was to donate the original 1905–1919 files to the Baseball Hall of Fame, as had been done with the 1891–1904 files. In the meantime, however, the 1905–1919 files were stored in a warehouse, which had a fire and apparently all of the 1905–1919 files were destroyed. I also asked Mr. Neft if there were any back-up files or printouts for the 1905–1919 files. He said that he was not aware of any. I then asked, "So, does that mean there are no data available to support your RBI numbers for the 1905–1919 seasons?" Mr. Neft answered, "That appears to be so."
21. Krabbenhoft, "Accurate RBI Records for the Players of the Deadball Era: Part 1—The Players on the 1906 Detroit Tigers," *The Inside Game*, Volume XIV, Number 1 (February 2014), 1.
22. Herm Krabbenhoft, "Accurate RBI Records for the Players of the Deadball Era: Part 2—The Players on the 1906 Detroit Tigers," *The Inside Game*, Volume XIV, Number 3 (June 2014), 4.
23. Herm Krabbenhoft, "Accurate RBI Numbers for the Players of the Deadball Era: Part 3—The Players on the 1919 Detroit Tigers," *The Inside Game*, Volume XIV, Number 4 (September 2014), 11.
24. Herm Krabbenhoft, "Accurate RBI Records for the Players of the Deadball Era: Part 4—The Players on the 1912 Braves, Cubs, Giants, and Pirates," *The Inside Game*, Volume XV, Number 1 (February 2015), 5.
25. Herm Krabbenhoft, "The Definitive Resolution of the 1912 NL Triple Crown Discrepancy," Research Presentation given at the annual Society for American Baseball Research Convention, Houston, TX, August 2, 2014.
26. Krabbenhoft, *The Inside Game*, Volume XV, Number 1. The Appendices to this article (available as a "Supplement" on SABR.org in the Deadball Era Committee Newsletters) provide (a) complete details for each run scored by each team: the identity of the player who scored the run, the run-scoring event, and the identity of the player who completed his plate appearance during the run-scoring event; (b) a game-by-game log of each run scored and each run batted in by each player on each team; (c) the text descriptions from multiple independent newspaper accounts for each run-scoring event in which a fielding error was involved for each of the top-six RBI accumulators.
27. For the text descriptions given in the various newspaper accounts for each of the 756 runs scored by the Chicago Cubs in 1912, see: Herm Krabbenhoft, "Accurate Runs-Scored Statistics for the Players on the 1912 Chicago Cubs," *The Inside Game*, Volume XIV, Number 6 (December 2014), 1.
28. Krabbenhoft, *The Inside Game*, Volume XV, Number 1. Krabbenhoft, *The Inside Game*, Volume XIV, Number 6.
29. Krabbenhoft, *The Inside Game*, Volume XIV, Number 1–4, Volume XV, Number 1. Herm Krabbenhoft, "Consecutive Games RUN Batted In (CGRUNBI) Streaks for Players on the Detroit Tigers—1914–1919," Research Presentation given at the annual Retrosheet Meeting, Houston, TX, July 31, 2014.
30. Herm Krabbenhoft, "Accurate RBI Numbers for the Players on the 1895 Philadelphia Phillies," Research Presentation given at the annual SABR Baseball Records Committee Meeting, Houston, TX, August 2, 2014.
31. Herm Krabbenhoft, email to Pete Palmer, November 2, 2014.
32. Pete Palmer, email to Herm Krabbenhoft, November 8, 2014.
33. Retrosheet's semi-annual release on December 14, 2014, includes the runs-batted-in information from Pete Palmer's updated data base of baseball statistics—which are in 100% agreement with my RBI numbers for all of the players on the 1912 Braves, Cubs, Giants, and Pirates.
34. Baseball-Reference.com, accessed on February 22, 2015.
35. The final draft of this manuscript was provided to Cory Schwartz (Vice President of MLB.com with the responsibility for the statistics presented on MLB.com).
36. As these conclusions are incorporated across baseball, biographical articles on Heinie Zimmerman will need to be updated as well. For example, the SABR BioProject entry on Zimmerman read as of February 22, 2015, "It was believed at the time that Zimmerman also paced the circuit with 103 RBIs, which would have made him the National League's first Triple Crown winner since…1894. Research conducted a half-century later, however, determined that his actual RBI total was only 99, ranking third behind Honus Wagner (102) and Bill Sweeney (100)."

Association Between Pelvic Motion and Hand Velocity in College-Aged Baseball Pitchers

A Preliminary Study

William T. Horlbeck, Talin Louder, Eadric Bressel

Baseball pitching is an intricate athletic skill requiring a complex and systematic activation of body segments to create maximal velocity at the distal aspect of the throwing arm.[1] The pitching motion can be divided into six phases: (a) wind-up, (b) stride, (c) arm cocking, (d) acceleration, (e) deceleration and (f) follow-through.[2] These phases are performed sequentially, and result in mechanical energy transfer through the segments of the kinetic chain, from the lower extremity to the throwing arm.[3,4,5]

Proper mechanics are crucial for injury prevention and facilitate consistent, successful pitching performance. Previous research suggests that erratic throwing mechanics decrease pitching performance and increase the likelihood of injury.[6] Studies that have investigated the pelvic region typically focus on mechanics during the later stages of the pitching sequence.[7,8,9,10]

Chaudhari et al. investigated the relationship between pelvic motion in the sagittal plane (Fig. 1) during transition from two-foot to single-foot stance and pitcher's total innings pitched, batting average against, strikeouts per inning, walks per inning, walks plus hits per innings pitched, and days missed due to injury.[11,12] These researchers observed that pitchers who exhibited less pelvic motion in the sagittal plane performed better through the course of a season and missed less time due to injury, indicating that pelvic mechanics are crucial to overall performance.[13,14] Moreover, a key benefit to the pelvic motion assessment utilized by Chaudhari et al. is the practicality of its implication as a field test to be utilized by coaches who aim to continuously improve pitcher longevity and throwing performance.[15,16] While Chaudhari et al. observed an association between pelvic motion in the sagittal plane and performance over the length of a season, the effect of pelvic motion on the pitch itself has not been addressed.[17,18] Additionally, while anterior-posterior (AP, Fig. 1) tilt is important, it is only one component of total hip motion. Therefore, the purpose of this study was to investigate the association between a field test assessment of biplanar pelvic motion (AP and medial-lateral (ML, Fig. 1) and hand velocity during the execution of a maximum effort fastball pitch.

METHODS

Participants

Nine National Club Baseball Association pitchers from a university club baseball team served as participants (Age: 21.33 ± 2.45 yrs; Height: 1.84 ± 0.04 m; Mass: 86.13 ± 18.05 kg; Arm Length: 59.75 ± 3.01). Pitchers were free from recent injury and had at least five years of competitive pitching experience.

Figure 1. Directional terminology

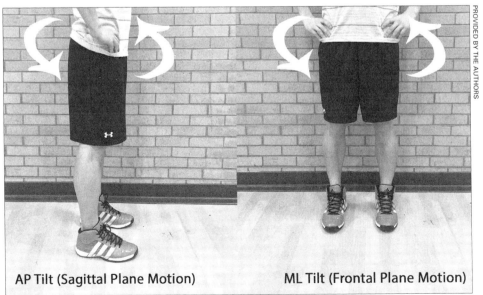

AP Tilt (Sagittal Plane Motion)   ML Tilt (Frontal Plane Motion)

PROVIDED BY THE AUTHORS

Data Collection and Analyses

A custom-built pitching mound was constructed to meet National Collegiate Athletic Association (NCAA) baseball regulations. From the mound, pitches were thrown into a net from a distance of 18.4 m. A rectangular target (0.64 m high x 0.38 m wide), with a small square in the middle, was secured onto the net.

Three-dimensional kinematic data were captured using a motion analysis system (Vicon Systems, Centennial, Colorado). Seven Vicon T-20 cameras sampling at 300 Hz tracked retro-reflective markers placed directly on the skin in accordance with the full-body plug-in gait model provided by Vicon. Three-dimensional raw position data were processed using Vicon Nexus software (Vicon Systems, Centennial, Colorado). Gaps were interpolated and data were smoothed using Woltring's quintic spline routine.[19]

The order of the pelvic motion test and the hand velocity test was randomized. All participants performed both tests. Prior to testing, participants were allowed unrestricted time to warm up ($\sim$ 10–15 min) as they normally would before a practice or game.

Pelvic Motion Test. Participants performed a modified pelvic motion test where they transitioned from a two-foot to one-foot stance by lifting and holding their kicking leg approximately 10 cm above the ground (Fig. 2). Participants repeated this test five times. Using bilateral ASIS and PSIS markers, Nexus defined the pelvis segment with an axis of rotation located at the midpoint between the two ASIS markers. Three-dimensional angular positions were computed for the pelvis segment by Nexus and exported into Excel. For each trial, AP and ML ranges were computed in Excel by taking the difference between the maximum and minimum values for angular position.

Pitching Hand Velocity Test. In addition to the warm-up, the participants performed 5 to 10 submaximal pitches to become comfortable pitching with reflective markers attached to their bodies. Once comfortable, pitchers were instructed to throw fastball pitches as fast and as accurate as possible from the wind-up position. They were asked to aim for a small square suspended in the middle of the target box. Participants repeated the pitching test for a total of 5 pitches. A 30–60 second rest was allowed between pitches. Three-dimensional position data for the throwing hand (third metacarpal) were differentiated with respect to time in Nexus, resulting in three-dimensional linear velocities. The three-dimensional velocity data were then exported into Excel and composed into a single, resultant vector for each time point using the Pythagorean Theorem. The maximum value for resultant velocity was selected and normalized to body weight (N) and arm length (cm).

Statistical Analyses

For each participant, five successful pitching trials and five pelvic motion trials were used to compute mean peak pitch velocity and mean pelvic tilt in the frontal and sagittal planes. Prior to statistical analysis, distribution of the data set was assessed using the Shapiro-Wilk test for normality. The Shapiro-Wilk test on mean hand velocity and mean pelvic tilt (AP/ML) revealed no significant deviation from normality. Empirical correlation coefficients (θ_o) between peak pitch velocity and pelvic tilt (AP/ML) were then computed using the Pearson's r method. The data sets (AP/Hand Velocity, ML/Hand Velocity) were then resampled using the Jackknife procedure in which single data pairs were excluded sequentially resulting in n estimates for Pearson's r.[20] The mean of resampled correlation coefficients served as an estimate of the true sample correlation ($\hat{\theta}$).[21] The distributions of Pearson's r estimates obtained from resampling were assessed using the Shapiro-Wilk test for normality. The Shapiro-Wilk test on the Pearson's r estimates revealed

Figure 2. Participant performing the Pelvic Motion Test

no significant deviation from normality. Variances of the Pearson's r estimates were then estimated using Equation 1.[22]

$$Var(\hat{\theta}) = \frac{1}{n-1} \sum_{i=1}^{n} (\hat{\theta}_{-i} - \theta_o)^2$$

Estimated 95 percent confidence intervals for the association between hand velocity and pelvic tilt (AP and ML) were then computed using Equation 2.[23]

$$\hat{\theta} \pm 1.96 \sqrt{Var(\hat{\theta})}$$

Reliability

Coefficients of variation ($C_v = 100 \cdot$ standard deviation/mean) on the sample and inter-trial variability of each participant were computed for hand velocity and both pelvic motion variables.

RESULTS

Mean hand velocity was 8.99 ± 2.27 m s^{-1} N^{-1} cm^{-1} ($C_v = 25\%$),

Mean AP tilt was $4.99 \pm 2.56°$ ($C_v = 51\%$), and

Mean ML tilt was $8.27 \pm 1.79°$ ($C_v = 22\%$).

Coefficients of variation assessing inter-trial variability ranged from 1% to 4% for hand velocity, 16% to 70% for AP tilt, and 3% to 38% for ML tilt.

Table 1. Results of jackknife estimation of Pearson's r between pelvic motion (AP / ML) and hand velocity (HV).

Jackknife Estimation	AP/HV	ML/HV
Empirical Pearson's r (θ_o)	-0.553	0.421
Estimated Pearson's r ($\hat{\theta}$)	-0.555	0.423
Bias	0.002	0.002

Results of the Jackknife estimation of correlation coefficients are presented in Table 1. Based on the estimated 95 percent confidence intervals, we observed a negative correlation between anterior-posterior pelvic tilt and hand velocity (Figure 3) and a positive correlation between ML pelvic tilt and hand velocity (Figure 3).

DISCUSSION

We observed a median AP tilt of 7.89°, while Chaudhari et al. reported a median tilt of 7°.[24] This is quite similar given the magnitude of movement variability in the pelvic region and the subtle modifications to the pelvic motion test used in the present study. In general, our results support the assertion that the pelvic region is a crucial component of the kinetic chain as evidenced by the plane-specific relationships reported in Figure 3.

Figure 3. Ninety-five percent Confidence intervals estimating the correlation co-efficient (Pearson's r) between hand velocity and pelvic motion in the AP: anterior-posterior (-0.42 < r < -0.69) and ML: medial-lateral (0.18 < r < 0.66) directions

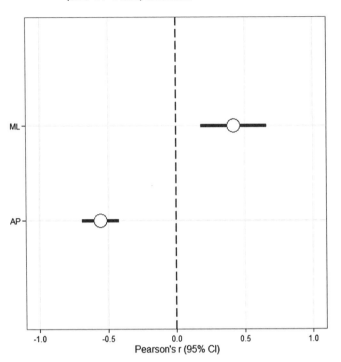

Optimizing control and position of the pelvis may contribute to pitching performance and longevity as evidenced by a significant increase in total innings pitched, a significant decrease in time missed due to injury, walks plus hits per innings pitched, as well as improvements in opponents' batting average, strikeouts per inning, and walks per inning.[25,26] Results of this study support this view and, although our predicted confidence intervals are descriptive and should be considered preliminary, they suggest a positive correlation exists between ML tilt and hand velocity, and the opposite for AP tilt.

CONCLUSION

While preliminary, this study does provide evidence that the pelvis plays an important role in pitching mechanics and performance. The pelvic motion assessment utilized in the present study is a practical field test accessible to coaches aiming to improve upon the longevity and performance of the pitching staff. Also, pitchers and coaches could implement directed practice focusing on pelvic position and motion by providing feedback regarding pelvic position, practicing in front of a mirror, or utilizing video recordings of pelvic motion. ■

References

Chaudhari, Ajit MW, Christopher S. McKenzie, James R. Borchers, and Thomas M. Best. "Lumbopelvic Control and Pitching Performance of Professional Baseball Pitchers." *The Journal of Strength & Conditioning Research* 25, no. 8 (2011): 2127–32.

Chaudhari, Ajit MW, Christopher S. McKenzie, Xueliang Pan, and James A. Oñate. "Lumbopelvic Control and Days Missed Because of Injury in Professional Baseball Pitchers." *The American Journal of Sports Medicine* (2014): 0363546514545861.

Fleisig, Glenn S., *The Biomechanics of Baseball Pitching* (Unpublished doctoral dissertation). University of Alabama at Birmingham, Birmingham, AL (1994).

Fleisig, Glenn S., James R. Andrews, Charles J. Dillman, and Rafael F. Escamilla. "Kinetics of Baseball Pitching with Implications about Injury Mechanisms." *The American Journal of Sports Medicine* 23, no. 2 (1995): 233–39.

Fleisig, Glenn S., Steve W. Barrentine, Nigel Zheng, Rafael F. Escamilla, and James R. Andrews. "Kinematic and Kinetic Comparison of Baseball Pitching Among Various Levels of Development." *Journal of Biomechanics* 32, no. 12 (1999): 1371–75.

Seroyer, Shane T., Shane J. Nho, Bernard R. Bach, Charles A. Bush-Joseph, Gregory P. Nicholson, and Anthony A. Romeo. "The Kinetic Chain in Overhand Pitching: Its Potential Role for Performance Enhancement and Injury Prevention." *Sports Health: A Multidisciplinary Approach* 2, no. 2 (2010): 135–46.

Stodden, David F., Glenn S. Fleisig, Scott P. McLean, and James R. Andrews. "Relationship of Biomechanical Factors to Baseball Pitching Velocity: Within Pitcher Variation." *J Appl Biomech* 21, no. 1 (2005): 44-56.

Stodden, David F., Glenn S. Fleisig, Scott P. McLean, Stephen L. Lyman, and James R. Andrews. "Relationship of Pelvis and Upper Torso Kinematics to Pitched Baseball Velocity." *Journal of Applied Biomechanics* 17, no. 2 (2001): 164–72.

Wight, Jeff, James Richards, and Susan Hall. "Baseball: Influence of Pelvis Rotation Styles on Baseball Pitching Mechanics." *Sports Biomechanics* 3, no. 1 (2004): 67–84.

Wilk, Kevin E., Keith Meister, Glenn Fleisig, and James R. Andrews. "Biomechanics of the Overhead Throwing Motion." *Sports Medicine and Arthroscopy Review* 8, no. 2 (2000): 124–34.

Woltring, Herman J. "A FORTRAN Package for Generalized, Cross-Validatory Spline Smoothing and Differentiation." *Advances in Engineering Software* (1978) 8, no. 2 (1986): 104–13.

Zhou, Xiao-Hua, Nancy A. Obuchowski, and Donna K. McClish. *Statistical Methods in Diagnostic Medicine*. Vol. 712. John Wiley & Sons, 2011.

NOTES

1. Kevin Wilk, "Biomechanics of the overhead throwing motion." *Sports Medicine and Arthroscopy Review 8*, no. 2 (2000): 124–34.

2. Glenn Fleisig. "Kinetics of baseball pitching with implications about injury mechanisms." *The American Journal of Sports Medicine* 23, no. 2 (1995): 233–39.

3. Ajit Chaudhari. "Lumbopelvic control and pitching performance of professional baseball pitchers." *The Journal of Strength & Conditioning Research 25*, no. 8 (2011): 2127–32.

4. Ajit Chaudhari. "Lumbopelvic control and days missed because of injury in professional baseball pitchers." *The American Journal of Sports Medicine* (2014): 2734–40.

5. Shane Seroyer. "The kinetic chain in overhand pitching: its potential role for performance enhancement and injury prevention." *Sports Health: A Multidisciplinary Approach 2*, no. 2 (2010): 135–46.

6. Glenn Fleisig. "Kinematic and kinetic comparison of baseball pitching among various levels of development." *Journal of Biomechanics 32*, no. 12 (1999): 1371–5.

7. Glenn Fleisig. The biomechanics of baseball pitching (Unpublished doctoral dissertation). University of Alabama at Birmingham, Birmingham, AL (1994).

8. David Stodden. "Relationship of pelvis and upper torso kinematics to pitched baseball velocity." *Journal of Applied Biomechanics 17*, no. 2 (2001): 164–72.

9. David Stodden. "Relationship of biomechanical factors to baseball pitching velocity: within pitcher variation." *Journal of Applied Biomechanics 21*, no. 1 (2005): 44–56.

10. Jeff Wight. "Baseball: Influence of pelvis rotation styles on baseball pitching mechanics." *Sports Biomechanics 3*, no. 1 (2004): 67–84.

11. Chaudhari. "Lumbopelvic control and pitching performance of professional baseball pitchers." 2127–32.

12. Chaudhari. "Lumbopelvic control and days missed because of injury in professional baseball pitchers." 2734–40.

13. Chaudhari. "Lumbopelvic control and pitching performance of professional baseball pitchers." 2127–32.

14. Chaudhari. "Lumbopelvic control and days missed because of injury in professional baseball pitchers." 2734–40.

15. Chaudhari. "Lumbopelvic control and pitching performance of professional baseball pitchers." 2127–32.

16. Chaudhari. "Lumbopelvic control and days missed because of injury in professional baseball pitchers." 2734–40.

17. Chaudhari. "Lumbopelvic control and pitching performance of professional baseball pitchers." 2127–32.

18. Chaudhari. "Lumbopelvic control and days missed because of injury in professional baseball pitchers." 2734–40.

19. Herman Woltring. "A FORTRAN package for generalized, cross-validatory spline smoothing and differentiation." *Advances in Engineering Software* (1978) 8, no. 2 (1986): 104–13.

20. Xiao-Hua Zhou. *Statistical Methods in Diagnostic Medicine*. Vol. 712. John Wiley & Sons, 2011.

21. Ibid.

22. Ibid.

23. Ibid.

24. Chaudhari. "Lumbopelvic control and pitching performance of professional baseball pitchers." 2127–32.

25. Ibid.

26. Chaudhari. "Lumbopelvic control and days missed because of injury in professional baseball pitchers." 2734–40.

Join SABR today!

If you're interested in baseball — writing about it, reading about it, talking about it — there's a place for you in the Society for American Baseball Research.

SABR was formed in 1971 in Cooperstown, New York, with the mission of fostering the research and dissemination of the history and record of the game. Our members include everyone from academics to professional sportswriters to amateur historians and statisticians to students and casual fans who merely enjoy reading about baseball history and occasionally gathering with other members to talk baseball.

SABR members have a variety of interests, and this is reflected in the diversity of its research committees. There are more than two dozen groups devoted to the study of a specific area related to the game — from Baseball and the Arts to Statistical Analysis to the Deadball Era to Women in Baseball. In addition, many SABR members meet formally and informally in regional chapters throughout the year and hundreds come together for the annual national convention, the organization's premier event. These meetings often include panel discussions with former major league players and research presentations by members. Most of all, SABR members love talking baseball with like-minded friends. What unites them all is an interest in the game and joy in learning more about it.

Why join SABR? Here are some benefits of membership:

♦ Two issues (spring and fall) of the *Baseball Research Journal*, which includes articles on history, biography, statistics, personalities, book reviews, and other aspects of the game.
♦ One expanded e-book edition of *The National Pastime*, which focuses on baseball in the region where that year's SABR national convention is held (in 2015, it's Chicago)
♦ 8-10 new and classic e-books published each year by the SABR Digital Library, which are all free for members to download
♦ *This Week in SABR* newsletter in your e-mail every Friday, which highlights SABR members' research and latest news
♦ Regional chapter meetings, which can include guest speakers, presentations and trips to ballgames
♦ Online access to back issues of *The Sporting News* and other periodicals through Paper of Record
♦ Access to SABR's lending library and other research resources
♦ Online member directory to connect you with an international network of SABR baseball experts and fans
♦ Discounts on registration for our annual events, including SABR Analytics Conference & Jerry Malloy Negro League Conference
♦ Access to SABR-L, an e-mail discussion list of baseball questions & answers that many feel is worth the cost of membership itself
♦ The opportunity to be part of a passionate international community of baseball fans

SABR membership is on a "rolling" calendar system; that means your membership lasts 365 days no matter when you sign up!
Enjoy all the benefits of SABR membership by signing up today at SABR.org/join or by clipping out the form below and mailing it to SABR, 4455 E. Camelback Rd., Ste. D-140, Phoenix, AZ 85018.

- - - ✂ -

SABR MEMBERSHIP RENEWAL FORM

	Annual	3-year	Senior	3-yr Sr.	Under 30
U.S.:	❑ $65	❑ $175	❑ $45	❑ $129	❑ $45
Canada/Mexico:	❑ $75	❑ $205	❑ $55	❑ $159	❑ $55
Overseas:	❑ $84	❑ $232	❑ $64	❑ $186	❑ $55

Add a Family Member: $15 for each family member at same address (list on back)
Senior: 65 or older before 12/31/2015

All dues amounts in U.S. dollars or equivalent

Participate in Our Donor Program!
I'd like to designate my gift to be used toward:
❑General Fund ❑Endowment Fund ❑Research Resources ❑_____
❑ I want to maximize the impact of my gift; do not send any donor premiums
❑ I would like this gift to remain anonymous.

Note: Any donation not designated will be placed in the General Fund.
SABR is a 501 (c) (3) not-for-profit organization & donations are tax-deductible to the extent allowed by law.

Name _____

Address _____

City _____ ST_____ ZIP_____

Phone _____ Birthday _____

E-mail: _____
(Your e-mail address on file ensures you will receive the most recent SABR news.)

Dues $_____

Donation $_____

Amount Enclosed $_____

Do you work for a matching grant corporation? Call (602) 343-6455 for details.

If you wish to pay by credit card, please contact the SABR office at (602) 343-6455 or visit the SABR Store online at SABR.org/join. We accept Visa, Mastercard & Discover.

Do you wish to receive the *Baseball Research Journal* electronically?: ❑ Yes   ❑ No
Our e-books are available in PDF, Kindle, or EPUB (iBooks, iPad, Nook) formats.

Mail to: SABR, 4455 E. Camelback Rd., Ste. D-140, Phoenix, AZ 85018

10/14

Pros vs. Cons

Federal Leaguers versus Federal Prisoners at Leavenworth

Bob Rives and Tim Rives

In one way, everyone on the diamond was a prisoner. The nine Leavenworth federal prison convicts were obvious; those wearing the blue and gray road uniforms of the Kansas City Packers only slightly less so. The Packers were members of the Federal League, a 1914–15 major league peopled by players trying to escape from their own "prison"—organized baseball's reserve clause which bound players to teams throughout their careers. It was part baseball, part labor action.

On an 89-degree September 13, 1915, the Packers became the first major league team to play a squad of convicts inside a prison.[1] It also was near the end of the team's and league's existence. Bankrupt and unable to win its lawsuit against the National and American Leagues that would have ensured parity, the Federal League would fold after the season as would its Kansas City franchise, also bankrupt.

The prison team, called the White Sox, would be more stable. It was an all star team of white players that would last until 1933 when the prison integrated the institution's ball clubs.[2]

The prisoners were ready for the game against the professionals. All 1,500 inmates were in the stands except for eight who were in solitary confinement.

Possibly among the solitaries was Robert Stroud, later well known as the Birdman of Alcatraz. Stroud spent most of his prison life locked up in solitary, although the record is silent on the date of the game. Also present at the ballpark that day was the Reverend A. J. Soldan, a Lutheran minister and prison chaplain, whose duties included oversight of the baseball program. Probably there was Dr. Walter Cronkite Sr., prison dentist and future father of the legendary CBS newscaster.[3]

The crowd seemed awe-struck as they watched the Packers enter the prison's sally port. The *New Era*, the prison newspaper, noted:

> As the giant Packers rolled in through the Sally-port gate, they sure did look formidable. Each man was about the size of two of ours with arms and legs like centipedes. It was a question of whether they'd come to make a barbeque of the White Sox or trim 'em on the diamond.[4]

Even Warden Thomas W. Morgan had little faith in his charges' fortunes when he saw the size of the professionals. As convict umpire Bert Felt passed the warden's box before the game, Morgan said to him, "Felt, it looks like it's up to you."[5]

The view from center field of the prison's ballpark. Leavenworth's famous Big Top dome is visible in the background.

U.S.P LEAVENWORTH, KANSAS. BALL PARK.

Bert may have had some experience in affecting outcomes. When he was president of the Nebraska State League, he had been accused of fixing games and inflating players' batting averages. But those weren't the reasons he was in Leavenworth. Money disappearing while he was president of a bank in Superior, Nebraska, had forced him to take his baseball role to Kansas.[6]

Felt became umpire that day when two Federal League officials did not appear. Two days after the game, The *New Era* said they refused to enter the prison. But on October 1 the newspaper apologized, saying the umpires, Fred Westervelt and William Finneran, had wanted to attend but had not been invited. "They tried to make the train that brought the Packers over and would have been here as spectators if not as umpires had they not been too late. Both umpires wish the statement that they declined to come corrected in The *New Era* which is most cheerfully done," the paper reported.[7]

Actually the size of the Packers was relative, even small by today's standards. Of the 15 "formidable" men who performed that day for Kansas City, only one was taller than six feet and none weighed as much as 200 pounds. The 15 averaged a bit over 5'8" and 175 pounds. By contrast, the shortest 21st century major leaguers are about 5' 8".[8]

Typical of the prisoners' size, though, was that of Irish O'Malley, a career convict, who pinch hit that day and in later seasons was the White Sox' regular catcher. O'Malley was just 5'6" and weighed only 130 pounds. William Basore, the prisoners' pitcher, was more nearly Packer-sized at 5'8" and 150 pounds.[9]

Basore was probably living out the dream of every American boy, pitching to a major league baseball team. Unfortunately, his parents and friends back in

BAIN COLLECTION, LIBRARY OF CONGRESS

Team manager George "Firebrand" Stovall told the Leavenworth Times his team had a "fine experience. I'm in favor of making this an annual event."

Neodesha, Kansas, were not on the invitation list. Some 300 local residents along with the major league players' wives were allowed to watch—although the women were kept outside and could see only through a gate. Most women had been banned from inside since a near riot two summers earlier when a woman entered the prison wearing a slit skirt.[10]

The Kansas City delegates had arrived at the prison in a special rail car arranged by Phillip J. McCarthy, a Kansas City businessman who also had arranged the game. Known as the city's "chief goodfellow" to some, McCarthy supported prison charities and getting the Packers together with the White Sox resulted from his efforts.[11]

Convicts at Leavenworth were there for every conceivable crime including serial killings. But pitcher Basore's was literally a nut case. A 22-year-old barber who apparently decided he needed more cash flow, Basore began placing ads like this one from the Omaha, Nebraska, *World-Herald*:

PARCEL POST

For Sale—Pecans, by parcel post, prepaid, anywhere; fresh, fine, eighteen pound sack $1 currency.

– Charles Wagner, Kansas City, Kansas, Armour Station

From Omaha, Basore received an order from the Mercantile Protective Bureau, provider of "law and collections, Our Past Record is our Future Guarantee." He also heard from Dresher the Tailor in Omaha, a dairy farmer at Parsons, Kansas, and Charles O. Follett at Petrolia, Kansas, among others. Unfortunately, the promised pecans were never delivered and that led Francis M. Brady, assistant U.S. attorney, to haul Basore into Federal court. Charged with using the mails to defraud, he was sentenced to two years in Leavenworth.[12]

Once there he was a model prisoner. When his minister, the Reverend John Hopping of Elk Falls, Kansas, wrote the warden about Basore's conduct, the prison official replied, "He [Basore] has made an excellent record here and has been in no trouble of any kind since his arrival at the prison…. He is the pitcher for one of our best baseball teams."[13]

Basore was a sandlot product, but with promise. In his lone season pitching in prison, he won 7 games, lost 2, and tied 1. In the season's opener against a Catholic high school team, he struck out 18, including a clean-up hitter named Christ.[14]

Shortly after pitching against the Packers, Basore went to a regularly scheduled parole hearing, made a strong case and was released after having served less than half his two-year sentence. Once free, he moved to Missouri, continued his career as a barber and operated a small resort.[15]

While the professionals were facing a sandlot pitcher, the toughness of the audience may have caused concern. Prison baseball was rough. "Do you think it is fair for a man in the bleachers to punch a third baseman in the ribs when he is trying to catch a fly?" asked the sports editor of The *New Era* after another game. Another Leavenworth prison team found itself on the wrong side of prison "fair play." It forfeited a game to the Kansas State Penitentiary nine rather than keep looking into the sharp flashes of light reflected from Kansas prison mirrors during the game.[16]

On that fateful mid-September day of 1915, though, it took little time for the Packers to show which team was made up of professionals and which of convicts. Kansas City second baseman Pep Goodwin led off by bunting safely. Art Krueger followed with a double. And when inning number one had ended, the Packers had scored four runs, two more than they would need all day, as it turned out.[17]

Newspaper coverage was widespread in the region. What the prison paper called "the crack sportswriters" from Kansas City and Leavenworth accompanied the Packers for the face off.

The *Kansas City Star* writer used an all-star lineup of prison clichés in his story. "Their Lone Run a Theft," the headline said of the White Sox' tally. "Stoves Invade Federal Prison and Within Committed all Known Crimes of Baseball—Krueger Drove One to Freedom—No. 9478 Stayed In," the sub-head noted. The *Star*'s box score used no prisoner's name, only numbers.[18]

The coverage was of a game that ended about as most had expected. The prisoners were no match for the professionals. Kansas City won 23–1 in 2 hours and 10 minutes, a game long for the time. "I guess we'll just have to accept that score as part of our punishment," one unnamed prisoner was quoted as saying.[19]

Amazingly, Basore pitched all nine innings, giving up 23 hits and 20 earned runs although he shut out the Federals in two innings. Packer George Perring was one of eight Kansas City players to have multiple hits, adding injury to insult by using a bat made from the scaffold at the old Ohio Penitentiary. Even under this uncanny attack, Basore's earned-run average was better than the only genuine Major League pitcher imprisoned at Leavenworth. Eul Eubanks, who had pitched in two games for the Chicago Cubs, and had an earned run average for his short major league career of 27.00. Eubanks would enter Leavenworth in

1933 for bootlegging, but was transferred to another penitentiary before he had a chance to play baseball for the prison team.[20]

Basore did field superbly, handling five chances including a pick-off and starting a double play, all without erring. "Basore pitched able, but unlucky ball," one sports page account said after the game.[21]

His teammates were less sure of hand, making seven errors and getting just four hits although two of them were doubles. The prisoners' only run came in the seventh inning. The Leavenworth shortstop singled and went to second when George "Chief" Johnson walked Basore. Johnson's wild pitch sent the convict runner to third. He then stole home while Drummond Brown was trying to throw Basore out at second.[22]

The run cost hundreds of prisoners their tobacco hordes. Tobacco was the currency of the prison's underground economy and most prisoners had bet their team would not score. Scores of sacks of Bull Durham furtively changed hands after the run came home.[23]

In that dead ball era (the leading home run hitter in the Federal League in 1915, Hal Chase, hit only 17 homers) only one was hit well enough to clear the prison's 40-foot walls. Art Krueger, the Packer left fielder, drove one of his four hits to freedom. "There was many a spectator who wished he could have been sitting on top of that pill when Art soaked it," the *Leavenworth Times*'s reporter wrote.[24]

Kansas City never let up. Stovall used five pitchers including Johnson with 17 wins and Nick Cullop with 22 and a 2.44 earned-run average. The team was bunting and stealing bases through the ninth inning.[25]

But not everything went the visitors' way. The prison team twice reeled off double plays. The right fielder played a line drive carom off the wall and threw out Packer Al Shaw at first base. At least three prisoners were cited by Packer manager George Stovall as good professional prospects—catcher Joe White, first baseman John Gilbert, and center fielder Clarence Gillis. Gilbert claimed professional experience in the International League before going to Leavenworth, but this was a cell house fiction.[26]

The inmates appeared to appreciate the Packers' take-no-prisoners approach to the game. The *New Era* said:

> One gratifying feature of the game was that the visitors showed no mercy at any time, starting off with four runs in the first inning, swatting all the balls that came their way and reaching out for any additional sparrows, crows or buzzards that happened to be motoring through the ozone or

nearby. When they rolled up seven in the seventh, a great groan shook the bleachers and all bets were off. It was no contest. No man in prison was so little sportsman as to collect wagers on that game.[27]

Even with the guards sitting among them unarmed, the prisoners behaved flawlessly. Deputy Warden A.J. Renoe called the crowd perfect and said he was well pleased with his charges' conduct. Packer manager George "Firebrand" Stovall told the *Leavenworth Times* his team had a "fine experience. I'm in favor of making this an annual event."[28]

But it was not to be. Even though the Packers were successful on the field—finishing fourth only five and a half games out of first—the league folded after the season. Its players for the most part returned to the other major leagues and high minors where they had performed before moving to the Federal League.

Stovall did take home a bouquet of flowers grown in prison flower beds. White Sox captain and catcher White presented them to him before the game, while Native American inmates gave a buttonhook to Packer pitcher Chief Johnson, a Nebraska Winnebago tribe member. Between innings, Stovall won prisoners' respect by chatting and telling them baseball stories. After the game he handed the ball to the groundskeeper, a 15-year convict identified only as "Number 84––", who quickly stuffed it into his pocket.[29]

At season's end, the news got better for the prisoners. The Packers had announced early that they would give their uniforms to the prison team. Several players contributed their gloves, shoes, catcher's gear, and other needed items. The *New Era* hailed the gifts in its October 1 edition:

Last Wednesday a shipment of ten pairs of shoes, mask, chest protector, shin guards, three finger mitts and catcher's gloves arrived from Jack Enzenroth, the Packers' famous catcher, and Manager Stovall of that team consigned to Joe White…. The goods were parceled out among the boys and all were delighted.[30]

A few days prior to the arrival White received the following letter from Enzenroth:

I am in receipt of your letter and present for which I thank you very much. You will receive shortly a box of shoes, gloves, etc., which we all hope you will be able to use, and our only regret is that we haven't more to send. Am sending to you so that you can first pick out what you want and distribute the remainder among your friends.[31]

While the Packers no doubt would have beaten any team the convicts put together, the prison did not send its best ball players against the professionals. The White Sox were the prison's white all-stars. Another team made up of black prisoners called the Booker T. Washingtons (Booker T's) regularly defeated the Sox in intramural play, winning 41 of the 59 games the two clubs played over the years. The Booker T's also twice won Kansas state independent semipro championships. In 1922 and 1924 they played the Kansas City Monarchs, losing but making the games competitive. In 1929 the African-American *Kansas City Call* described them as "one of the strongest colored baseball teams in the west."[32]

But there may have been a reason the prison didn't send the Bookers or an integrated team against the Packers. The *New Era*, shortly after the Jack Johnson-Jess Willard heavyweight boxing title fight in April 1915, editorialized:

The *New Era* suggests now this battle between two men of different races has been settled, all future fistic encounters of championship nature be between two men of their own color, thus eliminating the race feeling always attendant upon a white man and a colored man meeting in combat.[33]

In light of the riots across the county that followed the classic black vs. white boxing match, the prison administration may well have wanted to avoid any chance of a racially-inspired riot within Leavenworth walls. Coincidentally, Johnson would arrive at Leavenworth just a few years later to serve a year and a day for violation of the Mann Act. "Lil' Arthur" boxed and umpired baseball games during his time in Leavenworth, all without incident although his ring opponents were all African Americans.[34]

Baseball was important to the prison administration. When the sport was introduced in the prison system in the late nineteenth century, Leavenworth warden R. W. McClaughry summarized its place by saying, "Baseball takes the mind of the prisoner off his troubles, stimulates him to better efforts and…is one of the best diversions available."[35]

The sport had evolved at Leavenworth, perhaps owing its start to William ("Baseball") Wilson, a three-year big leaguer sent to prison for forging money orders. In 1910 he was allowed to receive the gift of a bat from an Omaha beer distributor. Using it during the occasional two-hour outdoor periods granted to prisoners who behaved, he likely boosted the game's start within the walls. While the sport may have lived on in the prison because of Wilson, he, unfortunately, did not. He died in a barroom fight a dozen years later in St. Paul, "the last chapter of his life…written with knives by his enemies" the *St. Paul* (Minnesota) *Dispatch* reported.[36]

Leavenworth was a logical place to begin games between a big league and prison league team. Perched on a bluff overlooking the Missouri River, the town of Leavenworth is the oldest city in Kansas. It and the surrounding Leavenworth County are to the corrections industry what Hollywood is to film and Silicon Valley to computers. No fewer than five prisons are located there, housing some 6,000 prisoners.

Best known—and the one where the game took place—is the United States Penitentiary-Leavenworth. Formidable looking with a capitol-like dome in the center called "the big top," it is surrounded by stone walls standing 40 feet high and extending 40 feet below ground level to discourage attempts at tunneling. Built with prison labor and opened in 1903, it holds 1,870, including 400 in a nearby minimum security camp.[37]

Four miles away is the United States Army's Disciplinary Barracks which opened in 1874 but moved into new buildings in 2002.[38] It houses up to 515 prisoners and serves as the military's maximum security prison. In 2010 a separate Joint Regional Correctional Facility for medium security offenders was opened nearby. Also at Leavenworth is a 460-bed facility operated by the Corrections Corporation of America for the U.S. Marshals Service.

In a suburb on the south side of Leavenworth stands the state of Kansas' Lansing Correctional Facility. Housing almost 2,500, it was opened in 1868 and for 20 years also was home for Oklahoma's offenders. The facility also housed female federal prisoners until a federal penitentiary was constructed in Alderson, West Virginia.[39]

With both the Packers and Monarchs a distant memory, there were further Leavenworth prison encounters with professional baseball. After World War II, the Leavenworth Braves of the Class C Western Association played pre-season exhibitions against the prisoners in 1946–48. The prisoners captured the final game, 9–6. Although box scores have not survived, the Braves roster that season included future star catcher and manager Del Crandall.[40]

COURTESY OF THE NATIONAL ARCHIVES AT KANSAS CITY. RECORD GROUP 129

Former Nebraska State League president Albert Felt umpired the contest between his fellow inmates and the Packers when Federal League umpires missed their train.

The Reverend A.J. Soldan left the prison in 1917. He spent much of his post-Leavenworth career in southern California where he served as minister of the Village Church in Westwood and as chaplain to the Los Angeles Police Department. Soldan was also on call to conduct funerals at the Westwood Memorial cemetery. As the baseball gods would have it, Soldan was called on August 8, 1962, to officiate at the funeral of Marilyn Monroe, a ceremony arranged by her former husband Joe DiMaggio, for one final unlikely brush with big league history.[41] ∎

Notes

1. Our claim that this was the first game played between a prison team and a major league team is based on a thorough search of online newspaper databases (*Proquest, Newspaper Archive, Chronicling America, The New York Times, Washington Post, Boston Globe, Chicago Tribune, Atlanta Constitution,* and *Los Angeles Times*), a discussion thread on SABR-L Archives, and research at the National Baseball Hall of Fame Archives and Manuscript Collection at Cooperstown in 2003. Harold Seymour and Dorothy Jane Mills note the Mutual Welfare League games at Sing Sing between inmates and the New York Yankees and New York Giants began in the 1920s. Harold Seymour, *Baseball: The People's Game* (New York: Oxford University Press, 1990), 414. We also consulted the Harold and Dorothy Seymour Papers, 1830–1998, Box 2, Folders 4–5, Division of Rare and Manuscript Collections, Carl A. Kroch Library, Cornell University.

2. Marc Okkonen, *The Federal League of 1914–1915* (The Society for American Baseball Research, 1989), 3; 24–5; The African American and white teams were occasionally combined for big games in the late 1920s. The merger became official in 1933 when the Great Depression reduced prison recreation budgets. "Baseball Ballyhoo," *New Era*, May–June, 1933, 8.

3. "Wind and Science," *New Era*, September 17, 1915, 4; Paul W. Keve, *Prisons and the American Conscience: A History of U.S. Federal Corrections* (Carbondale and Edwardsville: Southern Illinois University Press, 1991), 58; "Dentists Every Day," *New Era*, October 1, 1915, 4.

4. *New Era*, September 17, 1915, 4.

5. Ibid.

6. Bartholomew R. Burns, "Fielders' Choice: A Selected History of the Nebraska State League," Unpublished Honors Thesis, University of Nebraska, 1992, 33, 44; Andrea Faling, Nebraska State Historical Society,

email to Tim Rives, May 2, 2001; Albert Felt File; Inmate Case Files; United States Penitentiary-Leavenworth; Records of the Federal Bureau of Prisons, Record Group 129; National Archives at Kansas City. Additional Leavenworth files will be cited by inmate's name only.

7. "Prison Chatter," *New Era*, October 1, 1915, 3.
8. www.baseball-reference.com/teams/KCP/1915.shtml.
9. Irish O'Malley File; William Basore File.
10. Basore File; "Prison Chatter," *New Era*, May 7, 1915, 3; "Wind and Science," *New Era*, September 17, 1915, 4; "1,500 Convicts Attend Game," *The Leavenworth Post*, September 13, 1915, n.p.
11. "Prison Chatter," *New Era*, September 17, 1915, 4.
12. Basore File. *United States vs. William Basore*; Criminal Case Files; US District Court for the District of Kansas, First Division; Records of the US District Courts, Record Group 21; National Archives at Kansas City.
13. Basore File.
14. "Basore, Pitcher, an Enigma," *New Era*, May 7, 1915, 4.
15. Basore obituary, *Kansas City Star*, October 30, 1977, 16B.
16. "Clean Sportsmanship," *New Era*, June 27, 1919, 4.
17. "Wind and Science," *New Era*, September 17, 1915, 4.
18. "Their Lone Run A Theft," *Kansas City Star*, September 14, 1915, 8. William Basore was inmate 9478.
19. "Wind and Science," *New Era*, September 17, 1915, 4.
20. Eubanks File; "A Grewsome Bat," *New Era*, July 30, 1915, 4.
21. "Wind and Science," *New Era*, September 17, 1915, 4.
22. Ibid.; "Their Lone Run a Theft," *Kansas City Star*, September 14, 1915, 8.
23. "Wind and Science," *New Era*, September 17, 1915, 4.
24. "Their Lone Run a Theft," *Kansas City Star*, September 14, 1915, 8.
25. "Wind and Science," *New Era*, September 17, 1915, 4.
26. "Their Lone Run a Theft," *Kansas City Star*, September 14, 1915, 8.
27. "Wind and Science, *New Era*, September 17, 1915, 4.
28. "Make It Annual Event," *Leavenworth Times*, September 15, 1915, 5.
29. New Era, September 17, 1915, 4; "Prison Chatter," *New Era*, September 17, 1915, 3; "It's a Gala Day at Prison When K.C. Feds Play," *Leavenworth Times*, September 14, 1915, 3.
30. "Packers' Gift," *New Era*, October 1, 1915, 4.
31. Ibid.
32. "Baseball Season Ends," *New Era*, October 1927, 3; "Booker T's Win Final Game of Series 2 to 1," *Leavenworth Times*, October 7, 1929, 7; "Booker T's Meet Catholics Sunday," *Kansas City Call*, August 19, 1927, 6.
33. "A New Champion," Leavenworth *New Era*, April 9, 1915, 4.
34. Geoffrey Ward, *Unforgivable Blackness: The Rise and Fall of Jack Johnson* (New York: Vintage, Reprint Edition, 2006), 410–3.
35. "Penal Court in US Penitentiary Here is Unique," *Leavenworth Times*, May 18, 1913, 2.
36. Wilson File; "11 Men, 4 Women Shed No Tears at Funeral for Baseball Wilson," *St. Paul* (Minnesota) *Dispatch*, May 16, 1924, n.p.
37. United States Penitentiary-Leavenworth was established in 1895, but the inmates did not occupy the current building until 1903.
38. The original United States Disciplinary Barracks was located on the old Fort Leavenworth post about a mile north of the U.S. penitentiary site. It is now about three miles farther north.
39. Keve, 83.
40. Leavenworth *New Era*, April–June 1946, 87; Leavenworth *New Era* Annual Issue, 1947, 61; Leavenworth *New Era*, January-March 1949, 45; Del Crandall: www.baseball-reference.com/players/c/crandde01.shtml.
41. Albert T. Bostelmann, "Adolph John Soldan, 1877–1971," *Concordia Historical Institute Quarterly*, Winter 1985, 169-70; Soldan is visible in footage of Monroe's funeral on YouTube. He is the tall man in the clerical robe at the head of the procession: www.youtube.com/watch?v=3S3b9RJCfNw.

Dazzling Dazzy Vance in the "K-Zone"

Bryan Soderholm-Difatte

Rube Waddell. Walter Johnson. Lefty Grove. Bob Feller. Sandy Koufax. Sam McDowell. Nolan Ryan. Doc Gooden. Roger Clemens. Pedro Martinez. Randy Johnson. (There are others, of course.) Their names are synonymous with "overpowering strikeout pitcher." Even as time marches on, their names are not forgotten because each has been a standard against which subsequent generations of strikeout pitchers are measured. Relative to their peers, however, none of them, nor any other pitcher, was as dominant in the "K-Zone" in any single season as Dazzy Vance in 1924.[1] And he pitched in the toughest year to strike out batters.

Who was Dazzy Vance? His true name was Charles Arthur, but he earned the nom de guerre "Dazzy" because of the "dazzling" blazing fastball he was demonstrating early in his minor league career. Until breaking in with Brooklyn as a 31-year old rookie in 1922, however, Vance's career had been stalled almost entirely in the minor leagues because of chronic arm problems that contributed to an unacceptable lack of control, causing both the Pittsburgh Pirates and New York Yankees to give up on him in the middle-1910s. Bill James relates the story that Vance was cured of his sore arm when he was pitching in New Orleans in 1920 by a doctor who operated on his arm following an injury sustained in a hand of poker, after which he became the impressive pitcher who is today in the Hall of Fame.[2] Vance was extremely tough to hit. Not only did he have a terrific fastball and a wicked curve that broke sharply downward, and not only did he threw every pitch hard even as he paced himself to throw four or five pitches even harder when he most needed to, but Vance also was very deceptive in his windup and delivery. Dazzling Dazzy threw both his pitches with exactly the same motion, and—most famously—wore a tattered long-sleeve undershirt whose flapping as his right arm came around on the pitch made it more difficult for the batter to pick up the ball.[3]

WHEN STRIKEOUTS WERE RARE

In dramatic contrast to recent years, when strikeouts ratios have never been higher, strikeouts were at their lowest sustained level in the modern history of the game during the Roaring 'Twenties. Last year, major league pitchers set a strikeout record, kayoing 37,441 batters and averaging 7.73 strikeouts per nine innings (K/9 average). That broke the record of 36,710 strikeouts notched in 2013, which broke the record of 36,426 set in 2012.[4] There was no year between 1919 and 1930, however, in which the major league K/9 average was as high as even three strikeouts per nine innings. To put it another way, pitchers were striking out fewer than one batter every three innings, despite the fact that this was also the decade that Babe Ruth busted loose, giving swinging for the fences the good baseball seal of approval (although John McGraw, Ty Cobb, and a host of other "traditionalists"—including sportswriters who favored the practice of "scientific" baseball—surely did not approve).

The 1920s decline in strikeouts to 2.8 per game for each team from an average of 3.9 in the last decade of the Deadball Era can be attributed to various factors.[5] Major league baseball's institutional banishing of the spitball and other deviously treacherous pitches were probably most important to depressed strikeout ratios, as was the practice after the tragic hit-by-pitch death of Ray Chapman in 1920 of umpires ensuring that baseballs were removed from the game when grass and dirt stains made them too difficult to see. Moreover, it must be remembered that—in contrast to starting pitchers these days completing less than 3 percent of

Vance didn't "dazzle" in the minors while suffering from a chronic sore arm. In 1920, while pitching in New Orleans, he had surgery following a poker incident and found himself cured. He broke in as a 31-year-old rookie in 1922 with Brooklyn.

their starts and managers using an average of three relievers a game in which their starter does not go the distance—in the 1920s complete games averaged about 47 to 52 percent of starts and teams faced an average of only 1.5 relief pitchers in games the opposing starter did not finish. Finally, even though more batters took pleasure in adopting the Babe's slugger mindset, most (Ruth being an exception) were still embarrassed about striking out too often, and most were more concerned with putting the ball in play than swinging for the fences with two strikes.

No year since 1899 in which a full 154-game (or 162-game) schedule was played has had as few Ks in the official scorebooks as the 6,624 batters who went down on strikes in 1924. Babe Ruth led the major leagues with 46 home runs and 391 total bases. Brooklyn first baseman Jack Fournier led the National League with 27 round-trippers. In all, there were four players in the NL and two in the AL who hit more than 20 home runs, and there were an additional eight players with 15 or more triples—still the long-ball currency in the big leagues. In the midst of the Ruth-instigated Lively Ball Era, the power numbers in 1924—896 home runs, 1,175 triples, and 25 percent of all hits going for extra-bases—although down somewhat from the previous three years, suggested that big league hitters were swinging away at the plate. Yet major league pitchers averaged a record low 2.7 batters rung up for every nine innings of work since the pitching rubber was set at 60-feet, six-inches in 1893. Only 7 percent of the 95,391 plate appearances in the major leagues in 1924 resulted in a walk back to the dugout by a strikeout victim. Ruth's 81 strikeouts were by far the most in baseball. The Cubs' George Grantham came closest to the Babe's mark, striking out 63 times, and just five players struck out as many as 60 times.

Only six pitchers struck out more than 100 batters in 1924, four of them in the American League. The leading K-practitioner in the junior circuit was Washington's 36-year old Walter Johnson with 158 strikeouts in 278 innings giving him a 5.1 K/9 average. The preeminent strikeout pitcher of his era, and in the debate about whether his fastball was the fastest of any pitcher ever at least until the coming of Sandy Koufax, this was the last of twelve seasons in which The Big Train led his league in strikeouts. In his prime, Johnson had strikeout averages of 7.6 and 7.4 in the two seasons he fanned 300 batters—1910 and 1912, when he was much younger at 22 and 24. Finishing a distant second in strikeouts to Johnson in the American League in 1924 was Boston's Howard Ehmke with 119, and the Yankees' Bob Shawkey (114) and Herb Pennock (101)

In 1924, Vance's 262 Ks accounted for nearly eight percent of all National League strikeouts. Next in the league came his teammate Burleigh Grimes with 135.

were third and fourth. Shawkey was the only qualifying pitcher in the league to approach Johnson in K/9 average that season, with 4.9 strikeouts per nine innings; Ehmke averaged 3.4 and the lefty Pennock averaged 3.2 in the only season of his Hall of Fame career in which he fanned as many as 100 batters.

THE DAZZY VANCE PHENOMENON

While Johnson's 158 Ks came in the twilight of his career, baseball's premier strikeout pitcher in 1924 was Brooklyn's Dazzy Vance in his breakout season. Not much younger than Johnson at 33 years old, and long beset by arm problems, Vance had resurrected his going-nowhere career the two previous years with back-to-back 18-win seasons, leading the National League in strikeouts both times—with 134 and 197. But in 1924, he went 28–6, led the league in wins, earned run average (2.16) and strikeouts, with a phenomenal—for the time—262 in 308.1 innings pitched. His strikeout average of 7.6 per nine innings approached nearly three times the major league average for the year, and exceeded Johnson's by almost 50 percent.

Vance by himself accounted for nearly 8 percent of all punch outs by National League pitchers, and he struck out 104 more batters—the equivalent of three complete games and 7.2 innings of a fourth—than the major league pitcher with the next most, Walter Johnson. Second in the National League to Vance's 262 Ks in 1924 was his teammate Burleigh Grimes with 135, and third was Cincinnati's Dolf Luque with all of 86 Ks. A grizzled veteran of eight full seasons pitching in the major leagues but actually (at 30) two-and-a-half years younger than Vance, Grimes had the advantage of being grandfathered in as a practitioner of the spitball when the pitch was outlawed, which probably helped him in the K-Zone.

The fact that the Dodgers (known at the time as the Robins, after manager Wilbert Robinson) had the National League's top two strikeout pitchers goes a long way to explaining how Brooklyn was suddenly competitive in 1924, finishing second with a 92–62 record, a game-and-a-half behind the New York Giants, after coming home sixth with a 76–78 record each of the two previous years. Paced by 397 Ks courtesy of Vance and Grimes, Brooklyn's 638 strikeouts in 1924 accounted for 19 percent of the National League total. The fourth-place Reds were second with 451 strikeouts, 187 shy of the Dodgers. Getting 15 percent of their outs by way of the K, compared to less than 10 percent for the seven other NL teams, meant needing fewer outs in the field—about two per game, on average—reducing the opportunities for hits to sneak through or fall between fielders, and defensive miscues. This was important for Brooklyn because the Dodgers were not a good defensive team and had limited range; their 197 errors were the third-most in the league, consistent with their fielding percentage being the third-worst, and their .684 defensive efficiency average of making outs on balls put into play was well below the league average of .687.

The 1924 Dodgers actually did not make a run to derail the Giants' quest for a fourth straight pennant until late in the season. Brooklyn was as far as 14 games off the pace on August 9, but finished the season with a 36–12 run to force their New York City rivals from Manhattan into a fierce fight. The Dodgers spent most of September in a virtual dead heat with the Giants, typically half-a-game to a game-and-a-half behind, including one day when they were nominally tied, trailing by just .003 percentage points. Brooklyn's late-season surge was powered by Dazzy Vance. From the beginning of August till the end of the season, Vance made 14 starts, completed 12, won 11, and fanned 120 batters in 120.2 innings.[6] He also struck out six in a single four-inning relief appearance—his only time out of the bullpen that year—in which he was the winning pitcher. All told, Vance struck out 26 percent of the batters he faced in the final two months

Howard Ehmke of the Red Sox notched 119 strikeouts in 1924, while the Yankees' Bob Shawkey had 114. (American League leader Walter Johnson had 158.)

of the season. More significantly, Ks accounted for more than a third (33.7 percent) of his outs. Vance's pitching was so exceptional in 1924 that he was voted the National League's Most Valuable Player ahead of Rogers Hornsby, whose batting average was a staggering .424 that year. Hornsby was only two-for-fourteen in the three starts—all complete game victories—that Dazzy had against the Cardinals.

Dazzy Vance led the National League in strikeouts and K/9 average each of the next four years, three times striking out more than the American League's strikeout king for the season. The one year he did not, in 1926 when he had the third-most strikeouts in the big leagues, Vance was limited to only 22 starts and 169 innings because arm problems caused him to get a late start on the season, see limited action and pitch poorly in the first six weeks, and resulted in his being unable to pitch for ten days or more on five separate occasions. Still, his 140 strikeouts were 13 more than the National League runner-up in the K race, Chicago Cubs' right-hander Charlie Root, who threw 102 more innings. Even with a sore arm, Vance was the major league's most proficient pitcher when it came to strikeouts, disposing of 7.4 batters by way of the K per nine innings—an average 10 percent better than the major league leader in strikeouts that year, Lefty Grove. Major league pitchers averaged 2.8 strikeouts per nine innings in 1926.

DAZZY'S 1924 STRIKEOUT DOMINANCE IN HISTORICAL PERSPECTIVE

Dazzling Dazzy's dominance in the K-Zone in 1924

has no equal in two respects. First, his 262 strikeouts were nearly two-thirds more than the 158 racked up by his K-Zone rival—Walter Johnson—which is the largest difference in any season ever between baseball's strikeout king and the runner up (see Table 1). Within his own league, Vance had nearly double the 135 strikeouts recorded for second-best in the National League by his teammate, Burleigh Grimes. And second, no other pitcher's K/9 ratio in any given season has approached being 50 percent better than his closest rival for strikeouts-per-nine innings (see Table 2). Dazzy fanned 49 percent more batters per nine innings than the Big Train in 1924. Johnson would have needed 78 more Ks for the number of innings he pitched (277.2), or approximately two additional strikeouts per start, to match Vance in strikeout proficiency. Grimes,

whose strikeouts per nine innings were about half of Vance's, would have needed to fan 127 more batters (approximately 3.5 per start) to keep pace with Dazzling Dazzy in K/9 average in the National League for the 310.2 innings he pitched. The next year, Vance's average of strikeouts-per-nine innings was 41 percent better than runner-up Lefty Grove, giving him three consecutive seasons in which his K/9 average was at least one-third higher than the pitcher with the second-best mark (33 percent better than Walter Johnson in 1923).

Prior to Vance, the Philadelphia Athletics' eccentric Rube Waddell and the Washington Nationals' statesman-like Walter Johnson had been the most overpowering pitchers. There were others, of course. The Giants' Christy Mathewson led the National League in strikeouts five of six years between 1903 and 1908, but only once in K/9 average. The Philadelphia Phillies' Grover Cleveland Alexander (not yet "Old Pete") also led the NL in Ks in five of six years, between 1912 and 1917, and twice in strikeouts per nine innings. But neither was as feared with the fastball as the Rube and the Big Train.

When Waddell kayoed 349 batters in 1904, which would stand as the most since 1893 for 61 years, he had 46 percent more strikeouts than the New York Highlanders' Jack Chesbro, and his strikeout average of 8.2 per nine innings was 25 percent higher than his teammate Chief Bender's. Waddell's strikeout average was double the 4.1 Ks per nine innings for American League pitchers in 1904, and more than twice the major league average of 3.8, but still not close to Vance having a K/9 average in 1924 that approached three times the average for major league pitchers. In Walter Johnson's best strikeout year of 1910 when he fanned 313 (21 percent more Ks than runner-up Ed Walsh), his K/9 average of 7.6 was almost double the major league average of 3.9, but only 15 percent better than Smoky Joe Wood's 6.6 for the Boston Red Sox.

Lefty Grove displaced Vance as the premier power pitcher in the game in the late 1920s, and historically his fastball's fame has eclipsed that of Vance. But for all his acclaim in blowing batters

TABLE 1. Selected Pitchers' Best Single-Season Strikeout Differential

- Pitcher must have led the major leagues in strikeouts
- "Best single season" is the year he had the highest percentage difference over the pitcher with the second-most strikeouts and is not necessarily his career-high strikeout year
- *Italicized Pitchers* led the major leagues in strikeouts-per-nine innings
- **Bold strikeouts** indicates career high for the strikeout leader

% Diff	Year	Strikeout Leader		2nd in Strikeouts	
66%	1924	*Dazzy Vance*	**262**	Walter Johnson	158
59%	1940	*Bob Feller*	261	Bobo Newsome	164
48%	1973	*Nolan Ryan*	**383**	Bert Blyleven	258
46%	1904	*Rube Waddell*	**349**	Jack Chesbro	239
44%	1913	*Walter Johnson*	243	Tom Seaton	168
43%	1980	Steve Carlton	286	Nolan Ryan	200
40%	1979	*J.R. Richard*	313	Nolan Ryan	223
37%	1956	*Herb Score*	**263**	Billy Pierce	192
36%	1993	*Randy Johnson*	308	Jose Rijo	227
30%	1920	"Pete" Alexander	173	Stan Coveleski	133
26%	1966	Sandy Koufax	317	Jim Bunning	252
26%	1958	Toothpick Sam Jones	**225**	Early Wynn	179
25%	1987	Mike Scott	**306**	Mark Langston	245
25%	1986	Doc Gooden	268	Mario Soto	214
24%	1988	Roger Clemens	291	Mark Langston	235
22%	1960	Don Drysdale	**246**	Jim Bunning	201
22%	1933	Dizzy Dean	**199**	*Lefty Gomez*	163
22%	1926	Lefty Grove	194	George Uhle	159
7%	1970	*Sam McDowell*	304	Tom Seaver	283

Note: Feller's career high in strikeouts was 348 in 1946; Walter Johnson's was 313 in 1910; Carlton's was 310 in 1972; Randy Johnson's was 372 in 2001; Alexander's was 241 in 1915; Koufax's was 382 in 1965; Gooden's was 276 in 1984; Clemens's was 292 in 1997; Grove's was 209 in 1930; and McDowell's was 325 in 1965.

Pedro Martinez never led the major leagues in strikeouts. His career high in strikeouts was 313 in 1999.

TABLE 2. Selected Pitchers' Best Single-Season K/9 Differential

- Pitcher must have led the major leagues in strikeout average (strikeouts per nine innings)
- "Best single season" is the year he had the highest percentage difference over the pitcher with the second-highest K/9 average and is not necessarily his career-high in strikeout average
- **Bold K/9** indicates pitcher's K/9 average was a career high
- **Bold K** indicates pitcher led the major leagues in strikeouts

DIF	YEAR	K/9	RATIO LEADER	2ND IN K/9 RATIO	
49%	1924	**7.6**	Vance: 308.1 IP / **262 K**	W. Johnson: 277.2 IP /158 K	5.1
36%	1973	10.6	Ryan: 326.0 IP / **383 K**	Tom Seaver: 290.0 IP/ 251 K	7.8
33%	1993	10.9	R. Johnson: 255.1 IP/ **308 K**	Melido Perez: 163 IP/ 148 K	8.2
30%	1907	7.3	Waddell: 284.2 IP / **232 K**	Red Ames: 233.1 IP / 146 K	5.6
30%	1962	**10.5**	Koufax: 184.1 IP / 216 K	Ken Johnson: 197 IP / 178 K	8.1
27%	1955	**9.7**	Score: 227.1/ **245 K**	Bob Turley: 246.2 IP / 210 K	7.66
26%	1938	**7.8**	Feller: 277.2 / **240 K**	B. Newsom: 329.2 IP /226 K	6.2
18%	1984	**11.4**	Gooden: 218.0 IP / **276 K**	Ryan: 183.2 IP / 197 K	9.7
15%	1910	**7.6**	W. Johnson: 370.0 IP /**313 K**	Joe Wood: 196.2 IP / 145 K	6.6
14%	1966	10.4	McDowell: 194.1 IP / 225 K	D. Boswell: 169.1 IP / 173K	9.1
9%	1999	**13.2**	Martinez: 213.1 IP / 313 K	R. Johnson: 271.2 IP / **364 K**	12.1
6%	1988	9.9	Clemens: 264.0 IP/ **291 K**	Ryan: 220.0 IP / 228 K	9.3

Note: Ryan's career high in strikeouts per nine innings pitched was 11.5 in 1987; Randy Johnson's was 13.4 in 2001; Waddell's was 8.3 in 1903; McDowell's was 10.7 in 1965; and Clemens's was 10.4 in 1998.

Lefty Grove, whose career high K/9 was 6.8 in 1926, and Dizzy Dean, whose career high was 6.1 in 1933, never led the major leagues in K/9 average.

away with a fastball some said was better than Walter Johnson's in his prime, and notwithstanding his leading the American League in strikeouts in each of his first seven years in the Big Time, Grove never struck out more than 32 percent more batters than the league's runner-up (183 in 1928, to 139 by the Yankees' George Pipgras). Grove led both leagues in strikeouts only four times, never had the best K/9 average in the major leagues (although he did in the American League five times), and only three times averaged as many as six strikeouts per nine innings. Despite completing two-thirds of his starts when he was in his prime with the Philadelphia Athletics, only once in his career did Grove reach 200 strikeouts in a season. Vance cracked the 200-K barrier in three different years, all when strikeouts were hard to come by for pitchers.

Next came Bob Feller, also known as Rapid Robert, whose fastest stuff was in rhetorical (as opposed to direct) competition with that of Johnson and Grove. Feller's most dominating performances in the K-arena relative to his peers were 1938 and 1939 when his K/9 average was 26 percent better than the runner-up both years. In 1946, his most dominating year in the K-Zone, Rapid Robert fanned 348 batters—one shy of Waddell's 1904 record—in 371.1 innings, and yet his average of 8.4 strikeouts per nine innings, while nearly

double the American League average of 4.3, was just a smidgen shy of Detroit southpaw Hal Newhouser, who fanned 275 in 292.2 innings. It is likely that the return of wartime veterans, many of whom had not faced major league pitching for as many as three years, made it easier for Feller to exceed his previous high strikeout total (261 in 1940) by such a large margin in 1946; strikeouts in the two leagues increased by 20 percent that year compared to the war years, and were 10 percent higher than they had been in 1941—the year before his patriotic impulse caused Feller to enlist in the Navy.

Those 348 strikeouts might have come at considerable cost to the 27-year old Feller, however, because although he led the league in strikeouts each of the next two years, Rapid Robert never again kayoed as many as 200 in a season. Indeed, the 1,640 strikeouts Feller accrued in eight years from his rookie year in 1936 to 1946 (during which time he missed three full seasons and most of a fourth serving in World War II) accounted for 64 percent of his career total, and he continued pitching for another ten seasons. More significantly, Feller's K/9 average in the years through his 348-strikeout 1946 season was 7.8, when the major league average was typically between 3.4 and 3.6 Ks per nine innings.

Feller's K/9 average during his prime years would likely have been even better had he not had such difficulty controlling his overwhelming fastball and sharp curve. In each of his first seven full seasons in the big leagues, Feller walked at least 100 batters, including 208 in 1938, 194 in 1941, and 153 when he came within one of Waddell's single-season strikeout record in 1946. Vance, by contrast, had very good control in an era when more batters walked than struck out, only once walking as many as 100 in a single season (which was not 1924). Had he been able to command his fastball with greater accuracy, Bob Feller, and not his 1955 teammate Herb Score, probably would have been the first starting pitcher to strike out at least one batter for every inning pitched.[7]

VANCE STILL UNMATCHED IN THE RISE TO DOMINANCE OF POWER PITCHERS

Beginning with Sandy Koufax in the 1960s, major league baseball has not been lacking in clearly identifiable, renowned power pitchers. The era of the power pitcher that can be traced back to Koufax has seen a sufficient number of pitchers with high K/9 averages that none has been able to outdistance his peers to the degree Dazzy Vance did in 1924. Although his 197 strikeouts in 1960 were only the third-most in baseball, the fact they were accrued in only 175 innings made Koufax the first ERA-qualifying pitcher to average better than 10 Ks per nine innings; the National League average was 5.5 that year. When Koufax surpassed Waddell's 349 tally with 382 in 1965, the Cleveland Indians' Sam McDowell had 325 of his own and actually had a higher K/9 average (10.7) than Koufax (10.2).

The pitcher who has come closest to Vance's 1924 record for outdistancing his runner-up in K/9 average was the California Angels' Nolan Ryan in 1973. The 1973 Ryan Express topped Koufax by one with 383 and might well have fanned more than 400 had this not been the first year in the American League that pitchers did not have to hit for themselves because of the new designated hitter rule. Ryan's K/9 average of 10.6 that year was exactly double the major league average but, at only 36 percent better than runner-up Tom Seaver's 7.8 strikeouts per nine innings in the National League, still far short of Dazzling Dazzy's 1924 standard of K-Zone dominance.[8]

Ryan worked 326 innings in 1973 and completed two-thirds of his 39 starts. This is significant because a strong argument can be made that, in addition to the rapid evolution to a fundamentally different hitting philosophy in which the risk of striking out has become an acceptable trade-off for the potential benefit of what a power swing might bring, a precipitating factor in so many pitchers in the last thirty years having such high K/9 averages is the dramatic decline of the complete game. In 1924—the year of Dazzling Dazzy in the K-Zone—major league pitchers completed nearly 49 percent of their starts; Vance himself finished 30 of his 34 starts. Bob Feller, for his part, completed 36 of his 42 starts in 1946 when he fanned 348 batters, while starting pitchers overall completed 42 percent of their starts. When Koufax struck out his 382 batters in 1965, complete games accounted for 23 percent of all starts, but he finished 27 of his 41. And when Ryan established the new—still current—American League record in 1973, American League pitchers, liberated from having to be

Herb Pennock was one of only six pitchers in the major leagues to top 100 strikeouts in 1924, with 101.

removed for a pinch hitter in close games, completed nearly a third of their starts, compared to only 23 percent in the National "non-DH" League.[9]

But when New York Mets' rookie Dwight Gooden earned the nickname "Dr. K" by becoming the first qualifying starting pitcher to have a K/9 average of better than 11 with 276 strikeouts in 1984, he pitched only 218 innings because he completed just seven of his 31 starts, which was still much higher than only 12 percent complete games in the National League that year. Doctor K's 1984 K/9 ratio was just 18 percent higher than that of Nolan Ryan—the only other starting pitcher that year who averaged better than a strikeout an inning. By now pitching for the Houston Astros, Ryan completed just five of his 30 starts and averaged just over six innings per start. First with NL Houston and then with AL Texas, Ryan led his league in strikeout average every year between 1987 and 1991 (and the major leagues four times), seeming to defy age as this streak began when he was already 40 years old, but he finished only 17 of his 156 starts, about the same as the 11 percent complete games in the league he pitched in during those years.

As the twentieth century began, major league pitchers were completing only 4.8 percent of their starts, and in 2014 that figure was down to less than 2.5 percent. Of the most proficient K/9 pitchers since

Ryan, Randy Johnson became the first starting pitcher to average better than 12 strikeouts per nine innings in 1995 with the Seattle Mariners; set the record for the highest strikeout average in history at 13.4 in 2001 with the Arizona Diamondbacks; fanned more than one batter an inning every year from 1991 to 2004; and averaged 10.6 strikeouts every nine innings over his entire 22-year career—during which he completed 17 percent of his starts lasting just under seven innings per start. During his sixteen-year career, Dazzy Vance finished 62 percent of the games he started and averaged about eight innings a start.

Today's prevailing pitching philosophy, made possible by the diminished importance of complete games that would leave pitchers of Vance's, Feller's, Koufax's and even Ryan's generation aghast, reliance on closers to save close games, and specialized relievers in large bullpens, puts a premium on getting the most out of a starting pitcher for as long as possible in a game—which is now defined by pitch counts. Power pitchers are expected to bring the heat in every inning. An appreciable drop in velocity is usually enough to trigger the bullpen into action and could mean the starting pitcher is close to the end of his day. With high-quality relief on the way, managers are satisfied when their starting pitchers can give six or seven high-quality innings. The same is true even for teams with less than high-quality relief.

Indicative of this era of dominant power pitchers with high strikeout rates, 14 of the 88 pitchers who qualified for their league's earned run average title in 2014 by throwing at least 162 innings averaged at least one strikeout per inning; five of those 14 led the way with averages of better than 10 strikeouts per nine innings; two pitchers missed a K/9 average of 10 by less than one strikeout. Clayton Kershaw led the majors with 10.8 strikeouts-per-nine innings, but outpaced Chris Sale's 10.76 K/9 average by less than one percent,

was only 17 percent better than Ian Kennedy whose 9.3 average was the tenth-best in baseball, and 20 percent better than Jon Lester, who was number fourteen on the list of starting pitchers striking out at least one batter an inning. It's safe to say, then, it seems certain that for the foreseeable future there will be no pitcher who will dominate in the K-Zone relative to his peers—or can be even expected to dominate—the way Dazzy Vance did in 1924. ∎

Notes

1. The "K-Zone" is a term popularized by ESPN in its televised baseball broadcasts to refer to the strike zone. ESPN uses exclusive technology that allows viewers to see the location of pitches in relation to the batter's notional strike zone, as defined by the rule book.
2. Bill James, *The New Bill James Historical Baseball Abstract* (NY: The Free Press, 2001), 869.
3. Bill James and Rob Neyer, *The Neyer/James Guide to Pitchers: An* (sic) *Historical Compendium on Pitching, Pitchers, and Pitches* (NY: Fireside Books, 2004), pp. 410–11, and Richard Goldstein, *Superstars and Screwballs: 100 Years of Brooklyn Baseball* (NY: Plume Books, 1992), 142.
4. All statistical data in this article are from the indispensible website for baseball research, Baseball-Reference.com.
5. Strikeouts in the years 1918 and 1919 were not included for the Deadball Era in this decade comparison because the exigencies of World War I caused major league baseball to play less than a 154-game schedule both years. Strikeouts in the Federal League—whose records count for the major leagues—in 1914 and 1915 were also excluded.
6. See splits data for Dazzy Vance in Baseball-Reference.com.
7. With 245 strikeouts in 227.1 innings in his rookie season, Herb Score became the first major league pitcher to strikeout at least one batter an inning. To prove it was no fluke, Score did it again in his second season (a K/9 average of 9.5 in 1956, compared to 9.7 the year before), and might have made it three in a row, going on who knows how many, were it not for a devastating line-drive to the face off the bat of the Yankees' Gil McDougald early in the 1957 season.
8. Ryan is the only pitcher to have outpaced his closest rival in K/9 average by at least 30 percent in four different years, also doing so in 1977 (by 34 percent over Bert Blyleven), in 1987 (32 percent over Mark Langston) and in 1989 (34 percent over Langston). Vance, as already noted, did so three years in a row from 1923 to 1925.
9. Ryan is the only pitcher to have outpaced his closest rival in K/9 average by at least 30 percent in four different years, also doing so in 1977 (by 34 percent over Bert Blyleven), in 1987 (32 percent over Mark Langston) and in 1989 (34 percent over Langston). Vance, as already noted, did so three years in a row from 1923 to 1925.

More Baseball in Non-Baseball Films

Rob Edelman

Back in the mid-1990s, I published *Great Baseball Films* (Citadel Press), which charts the manner in which the sport has been depicted onscreen from the late 1890s to early 1990s. Twenty years ago as today, even the most obscure films with obvious baseball themes were readily accessible to researchers. However, seeking out films in which baseball is referenced but does not play a central role in the storyline is more problematic. So compiling a definitive list of non-baseball-themed films which cite the sport is, in a word, impractical. Even today, in our Internet/information age, there is no source for such information.

Nonetheless, while researching *Great Baseball Films*, it became apparent that some of the most revealing baseball sequences exist in non-sports films.[1] Since the book's publication, countless additional examples have come to the fore. Take, for example, *The Man in the Gray Flannel Suit* (1956). The title character is Tom Rath (Gregory Peck), a harried suburbanite and World War II veteran who commutes into Manhattan every workday. One day, while passing time on the train, Tom's mind wanders and he recalls an incident from a decade earlier—and a world away from mid-1950s America—in which he killed a young German soldier. Then in an instant, he is thrust back into the reality of 1956 when the man sitting next to him grimly declares, "There's no use trying. I just can't get used to it."

"Used to what?" Tom asks.

His fellow commuter responds: "The idea of the Brooklyn Dodgers as world champions."

The world had indeed changed in the decade since the end of the war.[2]

Then there is *On Moonlight Bay* (1951), a nostalgia-filled romance that mirrors the role of women in American society during a bygone era. The year is 1917 and Marjorie Winfield (Doris Day) is a teenaged tomboy who can swing a bat as well as any male. However, one look at William Sherman (Gordon MacRae), the handsome boy next door, and Marjorie readily exchanges her mud-stained baseball flannels for the frilly pink party dress she will wear on their first date. As she prepares for the date, Marjorie's mother (Rosemary DeCamp) advises her to "try not to walk like a first baseman," and her father (Leon Ames) quips, "I hope he doesn't try to dance with her. He's liable to get spiked."

As they converse, William, a University of Indiana senior, describes his college experience as "a farce. All the fellas are interested in is playing football and baseball…"

"What's wrong with baseball?" Marjorie asks.

William responds: "Baseball! It's the national insanity. At a time like this, when civilization is crumbling beneath our feet, our generation is playing baseball…"

Who is the now-smitten Marjorie to disagree? For after all, the man is always right.

Before their date ends, Marjorie already is changing her worldview. At one point William asks her to dance, but she hesitates. "Oh, I guess I thought you were a southpaw," she says, but she quickly catches herself and declares, "I mean left-handed."

As the evening concludes and they kiss goodnight, Marjorie's white-gloved left hand pushes aside forever the cap and ball that are resting on the table behind her. She and William are now courting, and her father is worried about her because, as he explains, "Marjorie is young and inexperienced. All she knows about men is their batting averages."

Quips Stella (Mary Wickes), the family housekeeper: "In case you're interested, this one's batting a thousand."

Unquestionably, mere mentions of baseball abound in the most unusual non-baseball situations. For example, in one brief scene in *Grease* (1978), the Rydell High School athletic coach (Sid Caesar) attempts to explain the finer points of sports to Danny Zuko (John Travolta). This sequence will fascinate anyone who is captivated by the image of Travolta garbed in a Rydell jersey and awkwardly swinging a baseball bat. But there is no baseball-related cultural context here. What most fascinates is the presence of a larger context, which exists in *The Man in the Gray Flannel Suit* and *On Moonlight Bay*: films featuring baseball sequences that reflect on the eras in which they were made.

Some non-baseball films cite real-baseball scandals. For example, two Jewish gangsters—one fictional and one real—are featured and referenced in *The Godfather: Part II* (1974). At one point, Hyman Roth (Lee Strasberg) declares, "I loved baseball ever since Arnold Rothstein fixed the World Series in 1919." Others cite memorable in-season games. In *One, Two, Three* (1961), C.R. McNamara (James Cagney), a Coca-Cola executive who heads to West Germany to promote his product, reports, "On Sunday, August 13, 1961, the eyes of America were on the nation's capital, where Roger Maris was hitting home runs number 44 and 45 against the Senators. On that same day, without any warning, the East German Communists sealed off the border between East and West Berlin. I only mention this to show the kind of people we're dealing with—real shifty." And "real shifty" does not refer to any Senators hurler who might consider hitting Maris with a pitch rather than challenging him with a fastball down the middle.

Brooklyn-born Steve Rogers (Chris Evans), the hero of *Captain America: The First Avenger* (2011), starts out as a 90-pound weakling. The time is World War II, and the borough is introduced onscreen with the Brooklyn Bridge in the background and some kids playing baseball in a street: an image that links the sport to mom's apple pie Americanism. As the plot unfolds, Rogers is transformed into the muscular title character and, upon waking up after winning out in contemporary action-movie fashion over the megalomaniacal villain, he finds himself in a room. A Dodgers game is being broadcast on a radio. "Just an absolutely gorgeous day here at Ebbets Field," the play-by-play man declares. He reports that the Dodgers are battling the Phillies; the game is tied 4–4; the home team is at bat with the bases loaded; and the hitter smashes a drive into the outfield. "Three runs'll score," the broadcaster adds. "Durocher's gonna wave them in… Pete Reiser with an inside-the-park grand slam… What a game we have here today, folks."

Only there's a problem: Rogers has performed his heroics during World War II, yet this game was played pre-Pearl Harbor, in May 1941. How does he know this? Because he was in the stands that day. Something is amiss… and this knowledge on Rogers' part further propels the plot. And here is where "real" mixes with "reel." On May 26, 1941, Louis Effrat noted in *The New York Times* that, a month earlier, Reiser was hit by a pitch thrown by Philadelphia Phillies hurler Ike Pearson and ended up hospitalized, with his career—and his life—imperiled. But Reiser survived and, as Effrat reported, "At Ebbets Field yesterday, Reiser faced Pearson for the first time since the accident on April 23, faced him in a situation that couldn't have been more

Pete Reiser's heroics in a game on May 26, 1941 made their way into the superhero film Captain America: The First Avenger *(2011).*

dramatic if it were part of a Hollywood scenario." Effrat added that the score was tied at four and the bases were loaded when Reiser strode to the plate. "Was he frightened?" Effrat wondered. "Did he flinch? The result, more than anything else, answers these questions…" as Pistol Pete belted a 3-and-1 pitch against the center-field screen, ending up with an inside-the-park dinger. The fictional Steve Rogers was one of the 12,941 fans on hand that day—and one can see how Effrat's reportage might have inspired the screenwriters of *Captain America: The First Avenger*.[3]

Other sequences spotlight iconic baseball moments. Predictably, in the Boston-centric *Good Will Hunting* (1997), Sean Maguire (Robin Williams) explains to Will Hunting (Matt Damon) that, on October 21, 1975, he knew that he had met the woman of his dreams. Why? Because that was Game 6 of the World Series. "Biggest game in Red Sox history," he declares, because this was the one in which Carlton Fisk belted his now-legendary dinger. Maguire adds that he and his friends had slept on the sidewalk all night to cop tickets. However, before the game, he was sitting in a bar and "in walks this girl." He soon reveals that he never made it to the game and was not present to experience first-hand a slice of Red Sox lore. But Maguire has no regrets because the woman was such a "stunner"—as well as his future wife.

Hall of Famers are cited onscreen in a range of ways. *Whip It* (2009) features a roller derby player who nicknames herself "Babe Ruthless." There is comic irony in the following dialogue from *Father's Day* (1997). Here, Jack Lawrence (Billy Crystal) tells Dale Putley (Robin Williams): "You're a tragic hero. You're Lou Gehrig." Putley's one-word response is: "Who?" Lawrence tells him, "Lou Gehrig. Everybody knows Lou Gehrig. The baseball player. He died of Lou Gehrig's Disease." The still clueless Putley's rejoinder is "Wow, what are the odds on that?" The central character in *Ace in the Hole* (1951), also known as *The Big Carnival*, is Chuck Tatum (Kirk Douglas), a New York newspaperman who's been sentenced to media oblivion in

Albuquerque, New Mexico. While complaining to one of his new paper's unhip employees, Tatum observes that in the American Southwest there is "No Yogi Berra. What do you know about Yogi Berra, Miss Deverich?"

"Yogi?" she responds. "Why, it's a sort of religion, isn't it?" In a Ruthian swing for the fences, Tatum retorts, "You bet it is—a belief in the New York Yankees." Meanwhile, *Wall Street: Money Never Sleeps* (2010), made almost six decades after *Ace in the Hole*, also references the beloved Berra. This serves to mirror his longevity on the American scene.

From the following dialogue in *French Connection II* (1975), one can guess the age of "Popeye" Doyle (Gene Hackman), a New York narcotics cop who is working in Marseilles and conversing with French Inspector Henri Barthelemy (Bernard Fresson):

Doyle: "You know, I had a tryout with the Yankees. You know what the Yankees are?"
Barthelemy: "Yes. As in 'Yankee go home.'"
Doyle: "Yeah. NO! No, uh…uh…no, the Yankee baseball…baseball team. Yeah, I had a tryout with them and…they sent me down to the…the minors. And the…problem was that…there was a fuckin' kid there, and he was…the fastest bastard, he was fuckin' FAST. And he…he played shortstop at the time, and he…he could hit the ball a fuckin' ton. A fuckin' TON! You know what 'fuck' means?"
Barthelemy: "Yeah."
Doyle: "Yeah. Well, I was in spring training… and I saw this kid…and I just immediately took the test for cops. That kid was Mickey Mantle. You know who Mickey Mantle was?"
Barthelemy: "No, I can't say that I know."
Doyle: "You don't know who Mickey Mantle was? Huh? How about Willie Mays? Say hey! Willie Mays! The mighty Willie Mays! See?"
Barthelemy: "No."

Moments later, the subject returns to baseball.

Doyle: "Well, and…Whitey Ford. Goddamn. You know who Whitey Ford was?…He was a dandy little southpaw. That's what we called him. He was a dandy little southpaw."
Barthelemy: "Southpaw?"
Doyle: "Yeah. He was a lefty."
Barthelemy: "You mean a communist?"
Doyle: "No, he was a Republican. But he was somethin', I tell you. He was somethin'…"

A throwaway line in *On the Waterfront* (1954) links the year in which the film was released to the haplessness of one major league team at this moment in time. At one point, a downtrodden dockworker notes that his beat-up windbreaker is "more full of holes than the Pittsburgh infield." But there is another line in *On the Waterfront* that resonates. In the film, Terry Malloy (Marlon Brando) has been subpoenaed to appear before a waterfront crime commission and is conflicted as to whether he should testify against union hooligan Johnny Friendly (Lee J. Cobb). Terry explains to Father Barry (Karl Malden) that Friendly "used to take me to the ballgames when I was a kid." Father Barry responds: "Ballgames. Don't break my heart. I wouldn't care if he gave you a life pass to the Polo Grounds…You've got some other brothers, and they're getting' the short hand while your Johnny's gettin' mustard on his face at the Polo Grounds."

In the early 1950s, the "life pass to the Polo Grounds" reference was appropriate for a New York City-area scenario. When *On the Waterfront* was scripted, who knew that, in just a few years, the Giants would abandon Coogan's Bluff for San Francisco and a "life pass to the Polo Grounds" would be meaningless—and worthless?

Similar references are found in another mid-1950s New York City-centric film: *Sweet Smell of Success* (1957). Here, slimy press agent Sidney Falco (Tony Curtis) tells the secretary of ruthless newspaper columnist J.J. Hunsecker (Burt Lancaster), "Don't try to sell me the Brooklyn Bridge. I happen to know it belongs to the Dodgers."

Later on, Falco tells Hunsecker: "I won't get Kello," referring to a thuggish NYPD lieutenant. "Not for a lifetime pass to the Polo Grounds." Baseball citations permeate *Sweet Smell of Success*. As he argues with Steve Dallas (Martin Milner), the boyfriend of his kid sister (Susan Harrison), Hunsecker observes, "Well,

Carlton Fisk's iconic homer in the 1975 World Series serves as a Boston cultural touchstone in the film Good Will Hunting *(1997).*

son, it looks like we may have to call this game on account of darkness."

In referencing his sister, Hunsecker notes: "If Sidney ever gets anywhere near Susie, I'd take a baseball bat and break it over his head."

The latter lines are obvious examples of how baseball is occasionally employed in a manner that has nothing to do with athletics. In some, baseball is akin to fate—and poetry. In *Grand Canyon* (1991), Mack (Kevin Kline), an entertainment industry accountant, recalls an incident in which he was almost run over by a bus but was grabbed by a stranger and yanked to safety. He explains, "I thanked this stranger, this woman in a baseball cap, but I was pretty much in a daze. When I thanked her, she said, 'My pleasure.' I didn't notice till the last moment that the cap was from the Pittsburgh Pirates, my favorite team since I was a kid. I never got over the idea that I should have thanked that woman more, talked to her awhile, something."

Then he adds, "How come she was wearing a Pirates cap? I just wondered, later on, was she for real, you know? Was that a real person or was that something else, you know, sent from somewhere else, to grab me back from that curb?"

Then again, with Hunsecker's threat to Falco in mind, endless films feature baseballs and baseball bats as weapons. One of the characters in *Inglourious Basterds* (2009) is a Jewish GI who relishes killing Nazis by smashing their skulls with bats. (This is contrasted with the stereotype of the Jew as brainy rather than brawny, which is explored in *Liberty Heights* (1999) via the following bit of dialogue: "There are very few Jewish ballplayers. You'll never hear, 'Ground ball to short. Flo Ziegfeld moves to his right, scoops it to Leonard Bernstein at second, who fires to first. George Gershwin stretches. Double play.' It's not gonna happen.")

In *The Gambler* (1974), a character known as Hips (Paul Sorvino) warns Axel Freed (James Caan), a literature professor and gambling addict, that the "only thing that's standing between your skull and a baseball bat is my word."

Stand By Me (1986) features boys playing "Mailbox Baseball," in which they smash mailboxes with a bat from a moving car. Then in *The Client* (1994), a young boy (Brad Renfro) disparages the behavior of alcohol-abusing fathers by noting that "they come home wasted and beat on you and your mother so bad that you gotta hit 'em in the face with a baseball bat!"

In *Manhattan* (1979), Isaac Davis (Woody Allen), making conversation at a party, observes, "Has anybody read that Nazis are gonna march in New Jersey?... We should go down there, get some guys together,

Whitey Ford's left-handedness reinforces the cultural divide between an American cop and a French inspector in The French Connection II *(1975).*

y'know, get some bricks and baseball bats and really explain things to them." In *Blackboard Jungle* (1955), Richard Dadier (Glenn Ford), an idealistic teacher, takes a job in a tough inner-city New York high school. As he finishes writing his name on the blackboard, an unidentified student hurls a baseball at the board, smashing it and partially obliterating Dadier's name. But the teacher has the final word. "Whoever threw that," Dadier says, "you'll never pitch for the Yanks, boy."

Not all such perpetrators are male. In *Fried Green Tomatoes* (1991), Ninny Threadgoode (Jessica Tandy) observes, "I'm worried about my little friend Evelyn. She said her husband, Ed, would just be sitting around watching his sports on TV...and she has an urge to hit him in the head with a baseball bat."

In *Mr. & Mrs. Smith* (1941), Harry Deever (Charles Halton), referring to the wife of David Smith (Robert Montgomery), declares, "I guess she's changed some, huh?"

David responds, "Well, she's...changed a little."

Harry chimes in, "She once chased a dogcatcher half a mile with a baseball bat," and David quips, "Well, she hasn't changed as much as you think."

The potential of baseball bats as weapons is further alluded to in *Mississippi Burning* (1988). Here, two FBI agents arrive in the title locale to investigate the disappearance of some civil rights activists, and one of them (Gene Hackman) describes a baseball game as "the only time when a black man can wave a stick at a white man and not start a riot." But the sport is connected to the worst kind of violence in *Clear and Present Danger* (1994). One of the villains is Ernesto Escobedo (Miguel Sandoval), a wealthy Colombian drug lord who shamelessly brags about his omnipotence while hitting baseballs from a pitching machine in a room in his hacienda. Not surprisingly, Escobedo's bat eventually is transformed into a weapon, which he menacingly wields against a man who has betrayed him.

Occasionally, a bit of introspection accompanies the violence. In *The Untouchables* (1987), Al Capone (Robert De Niro) observes: "What is that which gives me joy? Baseball! A man stands alone at the plate. This is the time for what? For individual achievement. There he stands alone. But in the field, what? Part of a team. Teamwork…Looks, throws, catches, hustles. Part of one big team. Bats himself the live-long day, Babe Ruth, Ty Cobb, and so on. If his team don't field…what is he? You follow me? No one. Sunny day, the stands are full of fans. What does he have to say? I'm goin' out there for myself. But…I get nowhere unless the team wins."

Following these words, Capone beats one of his hoods to death with a baseball bat.

Thankfully, not all "poetic" baseball references are accompanied by aggression. An extra-special baseball homage occurs at the opening of Woody Allen's aforementioned *Manhattan*. With Gershwin's "Rhapsody in Blue" on the soundtrack, Allen opens the film with a visual homage to the title New York City borough. You see ever-so-brief shots of the Empire State Building, the United Nations, unidentified skyscrapers, apartment houses, restaurants, bridges, crowds, traffic, ferries, Washington Square, the Guggenheim Museum, the Plaza Hotel, Central Park, Broadway, Lincoln Center, the Radio City Music Hall, and Times Square. The next-to-last shot, which lingers, is Yankee Stadium—which of course isn't even located in the borough of Manhattan. (The final image consists of fireworks over the mid-Manhattan skyline.) Another, similar Yankee Stadium shot is found in *Serpico* (1973). When honest cop Frank Serpico (Al Pacino) affirms that he will not play ball—no pun intended—with his corrupt fellow police officers, the scene is played on a hill that offers a panoramic view of the House That Ruth Built.

One of the highlights of the musical *The West Point Story* (1950) is a "Brooklyn" production number. Of course, one of the first lines is: "They know my shield from Ebbets Field to Cheyenne…" *Once Upon a Honeymoon* (1942) features Ginger Rogers as a Brooklyn native who grew up near Ebbets Field and quips: "Foul balls used to light in my backyard" before sighing "Dem lovely Bums." The opening sequence in *Arsenic and Old Lace* (1944) features loudmouthed Brooklyn Dodgers fans and brawling players at Ebbets Field. New York baseball is touched upon in *Kramer vs. Kramer* (1979). Here, a father (Dustin Hoffman) who hails from Brooklyn tells his son (Justin Henry) about his childhood: "We listened to the radio… We didn't

have diet soda. We had egg creams… We didn't have the Mets, but we had the Brooklyn Dodgers. And we had the Polo Grounds. And we had Ebbets Field. Oh boy, those were the days."

But not all movie references glorify New York nines. The Chicago location of *While You Were Sleeping* (1995) is established via a series of city landmarks. One, of course, is Wrigley Field, which is as much a symbol of the town as Yankee Stadium is a monument to New York. The New York teams are not the only teams that are admired. In *Boys Town* (1938), Freddie Fuller (Frankie Thomas), one of the residents of the title home for juvenile boys, is showing off the facilities to Whitey Marsh (Mickey Rooney), a hoodlum-in-training.

Freddie says, "There's our baseball field…last year one of our players was drafted by the St. Louis Browns."

Whitey responds: "Well, I like the Yankees"… and Freddie's rejoinder is, "You would!"

In so many films, baseball serves as a metaphor for healthy, thoughtful parenting and parent-child bonding. In *Stolen Summer* (2002), Joe O'Malley (Aidan Quinn), the father of a second-grader, wisely observes, "Baseball should be the only thing on an eight-year-old boy's mind." In *Critic's Choice* (1963), theater critic Parker Ballantine (Bob Hope) comically wrecks his back during a father-son game. While the sequence is played for laughs, the depiction of a post-World War II suburbia in which fathers toss horsehides to sons and parents cheer on their boys at Little League games is ever-present.

Baseball sequences also reflect on social interaction between children. In *The Happy Years* (1950), set in the 1890s, young Dink Stover (Dean Stockwell), an athletically inept prep-school student, is subjected to bullying. Upon entering a ballgame as a pinch hitter, Dink first hesitates while approaching home plate and then awkwardly holds the bat. The first pitch sails over his head and he falls to the ground, but his teammates taunt him. "Why didn't you let it hit ya?" one of them yells. "You'd have been on base. That's as good as a hit." The next pitch is a called strike. It's also a hit-and-run play, and the runner on base is thrown out.

A chorus of voices rings out at Dink: "What's the matter with you?" "Go on home to your mother." "Can't you play ball?" Next, Dink is stationed in the outfield. After dropping an easy fly ball, he is chased off the field by all his teammates. He ends up locking himself in his dorm room, donning a catcher's mask for protection and grabbing a bat, which he will employ as a weapon if the boys so much as touch him. In *The Happy Years* (which, given the film's scenario, is a purposefully ironic title), Dink's treatment is harsh and graceless. Still, his travails are depicted as a ritual of boyhood. In this regard, the film reflects the era in which it was made, rather than more contemporary attitudes toward bullying.

Other screen references mirror the manner in which baseball terminology has transcended the sport and become part of the culture. In *Crash* (2004), Flanagan (William Fichtner), an aide to the Los Angeles district attorney, tells Detective Graham Waters (Don Cheadle), "Actually, we were thinking of you until we saw that. It's your brother's file. Twenty-something years old and already three felonies. 'Three Strikes' Law, the kid's going away for life for stealing a car. Christ, that's a shitty law."

The following bit of action and dialogue is found in *Judge Dredd* (1995):

Mean Machine: "You got three strikes, lawman!"
(*The title character attacks Mean, but Mean blocks the blow with his mechanical arm.*)
Mean Machine: "Strike one! He-he-he..."
(*Dredd strikes back and, again, Mean blocks the blow.*)
Mean Machine: "Strike two!"
(*Dredd smashes a bar on Mean's head: a blow that would crack a human skull but leaves no impression on Mean.*)
Mean Machine: "Strike three. You're out, lawman!"

Other references, which are clever attempts to incorporate baseball into casual conversation, are reflections of how the sport has become engrained in American culture. In *Meet Me in St. Louis* (1944), set just after the turn of the 20th century, seventeen-year-old Esther Smith (Judy Garland) offers some advice to her lawyer-father (Leon Ames):

"Papa, if losing a case depresses you so, why don't you quit practicing law and go into another line of business?"

"That's a good idea," he says. "Starting tomorrow, I intend to play first base for the Baltimore Orioles."

In *Back to Bataan* (1945), Americans and Filipinos are battling the Japanese at the title locale. During the heat of combat, Col. Joseph Madden (John Wayne) calls to a fellow GI (Paul Fix), "Hey, Bindle...How's your pitchin' arm?" Bindle then heaves a grenade at the enemy, and it's the equivalent of a 100-mph strike. In *Vital Signs* (1990), a doctor (Jimmy Smits) observes, regarding the hazards faced by third-year medical students, "Third year is like being a rookie pitcher called on to pitch the seventh game of the World Series... blind-

folded." In *The Odd Couple II* (1998), Brucey (Jonathan Silverman), the son of Oscar Madison (Walter Matthau), tells his father, "Mom was married three times. You were married one time, and then never again for 30 years. Hers were too many, yours were not enough. So tell me...What is it about marriage that frightens everybody so much?"

Oscar answers, "I don't know, Brucey. It's like baseball: Either you can play or you can't play. Your mother could play; I couldn't play. Trouble with your mother was she kept getting traded all the time."

Examples of how baseball terminology has entered the culture are endless. One example: In *Ziegfeld Girl* (1941), wannabe stage performer Susan Gallagher (Judy Garland) casually observes, "This is Annie's night out, so I'm pinch-hitting for her." Plenty of these have sexual connotations. In *That Hagen Girl* (1947), a guy named Dewey Koons (Conrad Janis) hits on a gal named Sharon Bailey (Jean Porter) by asking her, "How 'bout it? C'mon, let's hit the high spots." Bailey is not impressed. "Why don't you go somewhere and catch yourself, you foul ball!" she says.

In *Follow the Fleet* (1936), Kitty Collins (Lucille Ball) asks a sailor who is trying to pick her up, "Tell me, little boy, did you get a whistle or baseball bat with that suit?"

A decade later, Ball spoke similar dialogue in *The Dark Corner* (1946). Here, her character is Kathleen Stewart. After her boss makes a pass at her, Kathleen responds, "I haven't worked for you very long, Mr. Galt, but I know when you're pitching a curve at me—and I always carry a catcher's mitt."

A defensive Mr. Galt replies, "No offense. A guy's gotta try to score, doesn't he?"

Kathleen's response is: "Not in my league."

And then in *Storm Warning* (1951), Marsha Mitchell (Ginger Rogers) is propositioned by her boss. "I thought...we could have a quiet dinner together," he tells her. "Just you and me. There's a cute French restaurant in Riverport." But Marsha will have none of it.

"Look, Cliff," she responds, "don't ya ever give up? You made a pitch in Baltimore, a wrong play in Mobile, and you fouled out in Atlanta. Cliff, in any league, three strikes is out."

Not all such baseball references are put-downs. In *Lethal Weapon 2* (1989), Riggs (Mel Gibson) and Rika (Patsy Kensit) are having fun between the sheets. At one point, Riggs observes, "I think it's time for the seventh-inning stretch." After a pause, he explains, "That's a baseball expression."

"I know," Rika says. "But we're only up to the fourth inning."

To which Riggs replies, "Batter up!"

The phrase "getting to first base" has come to refer to kissing—or, the initial stage of romantic or sexual intimacy—and it has been written into endless scripts. In *Lost in a Harem* (1944), an Abbott and Costello farce, the Abbott character chides Costello by telling him, "Oh, come on, you wouldn't get to first base with a beautiful girl like that."

In more recent decades, with the demise of the Hollywood Production Code, onscreen language has become more graphic—and raunchier. In *1941* (1979), United States Army Captain Loomis Birkhead (Tim Matheson) observes, "No man has ever gotten to first base with her on the ground. But get her up in a plane, she'll bat your balls right out of the park."

Other films simply offer snapshots of Hollywood at a moment in time: Who the popular stars were, and how baseball was woven into the social fabric of the era. In *Hollywood Hobbies* (1939), a one-reel short, two females take a "movie guide tour" through Tinseltown. After spying on a number of celebrities at work and play, they end up at a "big movie baseball game" (filmed on location at Gilmore Field in Los Angeles) whose participants are celluloid royalty.[4] Truman Bradley, then a popular radio broadcaster, announces from the press box and describes the charity event as "the world's screwiest baseball game" pitting the "Comedians" against the "Leading Men." Attending the game are James Stewart, George Murphy, Cesar Romero, Joan Davis, Spencer Tracy, Virginia Bruce, Tyrone Power, Jane Withers, and James Cagney and his mother. The managers are Joe E. Brown and Harry Ritz. The players include Buddy Ebsen (wearing a "Sauk Center" jersey and NY cap); John Boles; Buster Keaton (described as "that frozen-faced comic"); and Milton Berle ("Hippity-hop with the hat of a cop, it's Milton Berle to play shortstop"). Mary Pickford throws out the first pitch. The Ritz Brothers (presumably minus Harry) are the umpires. Arthur "Dagwood" Lake joins Bradley in the press box, and "crooner" Dick Powell swings a bat and belts a dinger.

All these baseball-in-non-baseball-film citations are a tiny sampling of the films I've researched or stumbled upon over the years.[5] Such citations keep appearing onscreen to the present day.

Two examples: Baseball bats are a constant presence in *Neighbors* (2014); they are in the hands of some raucous frat boys, and they are not being used in a spirited intramural sporting contest. In *Fading Gigolo* (2013), a character named Murray (Woody Allen) teaches youngsters how to hit baseballs. It is no coincidence that Murray, who is Caucasian and Jewish, lives with an African-American woman, and the kids he is mentoring are her kids. One of the themes in *Fading Gigolo* is the importance of assimilating into the American melting pot 21st-century-style. Here, the baseball connection is employed to reflect the notion that all Americans, regardless of race or religion, can play—and love—our National Pastime. ■

A version of this paper was presented at the Cooperstown Symposium on Baseball and American Culture, held at the National Baseball Hall of Fame & Museum in 2014.

Notes

1. Among the many examples cited in Great Baseball Films are: *College* (1927); *Speedy* (1928); *The Cameraman* (1928); *Up the River* (1930); *A Night at the Opera* (1935); *Black Legion* (1936); *Manhattan Merry-Go-Round* (1937); *Brother Rat* (1938); *Brother Rat and a Baby* (1940); *Remember the Day* (1941); *Meet John Doe* (1941); *Woman of the Year* (1942); *The Talk of the Town* (1942); *Larceny, Inc.* (1942); *Hitler's Children* (1943); *Whistling in Brooklyn* (1943); *Guadalcanal Diary* (1943); *Mr. Winkle Goes to War* (1944); *The Naughty Nineties* (1945); *The Best Years of Our Lives* (1946); *Deadline at Dawn* (1946); *Boys' Ranch* (1946); *A Foreign Affair* (1948); *Sunset Boulevard* (1950); *About Face* (1952); *Strategic Air Command* (1955); *Three Stripes in the Sun* (1955); *12 Angry Men* (1957); *Escapade in Japan* (1957); *The Geisha Boy* (1958); *Experiment in Terror* (1962); *The Horizontal Lieutenant* (1962); *Boys' Night Out* (1962); *That Touch of Mink* (1962); *The Family Jewels* (1965); *Ship of Fools* (1965); *The Odd Couple* (1968); *One Flew Over the Cuckoo's Nest* (1975); *Chapter Two* (1979); *The Chosen* (1982); *Cannery Row* (1982); *Max Dugan Returns* (1983); *Zelig* (1983); Under Fire (1983); *A Soldier's Story* (1984); *Indiana Jones and the Temple of Doom* (1984); *Protocol* (1984); *Birdy* (1984); *Gung Ho* (1986); *Ferris Bueller's Day Off* (1986); *About Last Night…* (1986); *Brighton Beach Memoirs* ((1987); *Radio Days* (1987); *Ironweed* (1987); *Funny Farm* (1988); *Big* (1988); *Naked Gun: From the Files of Police Squad* (1988); *Rain Man* (1988); *Parenthood* (1989); *Hook* (1991); *City Slickers* (1991); *Bad Lieutenant* (1992); *Simple Men* (1992); *Dave* (1993); *Sleepless in Seattle* (1993)…

2. Even though *The Man in the Gray Flannel Suit* references the Brooklyn Dodgers, it was cited in "New York Mets in the Movies," a paper presented in 2012 at the 50th anniversary New York Mets conference at Hofstra University. Non-baseball films with Mets-related sequences and references include: *Alice in the Cities* (1974); *The Wiz* (1978); *Do the Right Thing* (1989); *3 Men and a Little Lady* (1990); *Mo' Better Blues* (1990); *Jungle Fever* (1991); *Men in Black* (1997); *Frequency* (2000); *Small Time Crooks* (2000); *Kate & Leopold* (2001); *Two Weeks Notice* (2002); *Old Dogs* (2009); and *Friends With Benefits* (2011). A version of this paper may be found at: http://sabr.org/latest/edelman-new-york-mets-movies.

3. Louis Effrat. "Dodgers Stage Rally in Sixth to Triumph Over Phillies," *The New York Times*, May 26, 1941, 25.

4. www.imdb.com.

5. Plenty of other non-baseball films may be added to those cited here. *Air Force* (1943), *Battleground* (1949), *Lafayette Escadrille* (1958), and *We Were Soldiers* (2002) link American GIs and baseball. *Mr. Hobbs Takes a Vacation* (1962) and *War of the Worlds* (2005) emphasize father-son baseball connections, while *It Could Happen to You* (1994) spotlights the importance of adults employing baseball as a tool for mentoring youngsters. *Smoke* (1995) and its follow-up, *Blue in the Face* (1995), wax nostalgic about the late, lamented Brooklyn Dodgers and mirror the manner in which the sport is linked to civic pride and identity. *The Big Picture* (1989) underscores the fact that baseball heroes are among the most recognizable figures in American history. *The Lady Vanishes* (1938) and *The Miniver Story* (1950) connect Brits and baseball. The talents of women ballplayers are emphasized in *Cass Timberlane* (1947). Baseball card collecting and collectors are referenced in *Girl 6* (1996) and *Marilyn Hotchkiss' Ballroom Dancing & Charm School* (2005). The list goes on…

William Hulbert and the Birth of the National League[1]

Michael Haupert

In 1916, former National League President Abraham G. Mills said at a banquet celebrating the fortieth anniversary of the National League, "I cannot doubt that all true lovers of Base Ball will always cherish and honor the memory of William A. Hulbert."[2] Twenty years later the first honorees were elected to the new Baseball Hall of Fame. Hulbert was not among them, nor would he be for another sixty years.

WILLIAM HULBERT

William Ambrose Hulbert, second president of the National League, owner and president of the Chicago White Stockings, and successful businessman, was passionate about Chicago and the White Stockings. Not so much the latter because he was a devoted baseball enthusiast, but because he was a visionary. He saw what the future for baseball could be, and he recognized the changes that needed to be made to ensure that future. That future revolved around the quality of the game itself, but primarily it focused on the potential profitability of the sport of professional baseball. This is the story of how Hulbert turned a pastime into a business juggernaut.

William Ambrose Hulbert was born on October 23, 1832, in Burlington Flats, New York, a country crossroads located 15 miles west of Cooperstown. His parents moved to Chicago in 1836, where William was raised, along with two brothers. He briefly attended Beloit College, but his primary education was on-the-job training. He worked for his father's grocery business and a local coal merchant before establishing his own grain trading offices and obtaining a seat on the Chicago Board of Trade.

Hulbert grew up with the city of Chicago. When his family arrived, Chicago was a Midwestern outpost of fewer than 5000 souls. By the time he bought his first shares in the White Stockings in 1870, it had grown to the fifth largest city in the country with a population of just under 300,000. Most of that growth had occurred as he was moving up in the business world. Hulbert celebrated his 18th birthday in a city of 30,000. The tenfold population increase over the next twenty years was astounding. While Chicago grew in size, it did not grow in stature, at least from the viewpoint of the business community. Despite its standing as the fifth largest city, the business community had an inferiority complex, and felt that the eastern cities did not take Chicago seriously. The Chicago business elite were anxious to change that, and a group of them, including William Hulbert, decided that baseball would be one way to accomplish that change. They took notice of the national attention the Cincinnati Base Ball Club's 1869 tour had drawn to the Queen City, and decided a professional team would help draw the attention and respect they felt Chicago deserved.

Hulbert purchased three shares of the White Stockings ball club, which entered the National Association of Professional Base Ball Players, the first professional sports organization in the United States, which began play in May of 1871. The White Stockings inaugural season in the association was derailed by the great Chicago fire that burned 3.3 square miles of the city in October of that year. Among the victims of the fire were the team's home field, Union Baseball Grounds at Lake Park, along with the team's uniforms and equipment, and the homes of most of the players. Despite this disaster, the team finished out the season on the road, using equipment and uniforms borrowed from the rest of the league. However, it was the last championship game they would play until 1874. By then Hulbert had risen from minority owner to team secretary, a position that included responsibility for marketing and publicity. Hulbert demonstrated a flair for this, especially after the team moved into the National League. After one year as secretary, Hulbert was named president of the club. It was from this position that he made his most dramatic and important changes, not just to the team, but to professional baseball as an institution.

THE NATIONAL ASSOCIATION

The National Association (NA) was the first professional baseball organization. As such, its founders recognized the potential of baseball as a profitable business. Unfortunately, the way in which it was organized would prove to be too unstable to produce the expected profits. The NA was organized in March

William A. Hulbert, whose pride in Chicago ultimately led to the formation of the National League, proclaimed that he would rather be a lamppost in Chicago than a millionaire in any other city.

1871. The clubs had to visit each other during the season, but they were on their own to schedule the specific dates of the matches. This would prove to be problematic. The entry fee was only $10 per team. This proved to be another problem. The NA featured some clubs that were run as cooperatives.[3] These clubs were for the most part loosely organized and run more like the amateur clubs of old than a profit oriented business. Though they may have been small in number, an association is only as strong as its weakest franchise. This form of organization was the third strike against the success of the NA.

Cooperative clubs did not establish player payrolls. Instead, they split the gate, meaning that a poor turnout resulted in a meager payday. The low entry fee attracted clubs from small towns, which only exacerbated the low turnout problem. This not only resulted in low pay for the players, but made them a bigger target for gamblers looking for a little insurance on their bet. Hippodroming—the practice of throwing games—was perceived to be a widespread problem in the NA.

Low entry fees encouraged small, poorly financed teams to take a flyer on the association. They were unable to compete at the professional level however, and frequently folded before finishing the season. Twenty-four different teams played in the NA over the course of its five-year history, half of them appearing for only one year[4], including small towns such as Keokuk, Iowa, Fort Wayne, Indiana, and Middletown, Connecticut. Another five teams lasted only two years, and only three franchises survived all five years (Athletic, Boston, and Mutual).

In addition, small towns, which begat small crowds, proved unappealing to large town teams. This resulted in teams reneging on their agreements to play in small towns, finding it more profitable to stay at home and play exhibition games instead. An association without fixed schedules made it easier for teams to forego scheduling return games in smaller and more distant towns.

In 1875 for example, three of the nine eastern teams (Brooklyn, New Haven, and the Centennials), did not make a trip west to face any of the four western clubs. The Centennials folded after only a month of play, but the other two teams played the full season, hosting western clubs on multiple occasions. And the six eastern teams that did make a western swing did not always reciprocate the games the western teams played in the east. For example, the St. Louis Browns visited New York on two occasions, playing a total of six games there, but the Mutuals only played three games in its one St. Louis visit.

Gambling was not the only common vice associated with professional baseball. Alcohol flowed freely both in the stands and outside them, and all too frequently, it even spilled onto the field. Drunken behavior, which often led to rowdiness, was a common occurrence inside the ballpark.

Revolving was another issue that Hulbert abhorred. Revolving was the practice of players jumping teams from one season to the next. While he viewed this in itself as problematic, the bigger problem was that many players signed a new contract for the following season during the current season, while still under contract to another team. This led to credibility issues and further increased the attraction to gamblers. After all, if a player is contracted to another team for next year, it might be in his best financial interests to let up a bit when playing his future employers this year.

By 1875, after only five years in operation, the National Association was in trouble. It was weak and unable to play a complete schedule, or control the player jumping, rowdy behavior and gambling. The integrity of the games was so low that on occasion law enforcement officials were compelled to post signs at ballparks announcing that games played between the competing teams should not be trusted.[5] As the problems became more obvious the fans began to lose interest. Attendance declined each year of the organization's existence.[6] The time was ripe for a stronger, centrally governed league.

Hulbert was never comfortable with the National Association. As a businessman he recognized its many faults. As a proud Chicagoan, he believed that Midwestern teams, his White Stockings in particular, were slighted by the eastern-dominated organization. And as a club official, he was frustrated by the constant re-volving of players between teams. He complained that whenever Chicago signed a good player, he was likely to be stolen away by an eastern club. This complaint was bolstered by the fact that five members of his 1874 squad, including Davy Force and Levi Meyerle, the team's top two hitters, were signed by Philadelphia teams for the 1875 season.

Hulbert proved that he could give as well as take when it came to revolving. During the 1875 season he secretly signed Albert Spalding, Deacon White, Ross Barnes, and Cal McVey from Boston, and Adrian C. "Cap" Anson from the Athletics for his 1876 ball club. Both Boston and the Athletics were clubs that he intended to invite to be charter members in his new improved league—one that would outlaw the practice of revolving.

After organizing the new league, Hulbert did affect a dramatic decrease in revolving, even before the reserve rule was created after the 1879 season. A total of 211 players suited up during the five year history of the National Association, but only 138 of them played more than one season. Of those 138, only 19 percent played for only one team during their career. Half of the players changed teams three or more times, with four percent changing teams every year of the five year ex-istence of the organization. By contrast, in the first five years of the NL 27 percent of the players who were in the league for at least two years never changed teams, and only 22 percent changed teams more than twice.

As a businessman, Hulbert recognized an opportu-nity for profit and the shortcomings of the current structure in attaining that profit. The time was ripe to seize the initiative in the baseball market. Baseball was popular, familiar, and widely accessible to the general public. On larger fronts, the growth and development of the American economy was making the landscape for entertainment more inviting. Since the middle of the 19th century the average workweek had been declining and the average wage increasing. Increasing urbaniza-tion and the growth of intracity mass transportation meant that more people were in closer proximity to en-tertainment venues, and it was becoming cheaper and easier to get to those venues. Higher salaries and more free time meant Americans had the time and the money for entertainment, and baseball was well situated to satiate that growing demand. Hulbert knew that the cur-rent structure would not allow for it. Rather than let the opportunity pass, he did something about it.

William Hulbert was not the only person to recog-nize the troubles with the NA. Henry Chadwick had been publicly railing against gambling and rowdiness since before the NA even began. In the official associ-ation publication of 1873 he said that "when the system of professional ball playing as practiced in 1872 shall be among the things that were, on its tomb-stone—if it have any—will be found the inscription, 'Died of Pool-Selling.'"[7] And as early as 1867 he wrote that the model ballplayer was one who was "a gentle-man on all occasions, but especially on match days, and in doing so, he abstains from *profanity* [italics original] and its twin and evil brother obscenity."[8] Hulbert did not immediately come to the conclusion that the NA was broken and could not be fixed. While he may have been harboring such thoughts, he did not begin to act on them until after he had been appointed secretary of the White Stockings in the fall of 1874.

As the secretary, he was appointed to represent the team at the organization's annual meeting in Philadel-phia, where he was named to the league rules committee.[9] The *Chicago Tribune*, in announcing that Hulbert would represent the team, foreshadowed events under Hulbert's leadership when it commented that he held "some very pronounced ideas on the pun-ishment which should be meted out to "revolvers," and will make an excellent representative generally."[10] While there he "saw that a radical reform should be affected, and an entirely new departure made, to place the national game on an enduring footing. The idea of a National League originated then and there…and before he left Philadelphia he had thought out the general plan."[11]

THE NATIONAL LEAGUE

The concept of the National League may have begun with Hulbert's plans during the 1875 season, but the first concrete steps were taken on December 16 and 17 of that year when he convened a secret meeting with representatives of four NA clubs. Walter Newman Haldeman and Charles E. Chase, representing Louis-ville, Nathaniel Hazard and Charles A. Fowle of St. Louis, and John P. Joyce from Cincinnati met with Hulbert and Spalding in Louisville.[12] Hulbert was able to woo the westerners by appealing to their resentment over their poor treatment at the hands of the eastern clubs on issues such as revolving and the failure of east-ern clubs to make all their western swings.

The next step was to recruit the targeted eastern clubs. This was a more delicate process but Hulbert handled it masterfully. He needed to convince four east-ern clubs to join the league for geographic balance and marketing power. This would be tricky because unlike the western teams, the eastern clubs did not have a chip on their shoulder. The NA had worked well for them, so they weren't necessarily looking to go in a new direction. Hulbert had already identified the four eastern clubs he wanted. The eastern representatives who were invited were not aware of the extent of the agenda, save for Harry Wright who, for nearly a year, had been in correspondence with Hulbert, exchanging ideas for ridding the NA of its weaker clubs.[13]

The clubs were to send representatives to a meeting according to a letter to each dated January 23, 1876:

The undersigned have been appointed by the Chicago, Cincinnati, Louisville and St. Louis Clubs a committee to confer with you on matters of interest to the game at large, with special reference to the reformation of existing abuses, and the formation of a new association, and we are clothed with full authority in writing from the above named clubs to bind them to any arrangement we may make with you. We therefore invite your club to send a representative, clothed with like authority, to meet us at the Grand Central Hotel, in the city of New York, on Wednesday, the 2d day of February next, at 12n. After careful consideration of the needs of the professional clubs, the organizations we represent are of the firm belief that existing circumstances demand prompt and vigorous action by those who are the natural sponsors of the game. It is the earnest recommendation of our constituents that all past troubles and differences be ignored and forgotten, and that the conference we propose shall be a calm, friendly and deliberate discussion, looking solely to the general good of the clubs who are calculated to give character and permanency to the game. We are confident that the propositions we have to submit will meet with your approval and support, and we shall be pleased to meet you at the time and place above mentioned.

—Yours respectfully, W.A. Hulbert.
Chas. A. Fowle.[14]

While popular mythology has Hulbert taking the eastern representatives by surprise with his agenda and locking them in a room to present it, the actual invitation suggests something otherwise. By inviting them to confer about the "formation of a new association," it seems evident that he was tipping his hand.

The meeting of the National Association's Grand Council is considered as the founding meeting of the National League of Professional Base Ball Clubs (NL).

Each of the eastern teams, who were meeting with Hulbert on this topic for the first time, sent representatives. The west was represented by Hulbert and Charles Fowle. They held the proxy votes for Louisville and Cincinnati. Each of the eastern franchises was represented by owners: William Cammeyer (Mutuals), G.W. Thompson (Athletics), Morgan Gardner Bulkeley (Hartford), and Nicholas Taylor Apollonio (Boston) and William Henry "Harry" Wright, who was allegedly there to present the proposed changes to the playing rules. Also present were Lewis Meacham of the *Chicago Tribune*, the only reporter invited, and Nicholas Young, secretary of the NA, and soon to be secretary of the new NL.[15]

Dramatic accounts of the meeting tell of Hulbert locking the door and telling the assemblage, "Gentlemen, you have no occasion for uneasiness. I have locked that door simply to prevent any intrusions from without, and incidentally to make it impossible for any of you to go out until I have finished what I have to say to you, which I promise shall not take an hour." The story goes on to say that Hulbert mesmerized the gathered moguls and used his peerless salesmanship to convince everyone of his case, and then with a flourish, he produced an already completed league constitution, which was enthusiastically signed by everyone. While no eyewitness account has ever disputed the basic facts concerning who was invited, what was pitched, and that it was taken hook line and sinker, neither has any ever mentioned the locked door or the stirring sales pitch. Spalding tells this story complete with quotation, but he was not there.[16]

While the eastern clubs were necessary to the NL, each came with some baggage. Boston, the staunchest ally of the group, was a stock club, with more owners than players. A large ownership could mean a lack of involvement by any individual, since no one had sole control. A single-owner team, which Hulbert favored, was more likely to be the constant and sole focus of the owner. Hulbert himself was one of more than thirty stockholders of the White Stockings, which had been reincorporated just a few months prior. This would not be the first example of his believing that what was good for the goose was not necessarily also good for the gander.

Despite having recently raided the Boston roster of its stars, Hulbert needed and courted Boston for his new league. Boston's baseball history was rich, and Harry Wright's reputation was unparalleled in baseball. Having Boston and Wright aboard was critical to the success of the new league. Because Wright was so concerned about the glaring weaknesses of the NA and reforming baseball to save it, he was willing to overlook the loss of his stars and ally his interests with Hulbert.

The city of Philadelphia presented a problem. There were three NA teams, and the city had a reputation as a hotbed for gamblers and crooked players. The Athletics were Hulbert's choice. But their history of raiding each other's rosters would have to be papered over. The Athletics were not happy with Chicago for signing away Adrian Anson, their top player, and Hulbert still held a grudge against the Athletics over the signing of Davy Force the previous year.

The White Stockings and Athletics had been battling over players for years. In 1871 Ned Cuthbert signed with the White Stockings only to jump back to Philadelphia before ever playing a game in Chicago. He ultimately returned to Chicago in 1874. During the 1873 season Chicago signed Levi Meyerle to a secret contract for the following season. He tried to renege on the contract, but ended up playing in Chicago in 1874. The following year Meyerle and Davy Force were signed by Philadelphia clubs. Hulbert detested Athletics owner Charles Sperling so much that he swore they would not be allowed to join the NL unless he was expelled (which he ultimately was before the NL season began).[17]

Despite his personal animosity toward Philadelphia, Hulbert needed a team there. The market was too large and its baseball history too rich to leave to the NA. The Athletics needed Hulbert as well. There were several teams in the city, so joining the NL would give them geographic exclusivity at the top level, which was worth swallowing the fact that arch enemy Hulbert was involved. In the case of Philadelphia, Hulbert put the practical matter of league survival and business profits ahead of personal animosity. It was a decision he would ultimately come to regret.

The Mutuals had a reputation for employing shady players, and Hartford was smaller than the minimum sized city called for in the constitution. But New York was the largest city in the US and Hartford had Bulkeley, whose prestige and contacts would serve the league well. He was better known in business and political circles than baseball, having organized the United States Bank of Hartford in 1872 and served on the Hartford Common Council and as a city alderman. In 1879 he would take over leadership of Aetna Life Insurance Company, founded by his father in 1853. He was elected mayor of Hartford in 1880, governor of Connecticut in 1888, and then represented the state as a US senator 1905–11. Even though most of that was in the future, he already had a stellar reputation. He was from a prominent and wealthy New England family, and a successful businessman in his own

regard. Bulkeley's reputation, contacts, and business acumen were coveted by Hulbert for the new league.

Hulbert appealed to the owners, businessmen all, by using some simple economic logic. If the businessmen ran the teams and the players concentrated on playing ball, each party could concentrate on doing what they did best and everyone would be better off. The geographic exclusivity he promised to each club appealed to the owners as well. Exclusivity meant monopoly, and monopoly meant profit. Establishing the NL as the premier professional league, with entry strictly controlled by the monopolists themselves, also appealed to their sense of profits. If the new league was recognized as the premier assemblage of baseball talent then it would be able to attract a greater percentage of the better players, and with no equals to bid them away, it would lower the payroll burden, leaving a larger percentage of the revenues for the owners. Another reason to concentrate the quality of talent at the top was to reduce the number of poor drawing games played against low quality competition in small towns.

League membership was restricted to one team per city and mandated a minimum population of 75,000 (unless unanimously voted otherwise by the league—this is how Hartford gained admission). League teams were prohibited from hiring expelled players and under no circumstances could they play a game in another league city against anyone but the league team headquartered in that city. This was another means of reducing competition through geographic exclusivity.

Gambling was not tolerated by players or fans, nor was it allowed on the premises or any facilities owned by the member clubs. Teams were required to pay $100 annual dues—ten times what was required by the NA, and complete their season schedule. These two rules were the bedrock of the league and were enforced by the threat of expulsion.

Hulbert impressed upon those assembled that reforms were needed to prevent the demand for baseball from decreasing. Additional reforms included an end to revolving, a ban on alcohol at the ballpark, and no more Sunday ball. The latter item was the toughest sell because Sunday games were usually the best attended. Hulbert convinced his brethren that while a great deal of money could be realized in the short run by playing on Sunday, honoring the Sabbath would carry with it valuable moral cachet, which would result in greater long run profits.

The constitution was approved by the eight charter members at the meeting. Board members were chosen by lot. In order, the five names drawn were Bulkeley (Hartford), Apollonio (Boston), Cammeyer (Mutual),

Fowle (St. Louis), and Chase (Louisville). The legendary version of the meeting includes the detail that names were drawn from a hat, and it was decided that the first name drawn would be president of the league, which is how Bulkeley became president. Another story has Hulbert nominating Bulkeley to appease the eastern clubs. Like many legends, this one has a kernel of truth. The directors were indeed chosen by lot. This was already predetermined by Article IV, section 1 of the league constitution, which had been approved before the directors were chosen. According to the constitution the board would be determined by random drawing, and then the directors would elect a president from among their number. There is no specification that the first name drawn would be president. Since Hulbert was not a member of the board, it is more likely that his ally Fowle would have made the nomination.

It is unlikely that Hulbert would have allowed the league presidency to be determined by lot, as it would have left the leadership of the new league totally to chance, and nothing else he did was left to chance. It is possible that Bulkeley was suggested for the honor on the strength of his name having been drawn first. Bulkeley had a sterling reputation as a businessman, but only marginal and shallow baseball experience and interest. For those very reasons, Hulbert was likely to have wanted him as the figurehead president, thus allowing Hulbert to wield the real power from the background, which is exactly what happened. After the names were drawn a motion was resolved that the first name drawn be declared President of the League for 1876.[18]

An example of how Hulbert was perceived as the real power in the league can be seen in the appeal of the New Haven club. New Haven was shut out of the NL because it was too small. Hartford, which was even smaller, was allowed in because the exception clause required a unanimous vote, which they got. In February of 1876 New Haven sought to file a personal appeal, and sent their club secretary to Chicago to make the case to Hulbert. Hulbert was not the league president, nor even a board member, but New Haven knew who was pulling the strings. Without Hulbert's approval, there was no getting into the league. Their trip proved fruitless.[19]

The meeting concluded with the resignation of the invited teams from the NA and their formal inclusion in the new NL. The clubs did so in a formal declaration stating that "the abuses which have insidiously crept into the exposition of our National Game, and…the unpleasant differences which have arisen among ourselves growing out of an imperfect and un-systematized code" led to this action.[20] The break was simple and clean, no need to vote anyone out of a league. Just resign from the old organization and form a brand new one.

The new league differed from the NA in many ways, none more important than reputation. The constitution laid out very specific regulations pertaining to gambling, alcohol, and scheduling. It was important that the league live up to its constitution, and it would prove adept at doing so, thus slowly but surely rebuilding the damaged credibility of professional baseball. Over the first five years of the league each of these issues would become a high profile test of the will of the league to make very difficult decisions.

Hulbert supported a league wide requirement of 50 cent admissions because he felt lower prices cheapened the game. Higher admission fees allowed the teams to pay players higher wages, making them less likely to succumb to gamblers' entreaties. The NL established a 15 cent per ticket share for visitors. Hulbert preferred the percentage gate system to a flat fee system for visiting clubs because he felt it better supported weak clubs.

The success of the new league required that it attract the top talent. Hulbert claimed that eight was the most teams that could survive in an upper-echelon league given the quantity of available talent. The record of NL teams in exhibition games with non-league teams seemed to suggest otherwise. In 1876 NL teams lost 37 games to outside clubs, nearly one-third of the total they played. In 1877 the newly formed International Association squared off against NL opponents more than 100 times and won as often as they lost.[21]

A more compelling reason for limiting the size of the league was to insure financially stable franchises. Identifying eight such clubs proved to be a vexing problem. During its first decade of existence 21 teams were members of the NL at one time or another. In fact, by its third season only two of the original eight franchises remained in the league. The situation became so perilous that at one time Hulbert chaired a two man committee authorized to appoint any outside club in good standing as an emergency replacement in case a league team folded.[22]

The new league may not have been the knight in shining armor to baseball's maiden in distress that the folklore paints it, but it did do three important things that have made the baseball business the cash cow that it is today. First, they separated production (on field play) from management (front office). This not only took advantage of the different skills of two distinct groups of workers, but also concentrated the control and the profits in the hands of a small number of businessmen.

Second, using the puritanical arguments about observing the Sabbath and taking the moral high ground, the league cleansed the bleachers of the rough and rowdy crowd that gambled, drank, swore, and fought in the stands. Those same folks were less likely to attend games on other days because they were at work. Raising the ticket price to 50 cents from a quarter priced this lesser element out of the market. Covered grandstands, ladies in attendance, padded seats, and season tickets all operated as a form of conspicuous consumption that helped attract the coveted higher income classes into the ballpark.

Hulbert sought to make ballparks attractive to women. Not just any women, but upper class "genteel" women. Women would not visit the ballpark if there was rowdy behavior on the field and in the stands, which was the case when alcohol was commonplace before, during, and after the games. Less booze meant less fighting and hooliganism, which meant more women. And the more women in attendance, the more of a mollifying effect they were likely to have on the male behavior, further domesticating the ballparks. Hulbert was not a pioneer; he was following a profitable example set by eastern vaudeville houses, which had discovered that a family atmosphere appealed to a larger crowd.[23]

Finally, the idea of geographic exclusivity, now the bulwark of any professional league, was established. It was the innovation of Hulbert for the National League and it served two purposes. The first was to carve out monopoly territories for the owners, boosting their profit potential. Geographic exclusivity created the monopoly conditions that allowed the league to raise ticket prices to 50 cents. Second, once established, it helped the league keep interlopers out and profits up.

Hulbert also instituted the first fixed scheduling. This was an important innovation that helped the league control its requirement that all teams play their full schedules. By establishing a fixed schedule, in one fell swoop Hulbert eliminated the excuse that any team could not find a mutually agreeable date to travel to another city to finish its schedule. This made it tougher for teams to renege on their obligations and much easier for the league to monitor and enforce scheduling compliance. This issue was to come up much sooner than expected, and have dramatic results for the league. Hulbert also insisted on uniform contracts (though not right away), established a roster of umpires, and championed the reserve rule, though it was not strictly his idea.

Writing these things into the constitution and issuing press releases to brag about them was one thing. As the experience of the National Association demonstrated, enforcing them was quite another. The issue of enforcement was where Hulbert made his strongest stand. Over the first five years of the league his resolve was tested several times, but three incidents stand out above all others: the eviction of the New York and Philadelphia franchises after the 1876 season, the lifetime expulsion of four Louisville players in 1877, and the eviction of Cincinnati in 1880.

THE EVICTION OF NEW YORK AND PHILADELPHIA

The first hint of major trouble for the new league occurred toward the end of the inaugural season, when neither the Athletics nor the Mutuals completed its schedule. Neither was willing to make its second (and final) western swing. The Athletics told Chicago and St. Louis they could not afford a trip west but offered to host Chicago to complete the schedule. They offered 80 percent of the gate to Chicago and St. Louis if they would come east.[24] Hulbert refused.

Likewise, William Cammeyer reneged on the Mutuals' final western trip for reasons of financial hardship. Hulbert reacted differently to the Mutuals, whom he needed more desperately in his league. Chicago and St. Louis each offered Cammeyer a $400 guarantee for making the trip for a two-game series in Chicago and three in St. Louis. Cammeyer refused, and neither the Mutuals nor the Athletics finished its schedule, setting up a dramatic postseason showdown.[25]

According to the league constitution, both would be expelled. However, abandoning the two largest cities in the league would be a risky move. Hulbert felt strongly that the integrity of the league must be upheld, and he began posturing for expulsion well before the league meeting in December.

In reference to the upcoming meeting, Hulbert wrote to Boston owner Nicholas T. Apollonio about how important it was to the league that every club play out its schedule and that no club employ a man expelled from another club. "I know of no other possible use for a combination of clubs except to enforce these two things,"[26] said Hulbert, clearly stating his intentions before the meeting. Hulbert intimated that he intended to take a hard line, and was lining up support.

The first order of business at the annual meeting was the election of a new president. President Bulkeley was not at the league meeting, having previously offered his resignation in order to focus on his political career. After the board formally accepted his resignation, Hulbert nominated Nicholas Apollonio as his replacement. Apollonio refused, indicating that he was unsure he would still be involved with the team much longer. In fact, he was already in negotiations to sell the club, a fact that Hulbert was almost certainly aware of.[27] After Apollonio demurred, Hulbert was then unanimously elected to replace him.

As expected, the major topic of business was the fate of the New York and Philadelphia franchises. Taking the moral high road and holding strictly to the league constitution, Hulbert argued that expulsion was necessary for the survival of the league, its reputation hanging on the outcome of the expulsion vote. The *Chicago Tribune* called the meeting "the most important event in base-ball since the formation of the National League."[28] Hulbert carried the day, convincing the other owners that failure to enforce the constitution was tantamount to a death sentence. If the National League did not enforce its own rules, it would be no better than the organization it had abandoned just a year earlier, and would inevitably suffer the same fate as the National Association.

Cammeyer left the league without appeal. He did so, however, having already arranged to lease his Union Grounds to the Hartford club for the 1877 season, thus preserving his primary reason for being involved with baseball—profits. This also made it easier to expel the Mutuals, since the league would still have a presence in New York. Neither team was immediately replaced, and the NL played with six teams for the 1877 season.

THE LOUISVILLE FOUR

At the end of the 1877 season Hulbert presided over a moral crackdown on hippodroming, permanently banning Louisville players George Hall, James Devlin, Bill Craver, and Al Nichols from the league for throwing games during the season. He used the situation to his fullest advantage, proving once again that the league was serious about upholding its constitution. Shortly after the announcement of the Louisville debacle, he wrote to Hartford manager Bob Ferguson: "Certainly nothing can be lost to the legitimate game by the conviction and punishment of the thieves and scoundrels who infest it and by their presence as players bring disgrace and contempt upon it…Now it strikes me, the exposure and conviction upon their own confession of the four men named, makes our forthcoming League meeting an excellent time and place to strike an effective blow."[29]

At the league meeting in December of 1877 the directors unanimously expelled the players. It wasn't just the Louisville franchise that suffered from the scandal,

but St. Louis as well. They had contracted with Devlin and Hall for 1878. St. Louis had been in financial straits and looked to Devlin and Hall for redemption. When they were expelled, the team gave up and resigned from the league. Their resignation was accepted shortly after the league expelled the players for life. St. Louis would not return to the NL until 1885, three years after the St. Louis Brown Stockings established a franchise in the American Association.

Though Louisville was represented at the December meeting and participated fully in all deliberations, there was no news coming out of the city all winter about roster moves for the next season, and indeed, in March they withdrew from the league. The *Louisville Commercial* reported that the team folded because they "were so thoroughly disgusted with the conduct of the players last season that a call upon them now would meet with a cold response," adding that "the rascality of last year's players and the general conviction that dishonest players on other clubs were more the rule than the exception."[30]

If ever the new league was going to collapse, it should have been following the 1877 season. The NL had kicked out teams in the two largest cities after the first year, dropping membership to six teams. Then in 1877 it endured a player gambling scandal and the midseason bankruptcy of the Cincinnati club, followed by the loss of two more franchises before the opening of the 1878 season. Heading into its third season, the league had only two of its original franchises in the fold (Boston and Chicago), three of the four remaining franchises were in their first year of existence (Indianapolis, Milwaukee, and Providence) and the Cincinnati entry, while still in the same city, was a replacement franchise for the one that had folded in June. Hartford had also dropped out of the league after the 1877 season, having played that year in Brooklyn as the Brooklyn Hartford. And yet the league survived. Hulbert's moves, which directly caused the exit of the Mutual and Athletic clubs and indirectly led to the loss of Louisville and St. Louis, strengthened the league in the long run. Despite the short run chaos of musical franchises, the league was establishing credibility. Ousting teams and players for failing to abide by the constitution bolstered the reputation of Hulbert and the NL, which proved to be of great value in the long run.

THE EVICTION OF CINCINNATI

The 1880 season featured another team expulsion, this time the Cincinnati club. Cincinnati had been making a regular habit of leasing their ballpark out for Sunday games. This was a constant source of irritation to Hulbert, since it flouted the spirit of the Sunday prohibition. To make matters worse, beer was sold at those Sunday games—another Hulbert taboo. The final strike against the Redlegs was their desire to do away with the reserve rule that Hulbert championed.

Late in the 1880 season *Cincinnati Enquirer* sports editor O.P. Caylor blasted Hulbert in print for refusing to allow beer sales. He threatened to orchestrate Hulbert's ouster from the presidency, and failing that, to organize a whole new league.[31]

In a rant against beer and Sunday games, the *Chicago Tribune* chastised Cincinnati. The *Tribune* opined that "the question both of Sunday games and beer-jerking is not one of morals, but of sound business policy. Base-ball, outside of Cincinnati, is supported by a class of people by whom these practices are regarded as an abomination—a class of people whose patronage is of infinitely greater value in dollars and cents, let alone respectability, than that of the element to whom beer is an attraction and a necessity."[32]

At the league meeting in December the constitution was rewritten to prevent the playing of *any* [emphasis added] games at league parks on Sunday. It now read no "club shall take part in any game of ball on Sunday or shall allow any game of ball to be played on its grounds on Sunday."[33] At the same meeting Cincinnati was expelled for failing to satisfactorily guarantee that it would observe the new constitution.[34]

Caylor did not go quietly after the ouster of the Cincinnati franchise from the NL following the 1880 season. He threatened to start a new league, scheduling a meeting for its planning. However, nothing came of it that year. But the following fall the American Association (AA) was born. The AA was organized on an anti-Hulbert platform. It promoted Sunday games, beer sales, and discount admission prices of 25 cents. Hulbert would not live to see it.

THE INTERNATIONAL ASSOCIATION

In 1877, after abolishing the two largest cities from the league, Hulbert addressed another potential crisis when a competing organization was formed. In February 18 independent teams gathered in Pittsburgh and formed the International Association of Professional Baseball Players (IA) to replace the NA. Membership was $10 or $25 if the team wanted to compete for the championship. A total of 23 clubs signed up for the league, seven paying the higher fee to compete for the championship.[35] The IA wasn't interested in going to war against the NL. After all, its

clubs, all of which existed prior to its formation, profited greatly from the exhibition games regularly scheduled with the NL. Rather, the formation of the IA was in response to the demand for baseball in the many cities ignored by the NL. The IA included teams from towns ranging in size from Auburn, NY to St. Louis. Most of the clubs were run as cooperatives, and the players earned a share of the gate, not a salary.

Though it was a loose-knit organization, resembling the NA in its minimal membership fee and the size of its venues, the NL took it seriously. They allowed NL teams to schedule exhibition games with IA teams, but forbade the playing of those games on NL grounds.[36]

The "League Alliance" was the most effective response to the IA. The plan was actually conceived by Abraham Mills, a future league president and eventual employee of Hulbert's. In exchange for a $10 fee and their promise not to sign any player on an NL roster, alliance clubs received reciprocal respect for their player contracts and territorial rights. The alliance tied IA clubs to the NL with the promise of mutual respect for player contracts and bans on ineligible players. Twenty-nine clubs joined the alliance in its first year, including future MLB cities Minneapolis, St. Paul, Indianapolis, Milwaukee, Providence, Syracuse, Troy, and the once and future Philadelphia.

So who would join under such circumstances? Any team that saw the future: the National League was the standard bearer of quality baseball. The path had been blazed, and the future was the National League. Better to ally with it than be crushed underneath it. While the NL was not yet the behemoth that it would become, the impression that Hulbert gave about the inevitability of the success of the NL under his guidance was enough to convince several teams to ally with him.

Hulbert used the alliance approach as opposed to a more confrontational one for two reasons. The first was simple business: cooperation was more profitable than confrontation. After all, few IA teams were in NL cities, and those that were did not pose much threat. A secondary, though non-trivial reason for the cautious approach was that while NL players were better paid, the cooperative format of the IA offered players more control over their fate. The NL had to move slowly against this foe lest they force their hand and lose players to the more labor friendly league. Touting higher pay and the ability of players to concentrate on playing ball as opposed to front office details worked to the NL's advantage. After all, most ballplayers were not businessmen, and did not necessarily want to be.

Eventually the lure of higher salary won out over the ability to have more control, and the best players gravitated to the NL. As the NL increased its number of league games, leaving fewer opportunities to play exhibitions, it left fewer chances for IA players to compete against top notch competition, making the league even less attractive to the best players, and hence paying customers. The IA slowly faded away, folding in 1880.

THE HULBERT LEGACY

William A. Hulbert fell ill in the fall of 1881 and died of heart failure on April 10, 1882. Though it took 113 years after his death, William Hulbert was eventually inducted into the Hall of Fame. No inductee ever had to wait as long for the honor as Hulbert did. His enshrinement is a testament to his contribution to the game. But perhaps more than that, his legacy is the institution that still stands today. The National League, which in 2014 concluded its 138th season, has successfully beaten back the challenges of the International Association, the Players League, the Union Association, the American Association, and with American League, the Federal League. Furthermore, all major sports leagues in North America are built on the same foundation established by Hulbert: geographic exclusivity, separation of management and players, fixed schedules, a roster of umpires/referees, uniform contracts, and in the beginning, the reserve rule. William Hulbert may have been forgotten for a century after his death, but his imprimatur on professional sports yet endures. ∎

Notes

1. I would like to thank Greg Erion, John Thorn, participants at the 2013 Economic and Business History Society conference, the 2014 Popular Culture/American Culture Association annual meetings, the 2014 Society for American Baseball Research conference, two anonymous referees and Clifford Blau for helpful suggestions and comments, and Richard Smiley for valuable assistance in finding newspaper articles. Any remaining errors or omissions are solely my responsibility.
2. Abraham G. Mills papers and correspondence, National League, 1891–1926, series III folder, National Baseball Library.
3. Harvey Frommer, *Primitive Baseball: the First Quarter-Century of the National Pastime*, New York: Atheneum, 1988, 130–31.
4. Teams did not always finish the season that they started. And when they did finish, they didn't necessarily play a full schedule. In fact, in no season did all teams play even close to the same number of games. The best year was 1871 when Ft. Wayne played 19 games and New York played 33 (the average was 27.8). The worst was 1875 when Hartford played 82 games, Keokuk played 13, the league average was 51.5 and three of the 13 league teams played less than 20 games.
5. Bill Mooney, "The Tattletale Grays," *Sports Illustrated*, October 14, 1974, E6. www.si.com/vault/1974/06/10/616133/the-tattletale-grays.
6. Lee Allen, *The National League Story*, New York: Hill & Wang, 1965 [revised edition], 3.
7. Albert G. Spalding, [revised and re-edited by Samm Coombs and Bob West], *Base Ball, San Francisco*: Halo Books, 1991, 116.
8. Dean A. Sullivan, ed., *Early Innings: A Documentary History of Baseball*, Lincoln, NE: University of Nebraska Press, 1997, 66–7.
9. *Spalding Official Base Ball Guide*, Chicago: A.G. Spalding & Bros., 1883, 5.
10. *Chicago Tribune*, December 6, 1874, 2.
11. *Spalding Official Base Ball Guide*, Chicago: A.G. Spalding & Bros., 1883, 6.
12. *National League Meetings, Minutes, Conferences & Financial Ledgers*, BA MSS 55, National Baseball Library, 17.
13. Melville, Tom, *Early Baseball and the Rise of the National League*, Jefferson, NC: McFarland & Co., 2001, 79.
14. *Spalding Official Base Ball Guide*, Chicago: A.G. Spalding & Bros., 1886, 8–9.
15. *National League Meetings, Minutes, Conferences & Financial Ledgers*, 17.
16. This story is recounted in detail by Spalding in his book.
17. Neil W. MacDonald, *The League That Lasted: 1876 and the Founding of the National League of Professional Base Ball Clubs*, Jefferson, NC: McFarland & Co. Inc., 2004, 45.
18. *National League Meetings, Minutes, Conferences & Financial Ledgers*, 17.
19. Macdonald, 67.
20. *National League Meetings, Minutes, Conferences & Financial Ledgers*, 15–16.
21. Tom Melville, "A League of His Own: William Hulbert and the Founding of the National League," Chicago History, Fall 2000, 55.
22. Harold Seymour, *Baseball: The Early Years*, New York: Oxford University Press, 1960, 87.
23. Michael Haupert, *The Entertainment Industry*, Westport, CT: Greenwood Publishing, 2006, 11–13.
24. MacDonald, 194.
25. MacDonald, 194–95.
26. Chicago Cubs records, Chicago Historical Society, Hulbert letter to Apollonio, Nov 22, 1876.
27. True to his word, the brief baseball career of Nicholas Apollonio ended before the year was out. He sold the Boston franchise to Arthur Soden, who would become famous as the originator of the reserve rule.
28. *Chicago Tribune*, December 10, 1876, 7.
29. J.E. Findling, "The Louisville Grays' Scandal of 1877," *Journal of Sport History* 3, no. 2, (1976), 184.
30. Findling, 186.
31. David Pietrusza, *Major Leagues, Jefferson*, NC: McFarland & Co., 1991, 44.
32. *Chicago Tribune*, August 15, 1880, 12.
33. *National League Meetings, Minutes, Conferences & Financial Ledgers*, 132.
34. *National League Meetings, Minutes, Conferences & Financial Ledgers*, 132.
35. Lynn, London, Columbus, Pittsburgh, Guelph, Manchester, and Rochester were the seven who paid the steeper fee to contend for the championship.
36. Pietrusza, 49.

Michael Kelley's 1906–08 Woes with Organized Baseball

Dennis Pajot

Michael Kelley played only briefly in one major league season. Despite this lack of major league success he was a highly respected minor league player and manager. However, he found himself in extremely hot water with Organized Baseball for three years, starting in 1905. From being a part of a sham sale of the St. Paul franchise—a circumstance that actually placed him as chairman of the board of directors of the American Association—to later refusing to report in a trade to a major league team—thus challenging baseball's reserve clause. During this time Kelley's name appeared as many times in the newspapers' legal proceedings pages as in the on-field baseball pages.

Michael Joseph Kelley was born on December 2, 1875, in Templeton, Massachusetts. After high school he was offered scholarships to Dartmouth, Harvard, Brown, and Amherst. But much to the disappointment of his father, who hoped that Mike would pursue a career in law, Kelley chose baseball, signing with Augusta of the New England League in 1895. Thereafter, Kelley played with Newport, Ottawa, Rochester, and Hartford before being sold to Louisville of the National League in July 1899, where he had a .241 batting average in 76 games for the Colonels.[1] This would constitute his only playing time in the big leagues. In December 1899, Kelley was traded to the Pittsburgh Pirates in a multi-player deal that included future Hall of Famers Fred Clarke, Rube Waddell, Honus Wagner and Jack Chesbro. Then in March 1900, he was purchased by Indianapolis of the still minor American League. After two seasons in Indianapolis, Kelley became the first baseman and manager of the American Association St. Paul Saints from 1902 through 1905. During this period his clubs won two pennants, and finished third and fifth in the AA (1902: 72–66, third place; 1903: 88–46, first; 1904: 95–52, first; 1905: 73–77, fifth). In those years his batting averages were .272, .310, .298, and .285.[2] These accomplishments should project a cozy club/manager/player-type story. But things went sour between Kelley, the Saints, and the American Association.

The seeds of discord were planted on January 25, 1905, with the announcement that St. Paul owner George Lennon had sold the club to a stock company headed by Mike Kelley, who was soon elected president of the Saints. This gave Kelley the distinction of being the only player in the country to serve as a club president. Lennon also resigned his position as chairman of the board of the American Association, and Kelley assumed that position, as well.[3] Lennon still retained his half-interest in the AA Toledo Mud Hens, but sold same to J. Edward Grillo in March.[4] But it soon turned out that the St. Paul sale and Kelley's club presidency were only a front. Kelley had been named as president of the Saints solely in order to take over Lennon's position on the board of directors—a position Kelley could not hold as a player. Kelley later admitted he had never been elected president by the club, but had only acted as president for Lennon, with limited powers.[5]

Kelley and Lennon were having troubles during the season. It finally came to a head in mid-August, with Lennon offering Kelley for sale. The *Minneapolis Journal* commented, "Kelley is a splendid player, but it is said that internal dissensions in the direction of the business affairs of the club this year have been at the bottom of the poor showing of the team. Kelley is thought to have been a trifle listless and the club caught the fever." The day that this story was published the Saints were in sixth place with a 51–58 record.[6]

Exposure of the sham nature of Kelley's Saints presidency began with a report that Kelley wanted to manage the Toledo club in 1906. The St. Paul management issued the following statement regarding the situation:

> Mr. Kelly [sic] has no authority to negotiate with Toledo for next year without the consent of the St. Paul club. He was engaged only as a player and still remains under reserve to St. Paul. He does not own any stock in the St. Paul club whatever. He is for sale, however, to other Association clubs, or in fact any club. Clarence Huggins, secretary of the St. Paul club, will be released from further duties at once. George Lennon will again take hold of the affairs of the St. Paul club.[7]

Thereafter, Lennon stated that Kelley had been given an opportunity to become a part-owner in the club, but he had been unable to find backers and no stock was issued to him. Lennon said that if Kelley went to Toledo, it would cost the Mud Hens $4,000 for his services.[8]

Lennon moved quickly by selling Kelley to the St. Louis Browns of the American League on August 23.[9] (Lennon also sold shortstop Pete O'Brien, outfielder Charles Hemphill, pitcher Walt Slagle, and catcher Jack Sullivan to the Browns.[10]) Kelley refused to go to St. Louis, saying that he did not sign a contract with St. Paul, so he could not be held under their reserve clause. In addition, as Kelley was president of the club himself, Lennon had nothing to say about the matter. Kelley admitted that he wanted to manage Toledo in 1906, as this would be a stepping stone to managing a major league club.[11] To resolve the situation, Kelley appealed his sale to St. Louis to baseball's National Commission, and on September 1, the Commission put a temporary stop to the sale while the matter was under review.[12]

In front of the National Commission Kelley insisted that Lennon had sold him to St. Louis in retaliation for his collecting gate receipts to recoup some $6,000 in back salary due him. Kelley also offered proof that the $1,500 that Lennon had received from the Browns as purchase money was actually Lennon's own money, a fact concealed from public view to make the deal look sound. In addition to this "fake sale," Kelley claimed that he had never signed a contract with the Saints. He had only had an oral agreement with the club.[13]

On November 16, the National Commission ruled that Kelley must go to St. Louis and play ball for only about $1,500, compared to the $4,000 that he had made in St. Paul. The Commission stated that his acceptance of salary and continuous re-engagement without protest was the equivalent of a signed contract and carried with it all of the obligations and rights that inhere in contracts. In the ruling, American League president Ban Johnson and Commission chairman Garry Herrmann voted in favor of the St. Paul club, while National League president Harry Pulliam withheld his vote.[14]

At the same time, word was spreading that Kelley would become president of the Minneapolis American Association club, with the franchise's current president and manager William Watkins going to Indianapolis as a magnate. Watkins said that he wanted to dispose of the Minneapolis club due to business obligations in Indy.[15] The day after the National Commission's ruling, Kelley filed a petition in Federal District Court in Cincinnati seeking an injunction restraining the Commission from putting its decision into effect. Kelley claimed that under the present circumstances, if he did not report to St. Louis he would be blacklisted and deprived of his means of livelihood. He further alleged that the members of the Commission had a pecuniary interest in the situation and were therefore prejudiced against him. A temporary restraining order was issued until the case could be taken up for a full hearing.[16]

In December, Judge A.C. Thompson heard testimony on the case. He later determined that Kelley had signed a contract in 1901, but that this had occurred prior to the adoption of baseball's National Agreement. The reserve clause in that agreement could not, therefore, be held to have any bearing on the case. George Lennon contended that he had purchased Kelley in 1901 for $500 from Watkins, who owned the Indianapolis club of the Western Association at the time. Lennon always considered Kelley a player, paying him liberally, and considered him a valuable asset of the club. Kelley acknowledged that he had played for Indianapolis, but contended that the team's dissolution before the end of the season had released all the Indy players from their contract obligations. Kelley had merely promised Watkins that he would play for him in Indianapolis the following year. In the meantime, Kelley had gone to St. Paul to finish the 1901 season. There, Kelley was advised that his promise to Watkins was not binding because Watkins had no baseball rights at the time. But Kelley felt himself bound by his promise and told Lennon to make what terms he could with Watkins. Thus, any payment of $500 to Watkins by Lennon was in no sense a purchase, according to Kelley.[17]

Kelley's litigation ace in the hole was his election as chairman of the board of directors of the American Association earlier in the year. At the time, George Lennon had informed the other directors that he did not consider Kelley to be a player, and on this assurance, Kelley was elected to the board chairmanship, a position that he would have been ineligible to hold if he was a player. To substantiate his position, Kelley proffered affidavits to this effect submitted by AA directors to the National Commission and the federal court.[18]

At the hearing's end, Judge Thompson kept the temporary order in force, making things clear to organized baseball with the following directive: "The respondents are enjoined individually and as officers and members of the National Commission from making any finding or taking any action whereby any baseball club in the United States would be prevented from or placed under any penalty for playing or engaging said complainant [Kelley] as a player for the baseball season of 1906 or thereafter."[19]

While the temporary injunction was still in effect, Kelley announced that he had given up on managing in Toledo and was going to make an effort to purchase the Minneapolis Millers of the American Association.[20] His lawyer, Fred Hoffman, released this statement on December 6, 1905: "On account of the favorable decision of Judge Thompson [in keeping the temporary injunction in place until February] I have advised Manager Mike Kelley to go ahead with his business for next year, and he will undoubtedly sign a contract to manage the Minneapolis club in the American Association. The final hearing in the case will not come up until the February term of court, but Kelley cannot wait that long to arrange his affairs for the coming season, and will at once make an agreement with Mr. Watkins of the Minneapolis team, to take charge of the players for 1906. Of course, he runs chances of losing out in his fight against the national commission when the case is heard in February, but I feel certain that with the evidence at hand Kelley will come out on top."[21]

On December 17, it was announced that Kelley would be at the head of an organization of local capitalists that would take over the Minneapolis ball club from Watkins about January 1. Kelley made this statement:

I have an option on the team and franchise. The first of the week I shall start out to raise such cash as I need and I expect to close the deal with Mr. Watkins on his arrival here the latter part of the week. The franchise here is a valuable one and it will be little trouble to swing the deal. There is the nucleus of a good club here and I am certain I can make Minneapolis one of the strongest teams in the circuit. The Minneapolis public will do the rest if we get a good strong team. I want to come to Minneapolis and this is the first favorable opportunity I have had.

It was reported Kelley would put his own money into the deal and wanted to organize a local stock company of owners by having the entire franchise owned in Minneapolis, rather than by outside investors.[22]

On December 26, 1905, it was reported that Kelley had purchased the Minneapolis Millers from William Watkins. It was said that he had put his own money into the sale, and had the "backing of several prominent men of affairs of the Flour City."[23]

Within days, the American Association met in Chicago for its annual meeting. The owners of the Association had been split for some time on various issues. On one side of the divide were George Lennon, Kansas City Blues-Louisville Colonels owner George "White Wings" Tebeau, and Milwaukee Brewers owner Charles Havenor. They formed one voting bloc of the American Association. The other side contained William Watkins, Thomas Bryce of Columbus, J. Edward Grillo of Toledo, and now Mike Kelley of Minneapolis. When the meeting began Tebeau was nominated as temporary chairman for the year. According to George Lennon, a new chairman was needed because former chairman Mike Kelley was no longer a member of the American Association. He was property of the St. Louis Browns. A vote was taken, but only the three pro-Tebeau owners cast ballots. When Tebeau assumed the chair, Kelley rose and left the room with Bryce and Watkins, (for some reason Grillo was not in the hotel) stating that the "real director's meeting" would be conducted in another room. Tebeau and company paid no attention and demanded that Kelley—now former chairman of the American Association board of directors—turn over all league books, papers, and funds entrusted to him. Kelley refused and the newly installed directors adjourned. In the meantime, Kelley convened with his supporters in the other room. Kelley then resigned as AA board chairman, and Watkins was elected to succeed him.[24]

While all this was going on, American Association president Joseph O'Brien was waiting in the wings. He tried to call a meeting of the Association together, but he could not get a majority of club owners to attend. Finally, Grillo consented to join the pro-Tebeau group in the meeting, apparently to "protect himself against any frame-up." With five clubs now represented [keeping in mind George Tebeau owned two clubs], the meeting was called to order, but then immediately adjourned with no business taken up—including the transfer of the Minneapolis Millers to Kelley. Kelley was not overly concerned about all this, saying that it was only an internal matter, and would be resolved—with his side winning, of course.[25]

The next day things took another unusual turn. During the season it was the duty of the chairman of the board to collect a three-percent duty from all clubs to be used for any emergency that might develop. At season's end, club owners received a check for their share of any balance in the emergency fund. But when some presented their fund balance check for payment at the bank, they were informed that the check could not be honored. It turned out that during the season Mike Kelley had retained a bookkeeper who had asked for $125, but been refused. The disappointed bookkeeper subsequently garnished a portion of the emergency fund on deposit. The pro-Watkins/Kelley owners were able to get to a St. Paul bank before the others and were able to cash their checks. Upset pro-Tebeau men claimed that the cashed checks were illegally drawn from the account, as they were signed "Kelley, chairman," and Kelley was no longer a member of the Association, at least in their eyes. Kelley explained that all this was only an attempt to embarrass him. The bookkeeper would get his money when he completed his work, as Kelley was not about to pay him for a task not completed. Kelley then dismissed the tempest, saying that "it amounts to nothing."[26]

It appears that the American Association was beginning a war it had little hope of winning in the public mind. The sports writer who used the name O'Loughlin commented in the Minneapolis Journal: "The public has mighty little interest in the internecine fights between club owners of ball teams. …Both sides of this fight are firm, however, in the announcement that it is a fight to the last ditch. …It will take a legal battle to settle it if the magnates cannot agree. Legal battles cost a lot of money, and in this case such a fight would only concern seven or eight men." Then O'Loughlin got to the real point:

This is only a battle of bubbles, in reality, but the further the fight goes the more bitter it becomes. For their own protection, the protection of their pocketbooks and the good of the game these fellows should get together, break a bottle of milk and kiss and make up. It is a fight where all of them will lose in the long run, if it keeps up. Local sentiment is strong for Kelley and Watkins, and they will receive the full local support. It is to be presumed that similar conditions obtain in the other cities. The magnates should be spending the time they are using to talk fight in hunting up fast bush leaguers.[27]

On January 6, 1906, the transfer of the Minneapolis baseball club was formally completed. The sale price was reported to be about $30,000.[28] The new ownership syndicate consisted of Kelley (said to be one of the largest stockholders in the franchise) as president, director, and manager of the team. E.J. Westlake (of the Commercial Club) was elected vice-president. Walter D. Boutell (a member of the firm of Boutell Brothers, a big local furniture house) was named treasurer and a director. L.A. Lydiard (the city clerk of Minneapolis) was appointed secretary and a director, and E.G. Potter (a former state Senator), A.T. Williams (manager of the A.D.T. Company), John Van

Nest (alderman of the 13th Ward), and Wallace G. Nye (also of the Commercial Club) were named as directors.[29] The new ownership also signed a five-year lease on Nicollet Park and Minnehaha Park (where the Millers played Sunday games).[30] The team personnel went with the sale, except two players, Win Kellum and Mike Kahoe, who accompanied departing club owner William Watkins to Indianapolis.[31] One man who stayed with the club was Ed N. Dickenson, who had been with the Millers since he "carried bats for Perry Werden in the years gone by." He was now the superintendent of tickets, gates, peanut and pop concession, "and dictator of lineup on the scorecards." It was written that he "had been with the club so long that he is always listed as one of the immovable fixtures when the club is sold. He is right in the class with the grandstands, save that unlike them he never gets full."[32]

Kelley was given complete control of managing franchise affairs, including responsibility for the signing and releasing of players, and for signing all club checks. He was to report to the directors from time to time, but in general had a free hand in the general policy of the club. His first statement as president was one usually made by one in this position: "That I will give my best efforts toward making the club a playing and financial success seems hardly worth saying. I have a financial interest here now, and with an all-Minneapolis directorate behind me I feel that the club will do more business than ever before."[33]

Kind words were published for former club owner Watkins. The Minneapolis Journal wrote:

Today marks the end of the Watkins regime, and in leaving the club Watkins takes with him the friendship of almost every fan in Minneapolis. He came here two years ago, and while he did not win a pennant, he had good teams and was a stickler for fast, clean play and an uncompromising enemy of rowdyism in the field. The gentlemanly conduct of the Minneapolis teams on the field has been generally commented upon all over the circuit and it has been in a great measure due to the strictness of Watkins. He is a splendid business man, an astute manager and one of the cleanest men to be found in baseball today.[34]

In response to talk from St. Paul and George Lennon that the club sale was fake,[35] the Minneapolis Journal wrote of the new owners: "Men of the caliber of those in the new company are not mixing in fake sales, and this transfer will put an end to much of the chatter of the rebellious element in the American Association."[36]

With Kelley's American Association suit still pending disposition in federal court, the new Minneapolis manager brought a lawsuit against George Lennon in February alleging non-payment of his full compensation for services rendered to the St. Paul club in 1905. Kelley was seeking $2,369.69, with $1,000 attributed to unpaid salary and the balance for commissions on the sale of ball players. Kelley had originally brought suit against Lennon for the $1,000 in 1905, but discontinued the litigation when Lennon promised to settle. Not receiving any money, Kelley went to the courts again. In May a jury awarded Kelley a verdict of $889 and costs for his unpaid commissions.[37]

All along the central problem between Kelley and the American Association was his reserve as a player. As long as he did not play, it really did not matter. But on March 29, 1906, the National Commission promulgated a ruling that no player under reserve could become a bench manager. The Commission further decreed that Kelley would not be recognized as an owner.[38] The next day, Kelley supporters proposed that Kelley deposit $1,000 under protest with the National Commission, and then ask for a reopening of his case on the ground of a new development. Apparently this development was the claim that the St. Louis Browns had now offered to set a reasonable price upon Kelley's release. If true, such action would clear up Kelley's troubles. Kelley was not at the meeting, held in Chicago, where this strategy was unveiled, but club secretary Lydiard agreed it was an efficacious way to address the problem.[39]

The $1,000 was sent, but American League president Ban Johnson stated that John Bruce, a stockholder in the St. Louis Browns who had handled the deal, lacked the authority to act for the club. Therefore, Johnson would not accept the money for Kelley's release. It was now asserted that St. Louis had paid the St. Paul club $1,800 for Kelley, and that the Browns wanted that amount for his release. At this point, National Commission chairman Garry Herrmann said Kelley would be allowed to manage the Millers from the bench, but not be allowed to play until he secured his release.[40]

On April 17, the day before Opening Day, American Association president Joseph O'Brien sent a wire stating that Kelley could not manage his team from the bench. This left Kelley little recourse but a return to the courts. He had been willing to meet the Association half way, but it now appeared some were out to get him. O'Loughlin of the Minneapolis Journal saw only bad consequences from what lay ahead:

There is no doubt but that if the matter is thrown into court the whole bondage system of "organized baseball" will be knocked higher than a cocked hat in a Kansas cyclone. The contract, release and reserve system of baseball is farcical for justice and equity to the players, and once it is lined up against the regular law of contracts of almost any state the baseball law will go glimmering. Kelley has hesitated over involving himself and the American Association in a lengthy and expensive litigation, but there appears to be no other course left open to him.

O'Brien's act, if he has made the order attributed to him, means the beginning of a red-hot fight in the Association, and one that may mean the disruption of the league, the formation of a new one and a general rearrangement of western minor league baseball.[41]

Even in Milwaukee, where the Havenor faction was anti-Kelley, sentiment was with Kelley. Tom Andrews, sports editor of the Evening Wisconsin, wrote:

It may be organized ball wants to make a man pay nearly $2,000 because he wants to retire from the playing end of the game and become a business man himself, but it is not in keeping with American principles, and if the case is ever given a hearing in court there is not the slightest doubt that Mr. Kelley will be given his rights. If Kelley was a star player and he wanted to leave the St. Louis club and become a player-manager there would be some cause for asking a fair price for his release, but there is not a manager in the major leagues who would engage Mike Kelley at any kind of a salary to play first base (this is not intended to belittle Kelley's ability as a minor league player), and in this case Mike does not want to play ball, but simply to manage a team that he is interested in himself.[42]

Kelley sat in the grandstand on Opening Day in Louisville. It was reported that Garry Herrmann had issued a notice that Kelley could not participate, meaning as a player. However, O'Brien misconstrued this as meaning as a player or manager. It was said Herrmann called Kelley long distance and told him he could indeed manage from the bench, but as a favor asked Kelley to refrain from doing so. The report claimed that the National Commission chairman said he would notify O'Brien not to interfere with Kelley as a manager in any way, shape, or manner. Back on the field, the Colonels beat the Millers, 11–7, before 6,000 fans.[43]

The next day, Kelley took his seat on the Millers bench. Umpire Clarence "Brick" Owens told him that, under instructions from league president O'Brien, he was obliged to order Kelley to leave. If Kelley did not vacate the bench, the game was to be forfeited to the Colonels. Kelley replied, "If I go my team goes with me." The game was then declared a 9–0 forfeit win for Louisville. After the aborted contest, Kelley told the press, "I decided that the only way to fight the opposing faction is in their own style. I have always tried to be square and open in the game and avoid any Indian fighting, but I've got my back against the wall now; they can show their hand and I'll stay with them to the finish. Minneapolis is as good a baseball city as there is in the circuit, and if the other Association teams can afford to stand for this I can."[44]

Garry Herrmann informed the press that he had not given Kelley permission to sit on the bench, as Kelley claimed. Herrmann said, "I alone would not have the power to do such a thing. However, since the incident of yesterday Kelley has applied for permission to sit on the bench while his team is playing, and I am now having telegraphic correspondence with other members of the commission on the subject. Nothing definite has been done yet, but I believe the manager of the Minneapolis team will be granted the permission. There could be no harm in it."[45]

The next afternoon—April 20—Kelley sat on the Minneapolis bench undisturbed, and managed his team to a 9–3 loss. Herrmann had telegraphed Louisville owner George Tebeau that the Kelley situation came under a ruling made by Harry Pulliam and Ban Johnson some time back on the cases of Ned Hanlon, Connie Mack, and some other bench managers. Based upon that ruling, Herrmann stated that Kelley could manage from the bench, but he could not appear in uniform or be on the coaching lines. AA president O'Brien was compelled to abide by this direction, but ruled that the forfeited April 19 game would still stand.[46] Finally on May 8, 1906, the National Commission dismissed the controversy about Kelley's managing on the bench, stating that it would not interfere. A few days later, Kelley withdrew his lawsuit from federal court, and started negotiations with the St. Louis Browns to secure his release.[47]

In early June Kelley found himself in a little trouble with the law, but this time it had nothing to do with George Lennon, the St. Louis Browns, the American Association, or the National Commission. On June 6 the Indianapolis sheriff served warrants on Kelley and eight members of his team for playing a Sunday baseball game on the previous April 22. The warrants had been issued April 27, grounded upon a grand jury indictment, but this was the first opportunity that the sheriff had had to arrest the players within the jurisdiction. Kelley and his men posted a bond of $50 each and were released.[48]

Things appeared to be going smoothly between Kelley and the American Association, but cracks soon began to show. In the closing game of a series in Louisville on June 12, Kelley claimed that he and Colonels manager Suter Sullivan had agreed that the two teams would play until only 5:15 PM, in order to give the Millers time to get to the train station. Umpire Steven Kane understood this, Kelley maintained. But when it came time to call the game, the Millers were ahead on the scoreboard. Kane ordered the teams to continue playing, and the Colonels scored two runs in the ninth inning to win the game, 3–2. Umpiring with Kane was Brick Owens. Obviously, Kelley was not happy.[49]

Then on June 16, 1906, Toledo newspaperman Howard L. Spohn wrote that Kelley claimed that umpires Owens and Kane had relayed the signals of Minneapolis pitchers and catchers to the Louisville batters during the series in Louisville.[50] Here is what Kelley was alleged to have said:

When we landed in Louisville and the first day our pitchers were slaughtered, we naturally were greatly surprised. I talked to the boys and they were at a loss to explain the matter. They one and all said that the curves were breaking right, and they couldn't understand why they were being touched by everybody. That night a lurking suspicion was confirmed when Jesse Stovall came to the hotel and laughingly said: "Well, the buzzer from the house back of center worked pretty well today, didn't it?" Then he did his best to call our attention to that house and the possibility of signals being tipped from it.

His actions were so suspicious that I decided at once that he was stalling. I was still more firmly convinced of this when several other members of the team insisted on calling our attention to that same house, and I decided to watch closely the second day. I did so, and I found to my entire satisfaction that Kane and Owens were the boys who were doing the dirty work.

When a fast ball was signaled for, whichever umpire was behind the pitcher would draw his feet together and fold his arms. When the ball had passed the plate or been hit he would drop his arms. When a curve was called for he would step to one side with one foot for an out and with the other foot for an in. It was at first hard to believe that they would go so far, but I watched it closely and found out that every solitary ball was being tipped in advance. It wasn't occasional—it was the rule.

Then the next day we fixed up a deal. We arranged to cross every third or fourth ball, and the result was that they couldn't hit a little bit. It was downright funny to see the look on the faces of those batsmen when they would lean over and reach for a ball which had been tipped a curve out which came at them fast, straight for the head. Their look of surprise tipped the thing easily.

Well, on this same day, to make the matter strong, Claude Elliott was sent into the second story of this house and he would lean out of the window so far that everybody could tell just who he was. But it was all a stall. They wanted to get our attention to that house, while Kane and Owens got in their dirty work. Nothing could change my mind. I know I am right, and so does every man who was on the field. We had a fine chance against that game.[51]

The first game in Louisville was on June 9. The Millers lost 14–5, with the Colonels collecting 16 hits. The next game was again won by Louisville, 8–3, the home team knocking out 12 hits. The Millers won game three, 9–4, while the Colonels won the last game—the game that should have ended at 5:15 PM, 3–2.[52]

American Association president Joseph O'Brien was furious with Kelley and issued this statement from his office in Milwaukee:

Mr. Kelley has been making trouble for the Association all the year, first by fighting over his sale to St. Louis, and later about managing the team from the bench after the commission had refused him that privilege.

He has also been inciting fans at Minneapolis to roast umpires and the like, and now seeks to pass it off by charging crookedness on the part of the umpires. He has gone too far and must answer to the Association. The matter will be thoroly [sic] investigated, and Mr. Kelley will have a chance

to defend himself, but if guilty he may be put out of baseball. The charges are unfounded and ridiculous, and Kelley should be the last one to make such insinuations. He will get the limit of punishment, and he deserves it.[53]

O'Brien immediately started an investigation and suspended Kelley and both umpires, pending a hearing.[54] The *Minneapolis Journal* thought "this French style of pronouncing a verdict and then taking evidence will not go."[55] The newspaper was certainly on Kelley's side, commenting, "Kelley has not been a trouble maker and O'Brien knows it as well as anyone. Kelley only asked to be let alone in managing his club. His Toledo utterances may or may not have been intemperate, but he has been goaded past the point of endurance. He has not inspired the mobbing of umpires. The arbitrators alone are to blame, and Kelley should not be held responsible for the outbreaks of pinheaded thugs."[56]

Kelley denied making the inflammatory statements, but in Columbus he was quoted as standing by the story, only saying that as printed, it was far more elaborate than the way he had told it. At first, press accounts supported Kelley.[57] W.W. Landman, a director of the Toledo baseball club, told reporters what had happened. Landman said, "I met Mike in Toledo shortly after his arrival from Louisville. He was feeling very sore over the treatment he had received there, and in the course of a conversation told me that he believed the umpires had tipped the signals of the Minneapolis team. He said that he did not propose to make any row over it, or even make his opinion public, as he had no way of proving it, and he gave it to me as a personal belief, not as a fact. In some way the newspapers got hold of it and spread on it, with the result that it has made an ugly tangle."[58]

Within days, president O'Brien cleared umpires Owens and Kane to resume work. According to the *Milwaukee Journal*, "They are needed in the game, and as Manager Mike Kelley of Minneapolis is not a necessary article in the successful conduct of the American Association, he has been fitted with a bright tin can of double thickness pending an investigation."[59] On June 21, the American Association directors convened a special meeting in Chicago to hear the charges. The Louisville players had made sworn statements to the effect that neither Kane nor Owens "wigwagged" the signals to them. After a reading of affidavits from the umpires in which they denied unequivocally that they had ever been guilty of tipping signals, their suspensions were officially lifted. Kelley appeared in person, swearing that he never made such charges. Kelley claimed that his players believed that the umpires had it in for them, and the story began with that. The Colonels had even gone so far as to put a player in a window of a house across the street to keep the Minneapolis suspicions of signaling going. Kelley said that the Louisville scheme worked well, as it certainly distracted his players. Kelley further asserted that he told the reporter there was nothing to the talk of the umpires being involved, but the reporter "simply misconstrued the things which were said by the players and myself." The reporter who had broken the story refused to appear at the hearing, and after a discussion of more than two hours, Kelley was exonerated by the board.[60]

All remained calm for almost a month. Then in the eighth inning of a July 18 game with the Columbus Senators in Minneapolis, umpire Owens called a Miller runner out at the plate. The Millers vocally and physically disagreed, with Millers' first baseman Frank Freeman being ejected from the game. The Senators went on to win the game, 2–1, in 12 innings. Immediately after the game ended, fans from the bleachers swarmed onto the field and began throwing stones and clubs. Owens had to be escorted from the field and placed in a carriage by the police. The unruly crowd continued pursuit of the umpire until a police captain "mounted the seat and threatening to draw his revolver, lashed the horses out of the mob and to safety."[61] American Association president O'Brien immediately suspended Freeman and shortstop Andy Oyler for seven days and fined each $50 for an alleged assault upon Owens. In addition, Millers players Bill Fox, Lefty Davis, and Gene Ford were each fined $50 on a charge of rowdyism and inciting the fans. Manager Michael Kelley was reprimanded but not fined.[62]

Kelley was outraged at the suspension and fines, maintaining that his players were not responsible for the actions of the fans. He also felt that O'Brien should have come to Minneapolis and personally investigated the incident before imposing discipline.[63] Kelley immediately got a court injunction allowing Oyler and Freeman to play.[64] The next day, O'Brien gave umpire Owens orders that if either Oyler or Freeman played, the game was to be declared forfeited. Five thousand fans—an unusually large crowd for a Thursday afternoon game at Nicollet Park—were on hand, many armed with a large stock of eggs and the "avowed intention of 'getting' Owens'." Against the advice of police, Owens took his post, as eggs started flying across the field. None found their mark. Meanwhile, Oyler and Freeman took their positions in the field.

With the Senators' Ollie Pickering in the batter's box, Hank Gehring threw the first pitch of the game and Owens yelled out "strike one." O'Loughlin of the *Minneapolis Journal* later quipped, "No one knew whether he called a strike on Pickering or was referring to the egg that found such a splattering point upon his anatomy." At that, Owens immediately turned and ran toward the grandstand, bombarded by a broadside of eggs. Police escorted the umpire out of the park and to a waiting bus. Acting under instructions from president O'Brien, Columbus manager Billy Clymer refused to play without Owens as umpire and withdrew his team from the field. But the game was not called a forfeit at the time, as Owens had not called the game off while on the field. The crowd was given rain checks and left the grounds happy.[65]

President O'Brien declared the game a 9–0 forfeit win for the Senators and fined Kelley $100, suspending him until the fine was paid. The AA president also declared that Minneapolis was in danger of losing its franchise if it refused to abide by league rules. O'Brien then pulled Owens out of Minneapolis, sending him to Kansas City and replacing him with umpire Egan. The next day, Kelley paid his fine and the Columbus-Minneapolis series continued, without Freeman or Oyler on the playing field.[66]

Soon Millers secretary L.A. Lydiard got into the act, accusing umpire Owens of having bet $200 on the game of July 18. To support the charge, Minneapolis management secured affidavits from three "well known gamblers" which averred that they had an understanding with the umpire regarding when to bet on Columbus. According to one gambler's affidavit, he was approached by Owens who proposed to advance money to him to be bet on Columbus. In return, Owens would pay him a 25 percent commission on his winnings. The gambler stated that he refused to take the money, but acted on Owens's suggestion that Columbus was a cinch to win the game. The gambler placed his own bet on Columbus, later paying Owens 25 percent of his winnings. The other two affiants stated that Owens had approached them in the Brunswick Hotel and given each $100, directing them to bet at odds of 10 to 7 on Columbus. Each received a 25 percent commission on the money won by Owens from the bets placed by them.[67]

Owens emphatically denied the charge, saying that he did not have any money to waste betting on ball games. Owens asserted that he did not know any gamblers in Minneapolis, but he did know one man who had lost money on the July 18 game. The proprietor of the hotel where Owens lodged had lost $6 and was all over the umpire. Owens and others were certain that Michael Kelley was behind the allegations. Kelley said that he had nothing to do with them.[68]

Newspapermen in other cities were beginning to view Kelley in a different light. Manning Vaughan in Milwaukee wrote:

> Kelley, by his methods both on and off the ball field, has gained the title of trouble maker of the American Association, and his present step against Owens is but another step in the persecution he has heaped on the umpire all year. … Kelley has been going over the circuit hinting broadly that he would land his arch enemy sooner or later, and from then until now he has pursued the arbiter with a persistence which is sure to drive either one or the other out of baseball.

> But if anybody goes it will in all probability be Kelley. Not only has he defied all the laws of baseball, but by his actions two or three times this season he has cast a cloud of suspicion on the American Association, not only among the fans of the league, but all over the country. He has done more to hurt the game in the league than all the other rowdies taken collectively, and unless he is driven out of baseball the game as a clean sport in the Twin Cities will soon become a matter of history. …Lovers of clean sport can never and do not favor Kelley, and as long as he keeps up his fight against all that is right in baseball so long will he have thousands of fans wishing him out of the game.[69]

A scheduled July 31 AA meeting in Chicago to investigate the allegation was postponed when Milwaukee owner Charles Havenor and Louisville-Kansas City owner George Tebeau were unable to attend. St. Paul owner George Lennon held their proxies, but given the gravity of the charges, it was decided that the two owners should be present at the meeting.[70]

O'Brien had had enough of charges aimed at his umpires. He was quoted as saying,

> I called the meeting to clean all the dirty linen that has been accumulating in the Association for the past six months. The principal question to be considered will be the charges that Umpire Owens has been placing money on games in which he officiated. While we are at it, however, I intend to dig deep and to stop this constant charging and alleging that this or that other umpire, manager or player is playing dirty ball or acting against the rules. It has got to a point that can no longer be borne.[71]

Others agreed, deeming the charges no more than a vehicle for smearing the reputation of Owens, and could not be proven. Fuel was added to this suspicion when Lydiard lawyer Boutell said that he was very much in doubt if he could produce his witnesses.[72] Owens' attorney Henry J. Killilea of Milwaukee denounced the allegations made against his client, declaring, "The charges are preposterous, and the evidence that we will bring up against the Minneapolis charges in the morning will astound the directors who have doubted the character of Owens. If the Minneapolis directors are unable to produce their witnesses named in the affidavits I may help them, so you can judge for yourself how certain I am of the result of the meeting. If the umpire is found to be innocent nothing too severe can be meted out to the men who instigated the attack, and it is up to President O'Brien to sift the affair to the bottom."[73]

The meeting started at 9:00AM. on August 1, 1906. L.A. Lydiard was present with his attorney, as was Clarence Owens with his. Mike Kelley did not attend. The three gambler affidavits were read. They bore the signatures of "R. Smith," "Fred English," and "George Kusch." Norman W. King, a Minneapolis detective employed by president O'Brien, "threw a bomb into the camp of Owens' opponents" when he offered proof that "Smith" was in a sanitarium about twenty miles from Waukesha, Wisconsin, suffering from delirium tremens. And Smith was not his real name. Rather, he was identified as Emil Dulquist,[74] and he admitted that he got $20 for signing what was represented to him as merely a statement. Dulquist said that he was under the influence of liquor at the time.[75] King also furnished evidence that "Fred English" was another fictitious name. The true name of the man who signed the second affidavit was Byron, a gambler out of work and willing to do almost anything to make $20. It was further discovered that affiant "Kusch" was someone well known to the AA directors, but his real name was not disclosed at this time.[76] One of the affiants (probably the man known as George Kusch) sent a letter to Joseph O'Brien (that arrived on the day after the hearing) that stated that he was drunk and given $20 to sign the paper. This man (who did not give his real name) said he did not know Owens and had not seen a professional baseball game in ten years.[77]

Another hearing witness was an unnamed conductor on the Northern Pacific Roadway. He testified that a man named Fred Briggs had approached him in a saloon in Minneapolis and offered him $20 to sign a statement to the effect the Owens had wagered $200 on the game of July 18. The conductor testified that he turned Briggs down, but Briggs told him he already had two affidavits and wanted a third. According to Manning Vaughan of the *Milwaukee Sentinel*, Fred Briggs was a political constituent of Lydiard's and a gambler.[78] Thereafter, American Association umpire W.J. Sullivan testified that he was in Minneapolis on the day of the game in question, and that Owens was broke and had borrowed $10 from him until he got paid. To the directors, this seemed to prove conclusively that Owens had not placed a $200 bet on the July 18 game.[79]

At the conclusion of the proceedings, the American Association board of directors found the charges against Owens "wholly and entirely false." The following resolution was then passed:

Whereas, false and malicious charges involving the honesty and integrity of our national game as conducted in this Association were filed and published by a person or persons interested in the Minneapolis baseball club, and,

Whereas, said false and malicious charges have been a great injury and injustice to this, the American Association of professional baseball clubs, and to organized baseball in the United States, and realizing the duty we owe as officers of this Association to organized baseball to see that the guilty parties are properly and promptly punished for the wrong and injury done to this Association and to organized baseball; therefore, be it

Resolved, That the president of this Association be authorized and directed to immediately proceed to investigate and determine who is the guilty party or parties and report the same to this board, with the proper charge or charges to be preferred for a prompt and adequate punishment.[80]

Lydiard attorney Boutelle gave a detailed statement to the press when he arrived home from Chicago. He stated that after the July 18 Columbus-Minneapolis game, ugly rumors were flying about which needed to be looked into. According to Boutelle, if the rumors had any foundation, it was self-evident that they "must be run down amongst the class in the community that would be most likely to be engaged in gambling jobbery on the smaller scale. The management placed the investigation in the hands of a man whom they believed could trace the matter if it was susceptible of being traced at all." A few days later the man engaged reported that he had tangible evidence, and that three men were prepared to make affidavits or oral statements as to the facts of the matter. Lydiard had the witnesses give sworn statements at the attorney's office, and the Minneapolis management had no reason to assume that these parties were giving anything except the actual facts. Management then followed what seemed the only appropriate course to take, namely, to place the information in the hands of the National Commission as well of the president of the American Association. No charges were preferred by the Minneapolis people, and their sole intention was to present the information to the appropriate authorities for such action as they might deem warranted.

President O'Brien then called for a meeting to be held in Chicago on very short notice, and directed the Minneapolis management to procure the attendance of the men who swore to the affidavits. The time proved too short to comply with this directive. In the alternative, Minneapolis management proffered its version of the circumstances surrounding the assignment of umpire Owens to the Columbus series; what happened in the game (i.e. the fining of five players); the suspension of two players, and the refusal of O'Brien to come to Minneapolis to personally investigate the case. Management also claimed that it possessed a large number of affidavits from prominent businessmen and others "tending to disclose personal animus and hostility upon the part of Umpire Owens toward the Minneapolis team." The request of the Minneapolis management to have the case held in St. Paul was denied and they were forced to go to Chicago.

At the August 1 meeting, the Minneapolis management declined to act in the capacity of prosecutor of any charges made against Owens. They simply wanted to present the information that they had obtained. The AA board of directors refused to look at all the information, only being interested in the matter of Owens' purported betting on the game. When the Minneapolis team requested that the other matters be followed up on at a later time, the board refused that, as well. Boutelle concluded by saying: "They [Minneapolis management] do feel that it would have been a wise and better course to have taken less precipitate action in this matter and to have given it the benefit of a further and more complete investigation. The board, however, appeared to be satisfied to act on the evidence then before it and the charges were resolved then and there in favor of Umpire Owens, exonerating him fully."[81]

To add a strange twist to the case, the man who signed the affidavit as "R. Smith" died at the sanitarium within hours of Owens's exoneration by the board. Emil Dulquist had been drinking heavily, and a few days prior to the board meeting, he had been sent to the sanitarium for treatment. The *Milwaukee Sentinel* reported that Dulquist/Smith was a well known gambler in Minneapolis, who had formerly worked and lived in Milwaukee.[82] Then the day after the hearing, the *Minneapolis Journal* located the anonymous railway conductor who had testified at the proceedings. He gave the name F.W. Robinson, with a home address of 1322 Dupont Avenue. The superintendent of the Northern Pacific Roadway later said that no such man worked for the railroad out of Minneapolis. Nor was such a name listed in the city directories. The address was also bogus. 1322 Dupont Avenue North turned out to be a vacant lot, while there was no such address as 1322 Dupont Avenue South. To add to all this, no man by the name of Robinson was known at the saloon where the $20 offer was said to have been made.[83]

In a lengthy editorial on the "mistreatment" of Kelley by president Joseph O'Brien and the American Association, the *Minneapolis Journal*'s "The Dutch Uncle" wrote these lines in his Sunday "Boots and Boosts" column regarding the affidavits and Robinson:

O'Brien admitted to the writer, within two weeks, that this man [Robinson] was protecting his job by using an alias. Protecting the fact that he was an honest man so that his employer could not find it out and fire him for telling the truth!

O'Brien, Tebeau and the rest, if they knew this man was telling a lie about his name, residence and occupation, did not so inform the Chicago reporters, but apparently let it go forth as true with the possible intention of further besmirching the Minneapolis club. I do not know anything about the truth or falsity of the three affidavits accusing Owens. To knock him out, tho [sic] cleaner evidence should have been brought than that of a man, an anonymous man, skulking behind the alias. He was produced by a private detective, a relative of whom was offering for $50 an "exclusive story" to the effect that the three affidavits accusing Owens were false, to a St. Paul newspaper three or four days before the meeting in Chicago. A fair, impartial tribunal would not

go on such evidence. The innocence or guilt of Owens should have been established beyond all question, as the charge was a serious one and neither the Association nor the umpire can afford to have any cloud over the clean-up.[84]

Kelley protested that he was in no way responsible for the charges against Owens. "I have had absolutely nothing to do with this affair, although some people have tried to bring me into it. Mr. Lydiard acted entirely on his own responsibility in preferring charges against Umpire Owens. In fact, I did not know of the matter till the affidavits had been presented. This is a case for others to fight and not myself."[85] Kelley soon found out that he was wrong on this count.

Joseph O'Brien issued this statement: "It is now my duty to make a thorough investigation. I have no idea where it will lead to, but I will start immediately. We cannot submit to this sort of talk, as it does injury to everyone. An attempt was made to take Owens' bread and butter from him and ruin his otherwise good reputation as an umpire." Ban Johnson said that the National Commission might assume control of the proceedings from the American Association if justice were not done.[86] Owens let it be known that the matter was not forgotten by him either. He proposed to sue Lydiard, Mike Kelley, and the Minneapolis baseball club for criminal libel and seek damages of $100,000 for defamation of character.[87] Kelley did not seem fazed by all this commotion. Three days after the hearing, he was in Burlington, Iowa looking over a local squad for prospective players for his Millers. A few days later, he reported that he had signed four new players for his team.[88]

On August 12, 1906, O'Brien announced that he would hold a trial on August 22 in Milwaukee to air the evidence against Lydiard and Kelley in the Owens case. In the meantime, the two were suspended from all privileges in the American Association. O'Brien made it clear what the object of the "trial" would be by writing that Kelley and Lydiard were "to show cause why [they] should not be expelled by said American Association as an officer of the Minneapolis club."[89] With his team in Indianapolis, Kelley wrote back to O'Brien: "You have no grounds for suspending me as manager of the Minneapolis club, except personal prejudice. Your action in this matter is in line with your decisions in other cases in which the Minneapolis club was interested. In suspending me before trial you are simply taking advantage of your position as president of the American Association, and you are hereby notified that I shall take action immediately to protect my interests."[90]

Baseball people in Minneapolis were not taking all this very well. O'Loughlin of the *Minneapolis Journal* wrote the day after O'Brien's announcement:

The idea is held locally that Kelley is being made the butt of the Association for his every act, not because of any of his actions, but because he, in his fight for his rights, took baseball "law" into court and showed that it was worthless. He "showed up" some of the baseball leaders in a bad light. He has never been forgiven.

Minneapolis fans are tired of the whole business. They are angry at seeing one of the best cities on the circuit ruined and crippled to satisfy spites and grudges. They will not stand for more of it. If Mike Kelley is "Sloughed" by the board of directors without a full review of the whole affair, without an open, fair and impartial hearing, on that day professional baseball becomes a dead cock in the pit of Minneapolis. Kelley could organize an independent team and do more business in Minneapolis than could a Tebeau-Havenor dominated team playing in the circuit parks.[91]

It even appeared Kelley's action were causing friction among the parties usually on his side—including his own stockholders. The *Indianapolis Sun* wrote:

Kelley has not only been an expensive proposition for the owners of the Minneapolis team—and it is now said that Kelley does not own much of the stock—but he has gotten the team into all sorts of trouble. If Kelley is retained as manager and president by the Minneapolis stockholders it is said, it will completely rearrange the political alignment of the A.A. and the Watkins faction will be in the minority. The policy that Kelley has pursued has not been that of the real owners of the team, and it is said that he has gone against the instructions of those that have paid him his salary. Bryce of Columbus is now hot after Kelley's scalp, and it is understood that he has told the members of the so-called Watkins faction that unless Kelley is deposed he will desert the faction.[92]

Though suspended, Kelley was still running the team. On Sunday August 19, 1906, shortstop Andy "Pepper" Oyler did not show for the game, saying merely that he "did not care to play." The *Minneapolis Journal* observed that "as a result manager Kelley sent Graham, the utility man, in as shortstop and Oyler sought a cool spot at the clubhouse." The paper also reported that before the next day's game against Columbus, Kelley chose pitcher Gene Ford as his starting pitcher. "Michael J made up his mind to this at 3:30, yelled his decision thru a knothole in the left-field fence and then hiked out for a riverbank and a shade tree. He did—like Kelley did."[93]

The hearing was held on August 22. The evidence against Kelley and Lydiard was weak. The only person appearing in the flesh was a bartender named James McCarthy of Minneapolis, who told the directors that Lydiard asked him if he knew anything of gambling on the games in Minneapolis. McCarthy said that he did not. Fred Briggs testified about how he secured the gambler affidavits and swore that he did not pay a cent to anyone for making them. President O'Brien was asked about the persons whom he conversed with in Minneapolis about the affair, but George Lennon, chairing the meeting, sustained an objection to the question. Presented was a letter from "George Kusch" stating that the affidavit that he had made against Owens was false. It also came out at the hearing that the infamous F.W. Robinson's real name was Daly, and that he lived at 1333 [not 1322] Dupont Avenue North.[94]

In all, the testimony showed that Kelley knew that the club directors were getting affidavits together on Owens' suspected betting on games, but that Kelley did not take any part in securing the affidavits and that he did not know that they were sent to O'Brien until after the mailing. Kelley swore that he had nothing to do with these actions and that Lydiard had pushed the matter through. Kelley went so far as to say that president O'Brien had "been after" him all season and that he [Kelley] had refused to have anything to do with the Owens affair because he feared that league directors were "laying for just such an opening" in order to oust him from Organized Baseball. The proofs also suggested that the whole kerfuffle was sparked by a Minneapolis newspaper editorial about gambling on ball games, and the intimation that umpire Owens was mixed up in it. On a point of procedure, Kelley lawyer M.H. Boutelle thought it peculiar that the directors of the American Association had never recognized Kelley as president of the Minneapolis club, but still had summoned him to Milwaukee to show cause why he should not be expelled from that office.[95]

Nothing was done immediately to Kelley or Lydiard. On the same day as the proceedings, Milwaukee businessman August "Gus" Koch purchased the Minneapolis Millers from Kelley and his backers. According to an initial report, Koch had actually purchased all 300 shares of the club stock from William Watkins and Charles Ruschaupt, who had purchased the stock from Kelley and Lydiard when these two were suspended and could have nothing more to do with the club. At present, Watkins was the owner of the Indianapolis Indians franchise and Ruschaupt was a local businessman associated with the Indy team. The purchase price of the Minneapolis franchise was said to be around $20,000, or about $10,000 under what the club was thought to be worth.[96] (However, the *Milwaukee Journal* of August 23 stated the price was understood to be between $30,000 and $40,000.) Koch stated that he would like to have kept Mike Kelley as his manager, but was not sure if this would be allowed, as Kelley had apparently been "quietly" blacklisted by the American Association. For the time being, Millers captain Bill Fox would be in charge of the team until the Kelley issue was resolved.[97]

Gus Koch was a Milwaukee businessman who had been on the fringes of baseball for a number of years. For a long time he owned a saloon on East Water Street (now North Water Street) but had retired when Milwaukee became a "tight town." His obituary said that "for years he was proprietor of a gaming house on East Water Street, and that business is said to have netted him a large fortune." In the 1890s he also conducted vaudeville shows in the Exposition Building with future American Association president Joseph O'Brien, but the venture had sustained heavy losses that resulted in a lawsuit against O'Brien. At the time of his death in 1907, Koch was a wealthy man with considerable property interests on the west side of Milwaukee, in addition to property in other cities.[98]

Koch loved horses, but his hobby was baseball. In 1900, he was involved in the formation of a proposed major league to be called the National Association. Koch would be the holder of the nascent circuit's Philadelphia franchise. But when the American League took over Philadelphia and other cities that the association had intended to set up in, the National Association died stillborn. In early 1901, and supposedly with National League backing, a revived major league American Association was proposed, primarily to smother another newly-declared major, the American League. Koch and Joseph O'Brien were to head its Detroit franchise. But the anticipated financial backing of the National League never materialized, and by February this American Association was also dead. Reportedly, Koch lost $6,000 in the venture. An obviously bitter Koch later told the *Detroit Journal*,

Faro, poker, roulette and the horses are gentlemen's games compared to the game of the magnates. In the former a player has a chance; in the latter, you have no chance on earth. Now, a good, decent-looking porch-climber has my admiration. He will take a chance to get the coin, but when you deal with National League baseball magnates you are given the dope in a glass of sparkling champagne, and when you wake up you find the magnates have changed from Dr. Jekylls to Mr. Hydes. Oh, yes, I woke up all right.[99]

In the late summer of 1902 there had been talk of Detroit and Baltimore being jettisoned from the American League, with Pittsburgh and New York taking their place in 1903. Included in this report was the assertion that Boston American owner Henry J. Killilea (later the Milwaukee attorney for umpire Brick Owens) would take over the budding New York franchise, and that Koch would purchase the Boston club from Killilea. There was even a report that Killilea wanted to purchase the Detroit club and move it to Milwaukee.[100] These stories were empathically denied by Killilea who kept the Boston Americans, which won the 1903 AL pennant and then the World Series.

When Gus Koch purchased the team, the Millers were in fourth-place with a 62–61 record. The first game played under the new ownership on August 22 was a success, the Millers beating Bill Watkins' Indianapolis Indians, 1–0, before 500 fans at Nicollet Park.[101] Unhappily for Koch, the sale of the Millers was not met with favor by the Minneapolis fans. Mike Kelley was very popular in Minneapolis, and it was felt that he got the short end of the affairs with the American Association owners. Koch was also seen as allied with the anti-Kelley owners, and now that group had a majority in American Association councils.[102]

In his first statement to the press, Koch said all the right things:

The club is mine in its entirety. No one else has a dollar invested and if there is more stock issued or sold it will be to Minneapolis people. I am not a believer in the syndicate baseball idea and will not sell stock to anyone not a resident of the city.

It is my purpose before the beginning of another season to become a citizen of Minneapolis. I own several pieces of property and a residence in Milwaukee and as it is the slow season I do not want to sacrifice my holdings down there. It is my intention, however, to close out in Milwaukee and become an out-and-out citizen of this city. I regard this as my last move financially and will naturally want to be on the ground.[103]

To the accusation of being in the anti-Kelley camp, Koch had this to say: "The report that Havenor, Tebeau and Lennon are backing me or friendly to me is true to a certain extent so far as friendship is concerned. Had these men not been friendly to me I could not have taken hold of the club, as they control the board of directors and the board of directors say who shall and who shall not hold a franchise in the league. They are not interested financially with me. I will say that emphatically. I own every share of the stock."[104] Koch wanted Kelley to run the team, and expected him to be exonerated. Having attended the hearing in Milwaukee, Koch thought that he had heard nothing that could result in unfavorable consequences for Kelley. And Koch would use all of his influence to get Kelley back in good standing. In the meantime Captain Fox would continue to run the team.[105] Koch summed up his position by extending an olive branch. "Under the conditions prevailing in the league I believe I am the logical man to take hold here and am willing to give it a trial. I am going to treat everybody fairly and cannot ask the same treatment unless I do so. There will be no changes in the policy of the local club, as I can see no need for changes. I think things have been handled all right here so far as I can see."[106]

Within a week of Koch purchasing the team, there was a story published that he wanted to sign Bobby Quinn, presently the business manager of the Columbus Senators, to run his team. There were also suggestions that American Association president O'Brien wanted Quinn in Minneapolis. Koch was quick to deny all this, saying "I intend to retain personal charge of the club for the time being. It is possible that I shall select a manager later on, but not now. There is no truth in the story that Quinn has been offered the position."[107]

As we shall see, it appeared that Kelley did manage the team at times—from the grandstand. As would be expected, Koch stated that Kelley had not acted in the capacity of club manager since his suspension.[108] But immediately after the season was over, an article in the *Milwaukee Journal* divulged how Kelley had continued to manage the Millers:

The carpenter cut out a nice panel just back of the players' bench on the Minneapolis side of the grandstand. It was a panel 18 inches deep and 7 feet long. Then Kelley had wire screening tacked up. The carpenter built a house around about the atmosphere and the hole, and put on a door and lock. Then he constructed a bench for Michael, and the king of Nicollet Park mounted his throne.

It worked nicely. It gave a splendid view of the ball park in whole, and the manager could whisper to his players as they sat on the bench, and they could hear him. His head was not 10 inches from their caps. He could signal them when the team was on the field, or to the base runner, by changing the position of his hand on the screen.

He was complying with Joe's ultimatum that he could not sit on the bench and must keep out off the field. Joe was circumvented completely, and 'the coop' came to be a laughing post all around the circuit.[109]

But Koch maintained that he had only had Kelley scouting other teams for him.[110]

The Millers would end the 1906 season in third place, with an 80–71 record [according to the *Minneapolis Journal* and *Milwaukee Journal*. The 1907 Reach Guide gave the Millers an 81–68 record, while the Minor League Encyclopedia gives the Millers record as 79–66]. The team went 18–10 while Koch owned it.[111] About a week after the season ended, Gus Koch ran into trouble with city government. It was discovered that the fence on the east side of the team's Sunday playing grounds at the Minnehaha ballpark was located about 60 feet onto land that was to be used for a city street. That meant that the ballpark dimensions would have to be shortened and re-arranged. This expense, moreover, came on the heels of an increase of $25,000 in the tax assessment imposed by the city board of equalization.[112]

In October, Koch told the press that he was undecided who would manage the Millers in 1907. He wanted Mike Kelley, but with Kelley's suspension still in effect, Koch needed to act soon or go into the spring without a manager. Koch said that he had another man who could manage the club in 1907, and who would be just as good as Kelley, but Koch was not then at liberty to give out his name.[113] In the end, Koch never had to make any managerial decisions. On October 22, 1906, he sold the team to Michael and Joseph Cantillon. The Cantillon brothers were well-known in baseball circles. Joe had managed the AA Milwaukee Brewers for the past four years, while Mike was the president of the Des Moines team of the Western League. The reported sale price was $15,000, which meant at least a $5,000 loss in two months for Gus Koch.

Minneapolis Journal sportswriter O'Loughlin summed up Koch's role in Minneapolis: "Like almost every peacemaker, August received a heavy wallop for his pains. He found Minneapolis in a state of seething indignation at the league leaders for their conduct. He was tickled to death, evidently, to find someone to unload his club upon." Koch asserted that he had told American Association leaders that he wanted Kelley or he wanted out of Minneapolis. He was told that he could not use Kelley, the Cantillons were brought forward as purchasers, and the deal for the Millers was closed.[114] The next day, Koch said that he was looking to purchase another baseball team, thought to be the Indianapolis Indians.[115] This did not occur, as Gus Koch would only live another six months. He died in Milwaukee on May 3, 1907, age 47.[116]

Within days of the transfer of the Minneapolis Millers, Joe Cantillon was signed to manage the Washington Nationals of the American League, notwithstanding the fact that he still was co-owner of the Millers. Mike Cantillon would manage the Millers in 1907. In another twist, Jack Doyle, who had managed Mike Cantillon's Des Moines team in 1906, took over in Milwaukee as Joe Cantillon's replacement for the 1907 season.[117]

As neither Mike Kelley nor L.A. Lydiard was connected with the Minneapolis franchise any longer, the American Association board of directors was powerless to take further action against them. Accordingly, the AA owners decided to send all the hearing testimony to National Commission chairman Garry Herrmann for action "at the earliest possible opportunity." As for that maneuver, Kelley's lawyer said that "the meeting was acrimonious in the extreme and was marked by many clashes. The result was a fiasco for the prosecution, and sending the case to the National Commission was a clever way to end it without an open defeat."[118] Kelley was also outspoken, telling the press, "There is a big difference between civil law and baseball law. In civil law a man is innocent until proven guilty. In baseball, a man is guilty until proven innocent. At least, that is the way my case stands. The best I can get is the worst of it."[119]

The day after the hearing, gambler George Kusch had made a statement to Milwaukee newspaper reporters, AA president O'Brien, and a stenographer. Kusch said that he had expected to testify at the August hearing, but friends of Lydiard and others prevented him from leaving Minneapolis. Kusch further stated that he was paid $10 to say that he had received $100 from umpire Owens to bet on the ball game. He declared that Fred Briggs had paid him the money and took him to the office of an attorney where his affidavit was drafted.[120]

With Mike Kelley severed from Minneapolis ownership, it was now being said by some that the sale of the club to him and his investors by Bill Watkins earlier in the year had been a sham. Investor E.G. Westlake contradicted the assertion, saying that Watkins had been desirous of leaving Minneapolis due to bad health and his business interests in Indianapolis. Kelley, in turn, was interested in acquiring the Millers and had purchased over $5,000 in stock. Kelley wished to have a local directorate with him, and investors had put down their money, seeing the club as a good investment. The investors fully intended to complete the Watkins buyout, using anticipated club earnings for that purpose. In the meantime, Watkins held the unpaid-for stock, promising to sell none of it to any outsiders and vesting control of the club affairs entirely in the new board of directors of the Minneapolis Baseball Club. Watkins in no way interfered with the management or policies of the club. The stock that he retained served only as security for final payment of the full sale price for the club. Thereafter, the uncertainty of the Kelley-Lydiard situation prompted Watkins to advise some of the club investors to sell their holdings, as Watkins believed that was the best move that they could make. Ultimately, the investors turned over their stock to Kelley and Lydiard to make such disposition of it as they saw fit. Every stockholder recouped his money, so there was no "buncoing the public."[121]

People in and around Minneapolis were growing concerned that the American Association board of directors had little intention of lifting Kelley's suspension. There were rumors that unless the case was settled there would be reprisals, one being the prohibition of Sunday ball in Minneapolis and St. Paul, a move which would be very costly to the teams. Because Gus Koch was said to be a close friend of American Association president O'Brien and Milwaukee owner Charles Havenor, it was thought that he had joined the Havenor-Tebeau-Lennon brotherhood. Koch, however, said he wanted Kelley and that he wished to see the Kelley situation cleared up as soon as possible. But many fans viewed this statement as a "salve" or "bluff," and they were waiting for Koch to do something more than announce determination to see the Kelley controversy resolved. Attendance was falling off to a marked degree in Minneapolis, as fans were rapidly growing tired of the political machinations of the American Association's controlling body.[122]

The National Commission docketed the Kelley case for its September 1, 1906, session, but then decided that it had no standing in the case—for now. But that assessment would be reconsidered at the October Commission meeting, leaving Kelley in limbo during the interim.[123] Kelley officially spent his time scouting amateur players in the area, but unofficially he was no doubt managing Millers games. The September 8, 1906, *Minneapolis Journal* stated, "Banished Manager Kelley had a new man in the box for the Kochs." Reporting on the September 12 game in Kansas City, the same paper described a Millers pitching change as follows: "Kelley, who was in the grandstand, yelled out a name that sounded like Ford, and a moment later Eugene [Ford] took his place in the box." If this in fact was true, it might seem odd, as both AA president Joe O'Brien and umpire Brick Owens were also in the grandstand watching the game.[124]

When the National Commission met in October, chairman Garry Herrmann was displeased that the Kelley case had come before the body again, and had the matter referred to the National Association of Minor Leagues. In reassigning the matter, the three members of the National Commission added, "We strongly recommend, however, on account of the serious nature of the charges that that board thoroughly and carefully examine into the entire matter and that the men charged be either convicted or acquitted."[125] But the minor league office was also ill-disposed to deal with the Kelley case. It concluded that the matter was an internal league problem and dispatched it back to the American Association.

As this was all playing out, Gus Koch reiterated that he still wanted Kelley to manage his team in 1907. But as long as the suspension was in force he could not engage him. Koch told Kelley to talk to George Tebeau and Charles Havenor and try to settle the matter. "There is no reason why it cannot be settled if Kelley will go to the men in question and make his peace with them," said Koch. Yet Koch had to act soon on a manager or he would not have one come spring.[126] This, of course, became an irrelevant point for Koch on October 22, 1906, when he sold the Millers to Mike and Joe Cantillon.[127]

Finally on December 2, 1906, the American Association met in Chicago and declared that Kelley (and Lydiard) were ineligible to be an owner, manager, and player for any club in the American Association. In effect, Kelley was now blacklisted from Organized Baseball, as most likely no other club would hire him.[128] Days later, American League president Ban Johnson complicated Kelley's predicament by stating that no other club could hire Kelley, as he was still on the reserve of the St. Louis Browns. This was so, even though the Browns did not place Kelley on their reserve list, an oversight that ordinarily would have made him a free agent. Johnson, however, said "the fact that Kelley was not tendered a contract does not make any difference. The National Commission has decided that a tender of a contract is not necessary at a certain date. He is reserved just the same."[129] Kelley, who was not at the AA meeting, said he would contest the Johnson edict, which he called a farce. Minneapolis city clerk L.A. Lydiard was indifferent about the ruling against him, but thought that the entire controversy had been a blow at Kelley.[130] In some quarters it was believed that Kelley was declared ineligible because he had a two-year contract to manage the Millers and that AA owners were loath to see him make his $4,000 a year which former Minneapolis owner and present Indianapolis owner William Watkins would likely be responsible for.[131]

Few in Minneapolis believed that Kelley had gotten a fair shake. In the *Minneapolis Tribune*, sportswriter Frank E. Force observed, "At the meeting it was stated that $1,200 of Association money had been used in prosecuting the case, and fans here are wondering what was done with all this money. Perhaps it might have been wise to use a little of it in the search for Mr. 'Robinson', the gentleman on whose evidence Mr. Kelley was 'convicted', and yes who has never yet appeared to anybody's eyes."[132] "The Dutch Uncle" wrote in his Sunday column for the *Minneapolis Journal*, "The 'hearing' of Kelley was marked by more of vindictiveness than justice or impartiality. It will take years for the sting of it to wear away. In fact, it is doubtful if it ever wears away so long as the present governing clique of the American Association holds full sway."[133] It was even reported there was a movement on among fans in Minneapolis to raise a fund to help Kelley fight the AA in court, as well as was talk of organizing a boycott of Association games during the coming season.[134]

Even in Milwaukee, where Charles Havenor was a leader in the anti-Kelley camp, the AA "trial" was seen as a farce. The *Milwaukee Journal* wrote, "There was no hope for Kelley. The controlling faction demanded his removal and that settled it. He was a gone goose months ago and all that stood between him and final expulsion from the Association was some form of procedure that could be pointed to by the bouncers as indicative of a square deal."[135]

However, this sentiment was not felt in all cities. The *Cincinnati Post* believed that "ousting of the scandal makers is needed to ensure its [baseball's] safety."[136] To add a little more peculiarity to an already bizarre situation, Richard Meade, sports editor the *Toledo News-Bee*, printed an unflattering story about umpire Brick Owens. Before a game in Kansas City between the Blues and Mud Hens, Meade talked to Owens at the ballpark. Owens got a lot off his chest about his troubles with Kelley before the editor remarked that Owens was not looking well. Owens responded, "I'll tell you, I haven't been able to do myself justice for a week. I've hit it up harder than I should, and admit it has hurt my work. But I've cut out the booze, and I think you'll find my work better than ever." As Meade advised his readers:

And this was only four days after Owens had caused the trouble in Minneapolis. Through this statement Owens admits he was not himself during his session in the Miller City, and puts a rather shadowy complexion on the situation at that time. Now if Owens was drinking, as he says he was, he was not capable of handling a ball game where two clubs were fighting for the lead, as were Columbus and the Millers that fateful afternoon. As to the charges of "crookedness," the writer knows nothing, as the matter had not been brought up at that time, and subsequently, when it was put to Owens, he merely laughed and said nothing.[137]

Some newspapers thought the Owens interview was invented, but Meade stood by it. Meade noted that he had not written that Owens was intoxicated, only that Owens had not been himself for a week. Meade wrote "In justice to Owens, however, the writer will say that every time he saw him on the field, the umpire was in full command of his faculties. Thursday evening's story was not a tirade to discredit the umpire, he always has troubles enough, but it was simply done in justice to Mike Kelley."[138]

The *Milwaukee Sentinel* had this to say on things like the Meade report: "The attempts of Mike Kelley's friends to throw mud on the baseball reputation of Owens are becoming absurd. …Why the information, if it can be backed up with any substantial proof, has been kept under cover for such a long time is a mystery. William Sullivan accompanied Owens through the Minneapolis series and when the question was put to him he said there was not one iota of proof in the yarn."[139] The editor of the *Milwaukee Daily News* was particularly hard on Meade. He said that Meade was a personal friend of both Mike Kelley and Toledo owner J. Edward Grillo, and had it in for umpires who were disliked by either. The editor doubted that Owens

would have said such things to Meade, and found it odd that Meade should unveil his putative interview at this time, questioning why Meade had not reported what Owens said to AA president O'Brien or some other Association official earlier. "From this part of the country the alleged interview Meade had with Owens sounds 'fishy' as do most of the baseball stories that came from Toledo."[140] Owens, meanwhile, wrote a letter to O'Brien denying the story. O'Brien replied that he would take no notice of the Meade allegations.[141]

For his part, Mike Kelley wrote Meade a letter, revealing bits about the hearing and his current situation. He called the methods used "so one-sided they were ridiculous." Kelley added,

Lennon was judge, and the jury was composed of Lennon, Havenor, Tebeau, Watkins and Bryce. Both Watkins and Bryce are so frightened for fear their heads will be cut off by Havenor, Tebeau and Lennon that they haven't nerve enough left to vote against any proposition offered by the people in control. Mike Cantillon's actions at last Sunday's meeting prove that he doesn't control the Minneapolis vote. I have decided not to consider any offer from clubs outside of the league unless the suspension is raised by the members of the league, either by force or otherwise. If I'm not good enough to do business in a league controlled by men of the Havenor-Lennon-Tebeau type, then I certainly would not expect any other association to consider me in any capacity.[142]

On December 11, 1906, Kelley instituted a civil suit against the Minneapolis baseball club for $1,000 claimed to be due him as manager of the Millers in 1906. Kelley's contract called for $4,000 per annum, of which he was only paid $3,000. Gus Koch stated that when he took over the club in August, he was assured that former owner William Watkins would take care of Kelley's contract until the end of the season. Upon the sale of the club to the Cantillons, Kelley was not paid the remainder of his salary. In an amusing wrinkle to the suit, papers were served on Lydiard, who was still on the books as the secretary of the Minneapolis club. This little dispute would soon be straightened out. After the Minneapolis Baseball Company engaged an attorney to look into the suit, it was agreed by all that Kelley was due $1,000. The only remaining issue was whether he should be paid by Watkins, Koch, or the Cantillons.[143]

With Kelley's plight drawing national attention, the American Association decided to take up the case

Michael Kelley served as first baseman and manager of the American Association St. Paul Saints 1902–05, helming two pennant winners, but was soon embroiled in a scam that involved him acting as a front for club owner George Lennon. Lennon sold the Saints to a stock company headed by Kelley, who took the position of club president. Kelley took over Lennon's role as chairman of the board of the American Association, as well, a position no player was allowed to hold.

again. A number of AA club owners said they had not intended Kelley to be blacklisted from all of Organized Baseball, but only from their association. But there was doubtless even a bigger reason for the league resurrecting the matter. Fans in Minneapolis had become extremely hostile to the American Association, and there were a number of men "in position to make baseball in Minneapolis an extremely unprofitable venture." Within the previous few months a street had been opened through the first base bleachers at Minnehaha Park, the Millers Sunday playing grounds. The assessment upon the franchise and plant had been raised from a matter of a few thousand dollars to more than $20,000. Professional baseball had previously been taxed $600 per year for each ballpark, or only $1,200 in all. There was also talk of banning all Sunday baseball in the Twin Cities, and rumors of impending condemnation of grandstands and bleachers swirled about. In addition, letters written by fans to local newspapers urged a boycott of professional baseball games.[144] O'Loughlin of the *Minneapolis Journal* summed it up bluntly:

> Fandom is in a ferment of deep-seated anger against the whole league, and unless something is done to remove this feeling the Cantillon boys have an unpleasant reception awaiting them. The anger is not against Joe and Mike Cantillon, but against the men who have given the Minneapolis club, its president and stockholders so much the worst of it.

> Minneapolis is probably the most clannish city in the United States, barring none. This fact is

evidently not understood by the magnates of the American Association, whose teams come here to carry off large sums of money. Without Minneapolis, St. Paul could not have professional baseball for ten days, yet Minneapolis is enough of a ball town to join in any league in the country without St. Paul, and show a profit.[145]

At the December 30, 1906, meeting of the American Association, Mike Kelley was declared a free agent, able to sign wherever he pleased. However, there was also likely an unspoken "gentleman's agreement" among the magnates that Kelley would remain an "undesirable," either as a player or manager in the American Association."[146] Still, this made Kelley free to accept a contract to run the Des Moines club of the Western League—even though that club was owned by Mike and Joe Cantillon, the owners of the Minneapolis Millers. The offer from Des Moines was for $4,000 a season, the same salary that Kelley's contract called for with the Millers in 1906.[147] Kelley's unpaid back salary of $1,000 "for his services in the Gus Koch coop beneath the grand stand at the close of last year" was also satisfied.[148] Back at the AA meeting, it was further announced that umpires Brick Owens and Steven Kane would not be working in the American Association. Owens umpired 1907 in the Eastern League, but Kane remained in the AA.[149]

Shortly after the first of the year, Joe Cantillon met with Ban Johnson to clear a path for Kelley to manage in Des Moines. Johnson said he saw no problem, as long as Kelley could secure his release from the St. Louis Browns. As far as Johnson was concerned, Kelley was still on the Browns' reserve list. A little later, it was reported the Cantillons would purchase Kelley's release from the St. Louis Browns in order to speed his way to Des Moines.[150] But even with this, the Kelley ordeal was far from over.

A week later, Ban Johnson declared that Kelley was still not eligible to play in Organized Baseball. This was predicated on the fact that Kelley was still barred from playing in the American Association. According to Johnson, a player who was ineligible for one league was ineligible for all leagues in organized ball. Consequently, the American Association would have to declare Kelley eligible to play in their league before he could be employed elsewhere in the game.[151] Milwaukee Brewers owner Charles Havenor disagreed, declaring that he believed the American League president and National Commission member was wrong in his thinking. Said Havenor:

The National Commission in reporting the matter back, took the ground it was an internal affair of the American Association and refused to render a decision. By their action they placed the Kelley-Lydiard incident wholly in the hands of the American Association and out of their own jurisdiction. By the action of the Commission, unless it sees fit to reverse itself, it has no further interest in the matter. It is not and never has been the sense of the various owners in the American Association to place Mr. Kelley outside the ban of organized baseball. As far as the American Association is concerned, Mr. Kelley is at liberty to have the same privileges he enjoyed with the Minneapolis baseball club. There is nothing in the records of the National Association or before the National Commission which will stop Mr. Kelley from enjoying the baseball rights to which he is entitled. This is the sentiment of practically all the club owners of the American Association.[152]

In February 1907, Mike Cantillon was saying that Kelley would have absolute control of the Des Moines team. Kelley would be able to sign whomever he pleased and make whatever trades he thought would help the team.[153] Frank Hughes, secretary of the Des Moines club, announced a tentative line-up for the upcoming season that featured Kelley at first base. When the Western League season started, Kelley was indeed at the helm.[154] On March 5, 1907, the American Association met, but did nothing in regard to Kelley's blacklisting from their organization, president O'Brien saying the Kelley case was not on the agenda of the meeting.[155] The National Commission, however, held firm, prohibiting Kelley from acting as bench-manager of the Des Moines club. Kelley was still property of the St. Louis Browns, and thus ineligible to play with any other club in Organized Baseball but St. Louis. Kelley remained defiant, refusing to accept the decree, and on April 29, he had the Des Moines club in first place in the Western League, with a 7–3 record.[156]

On May 6, National Commission chairman Herrmann notified Kelley that he must vacate the bench of his team until notified that he had been reinstated by the Commission. Again, Charles Havenor voiced his opinion that the commission had no right to suspend Kelley, noting that if the Commission had ruled that Kelley could manage the Minneapolis team the previous year, why not Des Moines this year? Mike Cantillon was not pleased either, thinking that Kelley had been persecuted long enough. In a statement, the Des Moines club president said that a year prior, the

National Commission had adopted a rule [Ruling 43] stating that no player under reserve by one club could act as a manager of another club. However the rule plainly stated it would not be retroactive. Thus under the retroactivity clause, Kelley was in the clear to manage Des Moines even though on the St. Louis reserve list. Cantillon claimed that he had no notice of Kelley's suspension, only a letter from Herrmann stating that St. Louis wanted Kelley. Cantillon thought that St. Louis did not really want Kelley, but was only doing the bidding of a mean-spirited Ban Johnson, who wanted to continue the torment of Kelley. Cantillon concluded by saying, "We will never for a minute consent to any such work. He [Kelley] will play for Des Moines or the Commission will have a fight on their hands in the courts."[157]

A few days later, Garry Herrmann changed his stance, stating that the prior directive had been premised on an erroneous impression. Herrmann stated, "I felt, therefore, that it was my duty not only as a member of the Commission, but as a man, to immediately rescind that order, which I did, stating to Mr. Cantillon and Mr. O'Neill (president of the Western League) that there would be no interference pending action of the National Commission."[158] *Sporting Life* then weighed in with its opinion on the long-running Kelley controversy:

It is time he were brought to book, and with him the National Agreement magnates who have given, and are still giving, him encouragement in his contumacious attitude, for purely selfish and personal reasons, regardless of the general effect upon "organized ball." Personally Mike Kelley is one of the most lovable men in base ball, and why he has pursued his foolish course, and why he persists in, single-handed, pursuing it to the bitter end, is a mystery past finding out. He knows as well as any man the far-reaching power of "organized ball." He knows how much his obstinacy has already cost him; and he must know that, soon or late, he will meet with irretrievable defeat. Then, why not make his peace with the National Commission, which has never yet treated any man or case unfairly? As it stands Kelley's game is not worth the candle.

Apropos to the Kelley case, criticism of the National Commission and sympathy with Kelley from American Association magnates comes with poor grace considering that that organization has formally forbidden Kelley's employment by any club member in any capacity whatever. If Kelley is not fit for American Association company how can he be eligible in any other National Association league? If there is real sympathy or friendship for Kelley in the American Association he should be forthwith restored to good standing in the organization; so long as he is not reinstated discreet silence regarding all that relates to Kelley's controversy with the National Commission would best befit the American Association magnates, singly and collectively. Why look a gift-horse in the mouth?[159]

Within the week, it was reported that Joe Cantillon had purchased Kelley from the St. Louis Browns. It was therefore assumed by some that Kelley would play first base for Cantillon's Washington Nationals, but others believed that the Cantillons intended to keep Kelley in charge of the Des Moines team. Kelley actually suited up with the Nationals, but sat on the bench in a May 16 game in Chicago, Ban Johnson cautioning Cantillon not to play him. Umpire Silk O'Loughlin banished Kelley from the bench.[160] Kelley remained in uniform with the Nationals for some time, but saw no action on the diamond, as Johnson refused to let him play.[161]

On May 18, 1907, Joe Cantillon received a telegram from chairman Garry Herrmann, which stated that Kelley would probably soon be declared a free agent by the National Commission. Herrmann and National League president Harry Pulliam, a controlling two-thirds majority of the Commission, were of the opinion that as St. Louis failed to put Kelley on their reserve list the previous season, he was a free agent. A pleased Washington Nationals manager said that Kelley had been practicing daily and was hoping to get into excellent condition to play first base.[162]

Herrmann's inclination to reinstate Kelley came under heavy criticism from the editors of *The Sporting News*.[163] In a long statement, Herrmann had explained his reasons for Kelley's looming reinstatement. Herrmann had been told by an American Association club owner that at the December 2, 1906, meeting, the AA did not mean to banish Kelley from any league except its own. A copy of a letter from league president O'Brien to American League president Ban Johnson confirmed this. O'Brien wrote, "At the said meeting it was the consensus of the opinion of the various club owners, that it was to the best interest of the American Association that Kelley's connection with the American Association be terminated, but that he be not debarred from earning a livelihood with any other league in organized baseball." Herrmann revealed that

the National Commission had then told the AA that its action "would be a stigma against [Kelley] to any other association," and urged the AA to discuss the matter further and either find Kelley guilty or acquit him of the charges.[164]

As for Kelley being purchased by the Cantillons in order to be sent to Des Moines, Herrmann maintained that this could only be done if Kelley cleared waivers in both the American and National League. The Commission chairman also explained the basis of the St. Louis Browns' failure to place Kelley on their reserve list. Club president Robert Hedges thought that because Kelley was on the blacklist, it was not necessary to reserve him. Hedges also told Herrmann that if the Commission would keep quiet about the matter, he would fix the problem in a couple of days. Herrmann responded by saying that when club reservation lists were made (September 25, 1906), Kelley had not been blacklisted or suspended. That action had been taken on December 2. Herrmann further noted that if Hedges thought Kelley had been blacklisted, how could he sell such a player to Washington in May?[165]

Herrmann added that he and Harry Pulliam at first had serious reservations about voting against Kelley's reinstatement before doing so. Since that time, matters which Herrmann did not care to discuss had forced him to reconsider Kelley's ineligibility. Ultimately, it was decided that as long as Kelley pursued his suit in federal court and had not obtained his release from St. Louis, his case would not be heard by the National Commission. To resolve the impasse, Kelley's lawyer withdrew the federal court complaint and sent St. Louis a check for $1,000, the amount agreed upon between Herrmann and counsel for Kelley's release. But within a few days, the Kelley check was returned to Herrmann with a declaration that the St. Louis club would not accept it. Herrmann had no idea why the check was refused, and had written to Hedges to find out why.[166]

As for Johnson instructing his umpires not to allow Kelley on the field, Herrmann did not know what Johnson had based his decision on, unless Johnson had construed the action of the American Association in December 1906 to be a "permanent disability." Whatever the case, Johnson's position toward Kelley would not be addressed in any National Commission directive.[167]

On May 27, 1907, Kelley wrote a letter to Garry Herrmann that was published in *Sporting Life* under the title: "Michael J. Kelley's Manly Appeal." Kelley basically rehashed what Herrmann had expressed in his statement, but added some personal touches. Kelley wrote,

I realize that I have made some mistakes in baseball and that perhaps I have acted too hastily and unadvisedly in some matters, but I have a family depending upon me for support and realize fully that my only chance of earning a competent livelihood is through baseball, and, after settling my differences with the Commission in the early part of the season I have endeavored in every way to conduct myself in a manner strictly within the rules of baseball, and I feel that an injustice is being done me by not permitting me to play with the Washington club, and therefore, appeal to the National Commission so that I may be permitted to again earn my living through my efforts as a baseball player.

Kelley ended his appeal with these words:

I believe that I have suffered enough for mistakes which I may have committed during the year 1905, and that these matters should not be held continually against me, and should I be permitted to play with the Washington Club in the capacity in which Mr. Cantillon may desire, I assure the Commission that they will never have any cause to feel that I will in any way intentionally transgress or do any act which will be considered as inconsistent with the rules laid down by the National Commission for the government of baseball. Should the National Commission desire my presence or any further statement from me I will be glad to appear before them or send any such statement at any time.[168]

A rather unmoved Ban Johnson responded:

Without desire to discuss or dispute Mr. Herrmann's views of the Kelley case, I herewith give you my view of the case. Before processed further, however, I want to inform you that Mr. Pulliam unwittingly sided with Herrmann on the question of permitting Kelley to play, pending a decision in his case. Last week Mr. Pulliam wrote Chairman Herrmann that he felt that their position in the matter was entirely wrong, so Herrmann stands alone on the proposition. If we can't keep baseball clean, we might as well ring down the curtain. Kelley was found guilty of one of the worst crimes committed in the history of the game, and was expelled from the American Association. He was represented by counsel, there was a thorough trial, and the finding of the American Association in expelling him was clear and emphatic. Kelley had no appeal to the National Commission. The American Association through its constitution, reserves the right to govern its own affairs. The investigation and disciplining of club officials, is strictly an internal affair of an organization. The player is in no manner involved. It is my contention after carefully weighing the subject, that the National Association nor the National Commission can in no manner call to account, review or set aside this action of the American Association in regard to M.J. Kelley and L.A. Lydiard. His only appeal is to the American Association, as the acts for which he was punished were almost entirely detrimental to its welfare, integrity and good government.[169]

Most agreed the case had gone on long enough. Cincinnati sportswriter Ren Mulford, Jr. wrote that Kelley had "gotten so much publicity out of it that he'd be warranted in running for Vice-president. Bryan and Kelley would be a euphonious combination."[170] On June 10–11, 1907, the National Commission held a meeting in Cincinnati, and took up the Kelley case. The Commission determined that the St. Louis Browns had lost their claim to Kelley by failing to reserve him in the fall. It further ruled that Kelley could play in any league he desired, even though he was under a ban in the American Association. But inserted within the ruling was a clause that any league president could bar Kelley if he did not consider Kelley a desirable addition to any one of the league's teams. Thus, Kelley would effectively be barred from the American League, as Ban Johnson objected to him playing with Washington. The American League president also stated he would not withdraw his objection to Kelley. Indeed, Johnson disagreed with the other Commission members so strenuously that he refused to sign the papers issued by the body on the matter.[171]

Joe Cantillon was not happy, complaining that Ban Johnson was imposing his will on the other two members of the Commission. In fact, the Washington club was so upset with the ruling that it had decided to refuse to pass upon any waived American League player and block all AL deals with the minor leagues.[172] As can be imagined, Mike Kelley was also displeased with the ruling. He made this statement:

All the ball players and western people will see that the entire object of the qualifying clause of the decision was not to keep me out of the American League, but to bar me from the American

Association, where they think I might go to Minneapolis for the Cantillon brothers. If I were to sign with St. Paul today I could be playing in that city as soon as a train could get me there, and there would not be a single yelp. As it is they have that Minneapolis idea in their heads and I am barred. Johnson fought the case for the Milwaukee, St. Paul and other clubs that don't want me in the American Association, and had this power of the president's injected into the decision for their special benefit, hence, to make a pretense of saving his face, I am not permitted to play in Washington.[173]

Even the very pro-Havenor *Milwaukee Sentinel* thought that Johnson's disqualification of Kelley from play in the American League to be unfair. "From this point of view it appears that the powers that be, are rubbing it into Kelley. There is no doubt but that Kelley made serious and bad mistakes during this career in the American Association and that he fully deserved his expulsion from that organization. But there was little need for Johnson 'butting in' on the case. Baseball is the one means of livelihood that Kelley has and his expulsion from the Association was sufficient punishment to make him repent of this many baseball crimes."[174]

There was speculation that Kelley would make further appeals. A *Sporting Life* editorial commented, "The case will probably stretch out to Doomsday. It has become the 'Jarndyce vs. Jarndyce' case of baseball."[175] But the case was nearing an end, at least for 1907. Kelley had little choice but to report to Des Moines. The Washington club was out several hundred dollars because of the long delay in settling the case, as it presumably had paid Kelley's salary while he sat on the bench for the Nationals.[176] As of June 18, 1907, Des Moines was in second place in the Western League (29–20), behind Omaha (32–22). Enthusiastic Des Moines supporters thought that with Kelley back at the helm, the team might retake first place.[177] It was not to be. Kelley would manage the team to a (76–63) third place finish. He also played in 28 games at first base, hitting .245.[178]

In late July 1907, it had been reported that Kelley was offered the manager's job at Montreal of the Eastern League, but Mike preferred to stay in Des Moines, perhaps in hopes of going back to the American Association some day. This story surfaced again in October. Reportedly, Eastern League president Pat Powers was opposed to Kelley's presence in the Eastern League. Around December 1, however, Powers squelched the report, penning a letter saying that this was not true and that both Montreal and Toronto wanted Kelley.[179]

On December 14, 1907, club president James McCaffery of Toronto signed Mike Kelley to succeed Joe Kelley as his manager for the 1908 season. Joe Kelley had recently been hired to manage the Boston club of the National League, leaving behind the Eastern League champions of 1907. McCaffery originally wanted Jimmy "Doc" Casey to succeed Kelley, but Brooklyn demanded $1,000 and pitcher Jim McGinley (who had been 22–10 with the Maple Leafs in 1907[180]) for Casey's release. This was too dear a cost and Mike Kelley was hired instead. It was said that Mike would get $500 more a season than Joe had made in 1907 to manage the team. It was also reported that Mike Kelley would play first base for the Maple Leafs.[181]

In late June 1908, Clark Griffith resigned as manager of the New York Highlanders of the American League. Early rumors named Mike Kelley as a candidate for his replacement, but the job went to Kid Elberfeld. It was very doubtful Ban Johnson would have permitted Kelley to manage in New York, in any event.[182] On July 20, 1908, Kelley was released as manager of the Maple Leafs, captain Larry Schlafly taking over the job. However, two days later it was reported that Kelley had resigned. The team was in fifth place with a 35–39 record, owing much to injuries. Kelley had played in 32 games, with a .239 batting average. All but one of those games had been played at first base, where he made only three errors. Kelley had been roundly roasted by Toronto fans and he eventually found the job there "almost untenable."[183] Whether Kelley resigned or was released is not clear, but there was a report that before he left Toronto on July 30, a writ was issued on Kelley's behalf against the Maple Leaf organization for the sum of $1,700 in damages for alleged wrongful dismissal and breach of contract.[184]

On August 5, 1908, word came out that Thomas J. Hickey, former president of the American Association and now in the insurance business in Minneapolis, had made an offer to purchase the St. Paul Saints from George Lennon. If the deal went through, it was said that Hickey's first move would be to hire Mike Kelley as his manager. There were also reports that the American Association was going to expand into Chicago for 1909, and that Kelley would manage the new Chicago AA club. But the sale of the St. Paul franchise to Hickey never went through, and Lennon kept the Saints.[185]

A grass roots appeal by numerous St. Paul and Minneapolis fans was started to bring Kelley back. St. Paul mayor Daniel Lawler, all the city's common council members, and even Minnesota Governor John

A. Johnson "respectfully requested" the American Association to put Kelley back in good standing. The Commercial Club also asked for his reinstatement, and petitions said to contain over 5,000 names were sent to AA president O'Brien with the same appeal.[186] These petitions held as many as 13,000 signatures, according to some sources.[187] A meeting of the American Association owners was scheduled for August 5, 1908, but only five owners attended. Incredibly, George Lennon, the driving force behind putting Kelley out of the American Association two years prior, was now the head of the movement to re-instate him. Lennon even presented the Kelley clemency petitions to the board. Four AA directors voted in favor of reinstating Kelley, with William Watkins of Indianapolis reportedly casting the dissenting vote. Consequently league president O'Brien had to wait for either George Tebeau or Mike Cantillon to mail in his vote. The next day, Cantillon mailed in his yes vote, and Kelley was reinstated by the AA. (Tebeau also voted for Kelley). Lennon welcomed Kelley as his new manager-in-waiting.[188] The talk of the American Association entering Chicago died down, assuming that it ever was serious, and Kelley took over as manager of the Saints on August 9.[189]

Kelley took over a dismal last place team, with a record of 31–81. It was said that ousted skipper Tim Flood had been willing, "even anxious," to relinquish the managerial reins.[190] The Saints won the initial game played with Kelley sitting on the bench, their first win in 20 contests. Kelley's team won three of its first four games played under his direction, and attendance picked up. Still, the Saints finished the season in last place, with a 48–104 record.[191]

Kelley would continue to manage the St. Paul Saints through the 1912 season, taking the manager's job of the Indianapolis Indians in 1913. After serving as the business manager of the Saints in 1914, he again directed the Saints on the field from 1915 to 1923, winning American Association pennants in 1919, 1920, and 1922. At the close of the 1923 season, Kelley purchased a controlling interest in the Minneapolis Millers and managed the Millers until 1931. After his on-field duties ended, Mike remained the president of the Minneapolis club until he sold the franchise to the New York Giants in 1946. After the sale, Kelley was "honorary president" of the club for one year.[192] His minor league career managing record was 2,390–2,102.[193]

Mike Kelley passed away in a Minneapolis hospital on June 6, 1955, at the age of 79.[194] ∎

Notes

1. *Sporting Life*, July 22, 1899, 7; *The Sporting News*, June 15, 1955; Baseball-Reference.
2. 1903–1906 Spalding Baseball Guides; 1902 Reach Baseball Guide, 236, 241; Baseball-Reference.
3. *St. Paul Globe*, January 26, 1905; *Minneapolis Journal*, January 26, 1905; Sporting Life, January 2, 1905, 9, February 4, 1905 p9, February 18, 1905, 10.
4. *Sporting Life*, March 18, 1905, 6.
5. *Sporting Life*, December 9, 1905, 5, November 25, 1905, 10, December 16, 1905, 4.
6. *Minneapolis Journal*, August 15, 1905.
7. *Minneapolis Journal*, August 14, 1905; *Sporting Life*, September 2, 1905, 10.
8. *Sporting Life*, September 2, 1905, 10, 15.
9. *Minneapolis Journal*, August 24, 1905.
10. *Minneapolis Journal*, August 24, September 2, 1905; *Sporting Life*, September 9, September 16, 1905, 16.
11. *Minneapolis Journal*, August 25, September 2, 1905; *Sporting Life*, September 16, 1905, 16.
12. *Minneapolis Journal*, September 2, 1905.
13. *Minneapolis Journal*, January 3, 1906.
14. *Minneapolis Journal*, November 7, 1905, January 3, 1906; *Sporting Life* November 25, 1905, 2, 10.
15. *Minneapolis Journal*, November 17, 1905, January 7, 1906.
16. *Minneapolis Journal*, November 18, 1905; *Sporting Life*, November 25, 1905, 10.
17. *Sporting Life*, December 2, 1905, 10, December 9, 1905, 5, December 16, 1905, 5; *Minneapolis Journal*, December 17, 1905.
18. *Minneapolis Journal*, December 17, 1905.
19. *Minneapolis Journal*, December 17, 1905.
20. *Minneapolis Journal*, December 3, 1905; *Sporting Life*, December 2, 1905, 7.
21. *Minneapolis Journal*, December 6, 1905.
22. *Minneapolis Journal*, December 17, 1905.
23. *Minneapolis Journal*, December 26, 1905.
24. *Minneapolis Journal*, December 28, 29, 31, 1905; *Sporting Life*, January 13, 1906, 6.
25. *Minneapolis Journal*, December 29, 31, 1905.
26. *Minneapolis Journal*, December 30, 31, 1905; *Sporting Life*, January 13, 1906, 6.
27. *Minneapolis Journal*, January 4, 1906.
28. *Minneapolis Journal*, January 7, 1906.
29. *Minneapolis Journal*, January 6, 7, 1906.
30. *Minneapolis Journal*, January 7, 1906.
31. *Milwaukee Journal*, January 7, 1906.
32. *Minneapolis Journal*, January 7, 1906.
33. *Minneapolis Journal*, January 7, 1906.
34. *Minneapolis Journal*, January 6, 1906.
35. *Minneapolis Journal*, December 28, 1905, January 7, 1906; *Sporting Life*, January 13, 1906, 6.
36. *Minneapolis Journal*, January 7, 1906.
37. *Minneapolis Journal*, February 21, May 24, 1906.
38. *Milwaukee Journal*, March 29, 1906.
39. *Minneapolis Journal*, March 30, April 18, 190640.
40. *Minneapolis Journal*, April 13, 18, 1906.
41. *Minneapolis Journal*, April 18, 1906.
42. *Minneapolis Journal*, April 20, 1906.
43. *Minneapolis Journal*, April 19, 1906.
44. *Minneapolis Journal*, April 20, 1906.
45. *Minneapolis Journal*, April 20, 1906.
46. *Minneapolis Journal*, April 21, 22, May 11, 1906.
47. *Minneapolis Journal*, May 11, 1906.
48. *Minneapolis Journal*, June 7, 1906.
49. *Minneapolis Journal*, June 13, 14, 1906.
50. *Minneapolis Journal*, June 22, 1906.

51. *Minneapolis Journal*, June 16, 1906.
52. *Minneapolis Journal*, June 10, 11, 12, 13, 1906.
53. *Minneapolis Journal*, June 16, 1906.
54. *Minneapolis Journal*, June 16, 18, 1906.
55. *Minneapolis Journal*, June 19, 1906.
56. *Minneapolis Journal*, June 19, 1906.
57. *Minneapolis Journal*, June 18, 19, 1906, *Milwaukee Sentinel*, June 19, 1906.
58. *Minneapolis Journal*, June 20, 1906.
59. *Milwaukee Journal*, June 20, 1906.
60. *Minneapolis Journal*, June 20, 22, 23, 1906; *Milwaukee Journal*, June 22, 1906.
61. *Minneapolis Journal*, July 19, 1906.
62. *Minneapolis Journal*, July 19, 1906.
63. *Minneapolis Journal*, July 19, 1906.
64. *Minneapolis Journal*, July 20, 1906; *Milwaukee Journal*, July 20, 1906.
65. *Minneapolis Journal*, July 20, 1906.
66. *Minneapolis Journal*, July 20, 21, 1906.
67. *Milwaukee Sentinel*, July 28, 1906; *Milwaukee Journal*, July 28, 1906.
68. *Minneapolis Journal*, July 28, 30, 31, August 2, 1906; *Milwaukee Sentinel*, July 28, 1906; *Milwaukee Journal*, July 28, 1906; *Toledo News-Bee*, July 28, 1906.
69. *Milwaukee Sentinel*, July 29, 1906.
70. *Milwaukee Sentinel*, August 1, 1906; *Milwaukee Journal*, August 1, 1906.
71. *Minneapolis Journal*, August 1, 1906.
72. *Minneapolis Journal*, August 1, 1906; *Milwaukee Sentinel*, August 1, 1906.
73. *Minneapolis Journal*, August 1, 1906.
74. *Sporting Life*, August 11, 1906, 13; *Milwaukee Sentinel*, August 3, 1906.
75. *Minneapolis Journal*, August 2, 1906; *Milwaukee Sentinel*, August 2, 1906.
76. *Minneapolis Journal*, August 2, 1906; *Milwaukee Sentinel*, August 2, 1906.
77. *Milwaukee Sentinel*, August 3, 1906.
78. *Minneapolis Journal*, August 2, 1906; *Milwaukee Sentinel*, August 2, 5, 1906.
79. *Minneapolis Journal*, August 2, 1906; *Milwaukee Sentinel*, August 2, 1906.
80. *Minneapolis Journal*, August 2, 1906; *Milwaukee Sentinel*, August 2, 1906.
81. *Minneapolis Journal*, August 2, 1906.
82. *Minneapolis Journal*, August 2, 1906, *Sporting Life*, August 11, 1906, 13.
83. *Minneapolis Journal*, August 3, 4, 1906.
84. *Minneapolis Journal*, August 19, 1906.
85. *Toledo News-Bee*, August 1, 1906; *Sporting Life*, August 11, 1906, 13.
86. *Sporting Life*, August 11, 1906, 13.
87. *Minneapolis Journal*, August 2, 1906; *Milwaukee Sentinel*, August 2, 1906; *Sporting Life*, August 11, 1906, 13.
88. *Minneapolis Journal*, August 5, 8, 1906.
89. *Minneapolis Journal*, August 13, 1906; *Milwaukee Journal*, August 13, 1906.
90. *Minneapolis Journal*, August 14, 1906; *Milwaukee Journal*, August, 14, 1906.
91. *Minneapolis Journal*, August 13, 1906.
92. *Milwaukee Journal*, August 20, 1906.
93. *Minneapolis Journal*, August 21, 1906.
94. *Minneapolis Journal*, August 23, 1906; *Milwaukee Journal*, August 23, 1906, *Sporting Life*, September 1, 1906, 10.
95. *Minneapolis Journal*, August 23, 1906; *Milwaukee Journal*, August 23, 1906.
96. *Minneapolis Journal*, August 23, 25, 1906; *Milwaukee Journal*, August 23, 1906.
97. *Minneapolis Journal*, August 23, 24, 25, 1906.
98. *Minneapolis Journal*, August 22, 25, 1906; *Milwaukee Daily News*, May 4, 1907.
99. *Milwaukee Journal*, April 12, 1901.
100. *St. Paul Globe*, December 16, 1903.
101. *Minneapolis Journal*, August 23, 1906.
102. *Minneapolis Journal*, August 23, 28, 30, 1906.
103. *Minneapolis Journal*, August 25, 1906.
104. *Minneapolis Journal*, August 25, 1906.
105. *Minneapolis Journal*, August 25, 1906.
106. *Minneapolis Journal*, August 25, 1906.
107. *Minneapolis Journal*, August 31, 1906.
108. *Minneapolis Journal*, October 16, 1906.
109. *Milwaukee Journal*, September 26, 1906.
110. *Minneapolis Journal*, December 11, 1906.
111. *Minneapolis Journal*, September 18, 1906; *Milwaukee Journal*, September 17, 1906; *1907 Reach Guide*, 140.
112. *Minneapolis Journal*, September 23, 1906.
113. *Minneapolis Journal*, October 16, 1906.
114. *Minneapolis Journal*, October 23, 24, 1906.
115. *Minneapolis Journal*, October 24, 1906.
116. *Milwaukee Daily News*, May 4, 1907.
117. *Milwaukee Journal*, October 24, 1906; *Sporting Life*, November 3, 1906, 2.
118. *Minneapolis Journal*, August 23, 1906; *Milwaukee Journal*, August 23, 1906.
119. *Milwaukee Journal*, August 27, 1906.
120. *Minneapolis Journal*, August 24, 1906.
121. *Minneapolis Journal*, August 26, 1906.
122. *Minneapolis Journal*, August 28, 30, 1906.
123. *Minneapolis Journal*, September 1, 2, 1906.
124. *Minneapolis Journal*, September 7, 8, 13, 1906.
125. *Minneapolis Journal*, October 10, 16, November 2, 7, 9, 11, 1906; *Milwaukee Journal*, November 7, 1906.
126. *Minneapolis Journal*, October 16, 1906.
127. *Minneapolis Journal*, October 23, 1906.
128. *Minneapolis Journal*, December 3, 1906; *Milwaukee Journal*, December 3, 1906.
129. *Minneapolis Journal*, December 4, 1906; *Toledo News-Bee*, December 4, 1906.
130. *Minneapolis Journal*, December 3, 4, 1906; *Milwaukee Journal*, December 4, 1906.
131. *Minneapolis Journal*, December 3, 5, 1906; *Milwaukee Journal*, December 3 1906.
132. *Minneapolis Journal*, December 7, 1906.
133. *Minneapolis Journal*, December 9, 1906.
134. *Toledo News-Bee*, December 7, 1906.
135. *Milwaukee Journal*, December 3, 1906.
136. Milwaukee Daily News, December 7, 1906.
137. *Toledo News-Bee*, December 6, 1906.
138. *Toledo News-Bee*, December 8, 1906.
139. *Milwaukee Sentinel*, December 7, 1906.
140. Milwaukee Daily News, December 8, 10, 1906.
141. *Toledo News-Bee*, December 11, 1906; *Minneapolis Journal*, December 16, 1906; *Milwaukee Daily News*, December 10, 1906.
142. *Toledo News-Bee*, December 10, 1906.
143. *Minneapolis Journal*, December 11, 13, 26, 1906; *Milwaukee Daily News*, December 1, 1906; *Sporting Life*, January 5, 1907, 5.
144. *Evening Wisconsin*, December 8, 1906; *Minneapolis Journal*, December 27, 1906.
145. *Minneapolis Journal*, December 27, 1906.
146. *Milwaukee Journal*, December 31, 1906; Sporting Life, January 12, 1907, 6.
147. *Minneapolis Journal*, December 31, 1906; *Milwaukee Journal*, December 31, 1906, January 5, 1907; *Sporting Life*, January 12, 1907, 6, 10.
148. *Minneapolis Journal*, December 31, 1906; *Sporting Life*, January 12, 1907, 6, March 2, 1907, 7.
149. *Toledo News-Bee*, January 1, 1907; *Milwaukee Journal*, January 5, 1907.
150. *Milwaukee Journal*, January 3, 1907; *Sporting Life*, January 12, 1907, 6, March 9, 1907, 5.
151. *Milwaukee Journal*, January 10, 1907; *Sporting Life*, January 19, 1907, 8.
152. *Sporting Life*, January 26, 1907, 3.
153. *Sporting Life*, March 2, 1907, 7.
154. *Milwaukee Journal*, January 23, 1907; *Sporting Life*, March 2, 1907, 7

March 30, 1907, 12, May 4, 1907, 18.

155. *Sporting Life*, March 9, 1907, 5.

156. *Sporting Life*, May 11, 1907, 7, 23.

157. *Sporting Life*, May 11, 1907, 23.

158. *Sporting Life*, June 1, 1907, 6.

159. *Sporting Life*, May 11, 1907, 7.

160. *Sporting Life*, May 18, 1907, 6, May 25, 1907, 2, 4.

161. *Sporting Life*, June 1, 1907, 11, June 8, 1907, 2, 15.

162. *Sporting Life*, May 25, 1907, 2.

163. *The Sporting News*, May 25, 1907, 4.

164. *Sporting Life*, June 1, 1907, 5.

165. *Sporting Life*, June 1, 1907, 5.

166. *Sporting Life*, June 1, 1907, 5.

167. *Sporting Life*, June 1, 1907, 5, 6.

168. *Sporting Life*, June 8, 1907, 15.

169. *Sporting Life*, June 15, 1907, 6.

170. *Sporting Life*, June 15, 1907, 5.

171. *Milwaukee Sentinel*, June 16, 1907; *Milwaukee Journal*, June 12, 1907; *Sporting Life*, June 22, 1907, 2, July 6, 1907, 2; *Washington Times*, July 16, 1907.

172. *Milwaukee Journal*, June 13, 14, 1907; *Sporting Life*, June22, 1907, 2.

173. *Sporting Life*, June 22, 1907, 2.

174. *Milwaukee Sentinel*, June 16, 1907.

175. *Milwaukee Sentinel*, June 16, 1907; *Sporting Life*, July 20, 1907, 5.

176. *Milwaukee Sentinel*, June 16, 1907; *Sporting Life*, June 22, 1907, 13.

177. *Sporting Life*, June 29, 1907, 23.

178. *1908 Reach Guide*, 275, 277, 281.

179. *Sporting Life*, August 3, 1907, 24, November 2, 1907, 3, December 7, 1907, 2.

180. *1908 Reach Guide*, 209.

181. *Washington Herald*, December 12, 15, 23, 1908; *Washington Times*, December 26, 1907; *Sporting Life*, December 21, 1907, 3, January 11, 1908, 10.

182. *Washington Herald*, June 29, 1908; *Sporting Life*, July 4, 1908, 3, July 25, 1908, 4.

183. *Washington Herald*, July 20, 1908; *Washington Times*, July 22, 1908; *1909 Reach Guide*, 198, 199; *Sporting Life*, August 1, 1908, 15.

184. *Sporting Life*, August 8, 1908, 7.

185. *Milwaukee Sentinel*, August 6, 7, 1908; *Milwaukee Journal*, August 6, 1908; *Toledo News-News*, August 6, 1908; *Sporting Life*, August 15, 1908, 19.

186. *Toledo News-Bee*, August 7, 1908; *Milwaukee Journal*, August 7, 1908.

187. *Sporting Life*, August 22, 1904 (13,000); *Milwaukee Sentinel*, August 7, 1908 (11,000).

188. *Milwaukee Sentinel*, August 7, 1908; *Milwaukee Journal*, August 7, 1908; *Toledo News-Bee*, August 7, 11, 1908; *Sporting Life*, August 22, 1908, 14.

189. Washington Herald, August 16, 1908; *Sporting Life*, August 22, 1908, 1.

190. *Milwaukee Journal*, August 9, 1908; *Milwaukee Sentinel*, August 8, 1908.

191. *Sporting Life*, August 22, 1908, 1, 14; *1909 Reach Guide*, 183.

192. *The Sporting News*, June 15, 1955, 26.

193. Lloyd Johnson, ed., *The Minor League Register*. Durham, N.C.: Baseball America, 1994.

194. *The Sporting News*, June 15, 1955, 26.

The Chadwick Awards

IN NOVEMBER 2009, SABR established the Henry Chadwick Award, intended to honor the game's great researchers—historians, statisticians, analysts, and archivists—for their invaluable contributions to making baseball the game that links America's present with its past. In addition to honoring individuals for the length and breadth of their contribution to the study of baseball and their deepening of our enjoyment of the game, the Chadwick Award educates SABR members and the greater baseball community about sometimes little-known but vastly important research contributions, thus encouraging the next generation of researchers.

The roster of the previous 30 Chadwick honorees includes researchers from the past and present: Some are our colleagues, others our predecessors. All have contributed greatly to the field. This year we add five names to the ranks, and present their biographies, written by SABR members, here.

David Block by Andy McCue

David Block revolutionized the study of early baseball and the assumptions behind it. For decades, dating back to Henry Chadwick and the Mills Commission, baseball's roots were thought to be either in the English children's game of rounders or in the creativity of Abner Doubleday and his Cooperstown playmates. The Doubleday myth was shattered as researchers focused on its improbabilities, and on the Knickerbocker rules of 1845. Researchers found references to base ball or similar games decades before the Knickerbockers.

Block's path to undermining these assumptions was circuitous. Born in Chicago in 1944 and with a career in Information Technology, Block had been a collector of baseball ephemera and memorabilia. At first it was cards and other standard material, but then he began to branch into things that were more difficult to find.

There were nineteenth-century prints from *Harpers Magazine* and then photographs. Block said he was interested in depictions of college, high school, and sandlot baseball rather than the professionals. From there, he transitioned to early books and, with retirement, set out to do an annotated bibliography of them. Of necessity, he felt, the introduction to this book would have to discuss the origins of the game. But when he went to do his research, he was surprised to find how little was available, and how vague the available was. It was mostly rounders, and when he went to research rounders, he couldn't find anything.

He was traveling to some of the most heralded libraries in the U.S.—Berkeley, Stanford, San Francisco Public, UCLA, the American Antiquarian Society, the Library of Congress and New York Public. He worked with SABR members in the Bobby Thomson Chapter in England. He was looking in old dictionaries, booksellers catalogs and all kinds of books about sports.

His key discovery came in a 1796 German review of children's games—*Spiele zur Uebung und Erholung des Körpers und Geistes für die Jugend, ihre Erzieher und alle Freunde Unschuldiger Jugendfreuden* ("Games for

COURTESY OF DAVID BLOCK

the Exercise and Recreation of Body and Spirit for the Youth and His Educator and All Friends of Innocent Joys of Youth"). It included a short description of "Englische base-ball," with one player throwing a pitch to another, who had three chances to hit it. If he did hit it, he then ran counterclockwise around the bases attempting to score a run. Further research confirmed to Block that Chadwick's insistence on rounders as the foundation game was misplaced. Rounders was the name of base-ball when played in Devon, the western English county where Chadwick lived before emigrating to America.

The bibliography had been overtaken by the introduction. When Block's *Baseball Before We Knew It: A Search for the Roots of the Game* was published in 2005, it overturned the thinking about rounders and about who baseball's father was. It was clear baseball had no father. It had evolved.

Block's research in the wake of the book has been greatly aided by the spread of digitized databases of old newspapers and other materials. It has also been aided by the publicity his work has received, notably in England. He has made seven trips to the U.K. since the book, working at libraries in London, Oxford, and other cities, and making extensive use of the search capabilities of the British Newspaper Archive, a digitized collection of local and regional newspaper from around the island.

He calculates he has turned up about 250 references to base ball dating back to the middle of the eighteenth century, and including such notables as the Prince of Wales (1755). His next step is to turn all of these fragmentary mentions into some kind of narrative or annotated tool for future researchers. ■

Dick Cramer by Rob Neyer

Dick Cramer, recipient of a 2015 Chadwick Award, has been doing sabermetrics for just about as long as anyone alive.

Cramer grew up near Wilmington, Delaware, where his father worked as a chemist for DuPont. Young Dick turned to baseball early on. "I decided that following the Phillies," Cramer related in Alan Schwarz's book, *The Numbers Game,* "would be more fun and less costly than building and crashing model airplanes."

"In 1958," Schwarz wrote, "when he was 16, Cramer's parents went away for the weekend and left Dick $15 for expenses; he promptly mailed the cash to APBA for its baseball dice game. The Cramers were furious, but Dick was hooked." He wasn't shattered by the Phillies' collapse in 1964, and somehow managed to remain optimistic about them for a few more years. Maybe until shortly after 1966, when, Cramer says, "I started doing 'analytics,' and on the basis of computer simulations had reinvented OPS (as on-base average times, not plus, slugging average) by 1969. A squib in *The Sporting News* in 1971 introduced me to SABR, and Bob Davids then introduced me to Pete Palmer."

Along the way, Cramer had earned an AB in Chemistry & Physics from Harvard in 1963, and a PhD in Physical Organic Chemistry from MIT in 1967.

In the '70s, Cramer served one term as SABR's vice president and was on the board of directors for a spell. Cramer's first published article appeared in the 1975 *Baseball Research Journal.* But it was his second article, published two years later, that established a significant baseline for future analysts. In "Do Clutch Hitters Exist?" Cramer looked at batting statistics from 1969–70, and his conclusion was easy to grasp: "[T]here is no tendency for players who were clutch hitters in 1969 to be clutch hitters in 1970. True, a few of the 'clutch hitters' in 1969 were also 'clutch hitters' in 1970; but as many became 'unclutch' and most became average, ex-

COURTESY OF DICK CRAMER

actly as would be expected if 'clutch hitting' is really a matter of luck."

More than 30 years later, Cramer and Palmer teamed up for yet another study of clutch hitting, this time using oodles more data and different methods. Their conclusion? "Thus the results of the original study are yet again confirmed, this time by every analysis we can devise and based mostly on 50 seasons of major league play. Over this period there is no convincing evidence that any fluctuation of any batter's performance in tense situations had any cause beyond random variation."

In 1980, Palmer introduced Cramer to Steve Mann, who introduced Cramer to Matt Levine; in 1981, the latter two founded STATS, Inc. Over the following decade-plus, Cramer remained heavily involved as STATS became one of the leading providers of sports information in the world (which of course it remains today).

Following a decade-long hiatus from serious baseball work, Cramer reconnected with sabermetrics in 2004. "For the last ten years," Cramer says, "I've been greatly enjoying working with Retrosheet, as my interests and goals are much like Dave Smith's and he is so extraordinarily good at making things work together."

Outside of baseball, Cramer founded and led SmithKline's computer-aided drug design, holding a variety of positions. In 1983, he joined Tripos (now Certara Discovery) and until recently served as Vice President for *Science.* In 2000, Cramer moved to Santa Fe, where he lives in the Sand River cohousing development. ∎

Bill Deane by Lyle Spatz

Bill Deane joined SABR in 1982 at the suggestion of former Chadwick Award winner Cliff Kachline. In 1986, he was chosen by the National Baseball Library to be its Senior Research Associate. His service, which ran through 1994, helped earn the Library an international reputation for timely and accurate service to baseball fans, scholars, and media personnel. Perhaps his greatest contribution was the expansion of the library's research files, including historical documentation of the annual Hall of Fame Game and of the voting of the various Veterans' Committees. Bill became somewhat of a "boy wonder" (by SABR standards) when he was recognized with a SABR salute in 2001 at the tender age of forty-four.

Deane's personal research interests delve into both the game's numbers and its history. They include an ongoing list of players who homered in their final major league at bats (which he considers his best project), statistical charts such as most homers and RBIs in a season by a leadoff hitter, most hits and most homers in a player's first 1,000 at bats, and best performances before the All-Star break, an ongoing list of major leaguers who were murdered, committed suicide, or died accidental deaths, the documenting of successful executions of the hidden-ball trick, and the debunking and disproving of baseball myths.

Bill served as *Total Baseball*'s managing editor for the last edition, and compiled the Major League Baseball Calendar 1999–2006. His compilation of the voting breakdowns for every Most Valuable Player Award, Cy Young Award, and Rookie of the Year Award elections since 1911 formed the basis of his "Awards and Honors" chapter in *Total Baseball*. In the years before those awards were given, Bill created Hypothetical Awards, using his knowledge of voting patterns to determine who the likely winners would have been.

Deane is also considered the foremost expert on Hall of Fame voting, and baseball fans look forward to his annual HOF predictions, which have for the most part been amazingly accurate. He has been featured, acknowledged, or quoted in countless books, news-paper and magazine articles, and radio, television, and online interviews. He served on the Committee for Historical Accuracy for *Macmillan's Baseball Encyclopedia*, and is a regular contributor to SABR-L. His posts are often in multiple parts, which answer questions, correct previous responses, or add new information to a whole range of baseball-related subjects.

Bill became a baseball fan at age ten, and four years later had his first published baseball-related piece, in the nationally syndicated "Johnny Wonder" column. Since then, he has written many books and hundreds of articles in such publications as *Baseball America*, *Baseball Digest*, *The Sporting News*, *Street & Smith's Official Baseball Yearbook*, and *USA Today Baseball Weekly*. He recently turned two of his major research interests into books: *Baseball Myths: Debating, Debunking and Disproving Tales from the Diamond* (2012), and *Finding the Hidden-Ball Trick: The Colorful History of Baseball's Oldest Ruse* (due out early in 2015), both published by Rowman & Littlefield. Still, he considers himself a researcher first and a writer second. Bill, who was born in Poughkeepsie, New York, has lived within ten miles of the Baseball Hall of Fame since 1986. ∎

Jerry Malloy by John Thorn

COURTESY OF LARRY LESTER

Jerry Malloy (1946–2000) was a pioneer researcher who has been honored by the creation of an annual Negro League Conference named for him, as well as a book prize. SABR is honored now to count him among its Chadwick Award recipients.

His first great contribution to baseball history was "Out at Home: Baseball Draws the Color Line, 1887." This monumentally important essay was first published in *The National Pastime* in 1983, then anthologized twice more within the decade—in both Warner Books *The National Pastime* and Scribners' *The Armchair Book of Baseball*. It is not too much to say that this long essay transformed our understanding of black baseball.

When Jackie Robinson opened the 1947 season with the Brooklyn Dodgers, most baseball fans and writers believed that he was the first black to play in the major leagues. (Robinson himself believed that at the time.) It has turned out he was at least the fourth. William Edward White was the first, in 1879; Jerry Malloy died before this discovery. Who are the other two we know of? Moses Fleetwood Walker and his brother Welday Wilberforce Walker. For a few years in the 1880s, with slavery dead and Jim Crow not yet ascendant, a spirit of racial tolerance prevailed in America that permitted black and white to rub shoulders without strife. Many black players performed at all levels of Organized Baseball into the 1890s, but the color bar that Jackie Robinson broke was erected in the International League in 1887. How and why it happened was largely unknown until Malloy pried open century-old secrets.

A history major in college who worked as a retail clerk in Mundelein, Illinois, Jerry was particularly delighted that it won commendation from C. Vann Woodward, author of *The Strange Career of Jim Crow* (1955) and the preeminent historian of American race relations.

Malloy's subsequent work included articles for the *Baseball Research Journal* and *The National Pastime*. For University of Nebraska Press he edited a contextual republication of Sol White's *History of Colored Baseball with Other Documents on the Early Black Game,* *1886–1936*; his commentary was superb. The late Jules Tygiel, also a Chadwick Award recipient, said of him, "His articles for SABR were pathbreaking and exceptional and rank among the very best this organization has ever published. Even more so, I doubt that the best among us have ever been as generous with their research and support as was Jerry."

In the acknowledgment to his Seymour-Medal-winning *Fleet Walker's Divided Heart*, David Zang wrote: "In an unprecedented act of generosity, Jerry shared not only his thoughts on Walker but also his entire file of documents. They arrived at a point long after I thought this manuscript was complete. Their availability added detail and insight that would have been otherwise lacking."

Jerry Malloy died at the age of fifty-four, when he was immersed in further personal and collaborative research of the African American experience in baseball. What he left us was not voluminous, but it was choice and utterly indispensable. He had set the drawing of the color line in baseball at 1887, but then had found another instance, 20 years earlier, which he shared excitedly. With his typical modesty, Jerry emailed several colleagues about his discovery: "Appended is a transcription of a four-page, handwritten 'Report of a Delegate of the Pythian to the Pennsylvania State Convention,' dated October 18, 1867. It relates the events of the attempt of the Pythians, a prominent black club from Philadelphia, to join the Pennsylvania Base Ball Association, at a meeting held at the Court House, in Harrisburg, on October 16, 1867.... I know of several researchers who would be interested in this Pythians delegate report, as it documents baseball polity's early rejection of black ballplayers and teams. I thought I'd make it available to SABR's online membership. I did the best I could with the transcription, and any errors are mine." ∎

David Nemec by Christina Kahrl

Among the many avenues of curiosity for a baseball historian, perhaps none is more reliably arcane—even for SABR members—than the nineteenth century and the lessons it provides about the development of the game into a popular national pastime and a money-making enterprise. But among those happy few who have sought to dispel ignorance of the period and its importance, few rank as high or have earned as much recognition as SABR member **David Nemec** has.

A college ballplayer at Ohio State before he settled in California's Bay Area in 1983, Nemec got started writing baseball trivia books in the 1970s. He moved on to writing a history of the game's rules before starting to deliver his signature contributions in the '90s: *The Beer and Whisky League* (about the major league American Association, 1882–91; 1994) and *The Great Encyclopedia of Nineteenth Century Major League Baseball* (1997), still cited as the definitive treatment of the subject even before it was expanded and re-published in 2006.

In a sense, Nemec's career as a historian was made possible not simply by a love for the game's history, but the realization of how much had been left unwritten. Thinking back on the reference books available before the first *Macmillan Baseball Encyclopedia* was published in 1969, Nemec was inspired to fill in the blanks.

"I was caught irrevocably by the nineteenth century almost from the first moment I opened my copy of the original edition of Turkin and Thompson," Nemec reflected. "Since no team rosters were provided, I soon began compiling my own of every team from 1871 to what was then 1951, I believe. Long before I finished I realized that I would be left with many gaps, particularly with the National Association clubs—positions unfilled, a shortage at certain positions with regard to the number of games played, etc. It became an ambition even then to fill those gaps, find first names for the many players listed only as a last name, uncover birth and death dates, etc. From that grew a larger ambition to one day write about my discoveries. What form that would take I still had no notion, nor did I until the early 2000s, when I acquired box scores for almost every 19c major league game. But as I went through them, things gradually began clicking into place."

The culmination of his tireless pursuit and publication of information about the nineteenth century was his recent trilogy of books comprising biographies of every major league player, manager, principal owner, regular umpire, and league president prior to 1901. (The first two volumes, mostly on players, were published by Bison in 2011; the third, which added more umps and execs to the rolls, was a McFarland title in 2012.)

"The trilogy brought dimension to hundreds of figures that heretofore had only been ghostly wisps, some much fuller than others depending of what my research yielded," Nemec said. "I regard all these bios as works in progress; there is still much to be learned of interest and significance about each of these ghosts. Since these books were published I have continued to expand my bios as new research emerges, and some of the results now appear on the SABR BioProject site."

Nemec is quick to observe that SABR also played a significant, albeit brief, part in his original research: "My biggest break was SABR's acquiring the usage of ProQuest material for one full year—before ProQuest pulled the rug upon discovering how many hits the site was getting each and every day from SABR members."

Nemec's contributions to baseball research far transcend any single category, more regularly aiming at entertaining baseball fans of any era. His interests have also ranged far beyond baseball, as he's a playwright who also has eight novels and true crime nonfiction titles to his credit. But that creative breadth allowed Nemec the opportunity to create singular works like his nineteenth century baseball novel, *Early Dreams* (2004).

"*Early Dreams* paints a portrait not only of what it was like to be a struggling rookie player in the tumultuous 1884 season—the most interesting one in all of baseball history in my opinion—but also to serve as a prism through which life in 1880s America could be viewed," Nemec said. "Indeed, baseball has always been an excellent prism in that respect. It was a treat to find a vehicle in which I could combine the two. ...I started as a fiction writer and will probably end as one."

Reflecting on his Chadwick-worthy career, Nemec observed, "I take great pleasure in breathing new life into nineteenth century research and resurrecting the many individuals who played key roles in the game's early development, both on the field and off, but have never been given their due. ...I'll always be more drawn to the Sammy Vicks than to the Babe Ruths, and not only in baseball." ∎

SABR BioProject Books

In 2002, the Society for American Baseball Research launched an effort to write and publish biographies of every player, manager, and individual who has made a contribution to baseball. Over the past decade, the BioProject Committee has produced over 2,200 biographical articles. Many have been part of efforts to create theme- or team-oriented books, spearheaded by chapters or other committees of SABR.

THE YEAR OF THE BLUE SNOW:
THE 1964 PHILADELPHIA PHILLIES
Catcher Gus Triandos dubbed the Philadelphia Phillies' 1964 season "the year of the blue snow," a rare thing that happens once in a great while. This book sheds light on lingering questions about the 1964 season—but any book about a team is really about the players. This work offers life stories of all the players and others (managers, coaches, owners, and broadcasters) associated with this star-crossed team, as well as essays of analysis and history.
Edited by Mel Marmer and Bill Nowlin
$19.95 paperback (ISBN 978-1-933599-51-9)
$9.99 ebook (ISBN 978-1-933599-52-6)
8.5"X11", 356 PAGES, over 70 photos

DETROIT TIGERS 1984:
WHAT A START! WHAT A FINISH!
The 1984 Detroit tigers roared out of the gate, winning their first nine games of the season and compiling an eye-popping 35-5 record after the campaign's first 40 games—still the best start ever for any team in major league history. This book brings together biographical profiles of every Tiger from that magical season, plus those of field management, top executives, the broadcasters—even venerable Tiger Stadium and the city itself.
Edited by Mark Pattison and David Raglin
$19.95 paperback (ISBN 978-1-933599-44-1)
$9.99 ebook (ISBN 978-1-933599-45-8)
8.5"x11", 250 pages (Over 230,000 words!)

SWEET '60: THE 1960 PITTSBURGH PIRATES
A portrait of the 1960 team which pulled off one of the biggest upsets of the last 60 years. When Bill Mazeroski's home run left the park to win in Game Seven of the World Series, beating the New York Yankees, David had toppled Goliath. It was a blow that awakened a generation, one that millions of people saw on television, one of TV's first iconic World Series moments.
Edited by Clifton Blue Parker and Bill Nowlin
$19.95 paperback (ISBN 978-1-933599-48-9)
$9.99 ebook (ISBN 978-1-933599-49-6)
8.5"X11", 340 pages, 75 photos

RED SOX BASEBALL IN THE DAYS OF IKE AND ELVIS: THE RED SOX OF THE 1950s
Although the Red Sox spent most of the 1950s far out of contention, the team was filled with fascinating players who captured the heart of their fans. In *Red Sox Baseball*, members of SABR present 46 biographies on players such as Ted Williams and Pumpsie Green as well as season-by-season recaps.
Edited by Mark Armour and Bill Nowlin
$19.95 paperback (ISBN 978-1-933599-24-3)
$9.99 ebook (ISBN 978-1-933599-34-2)
8.5"X11", 372 PAGES, over 100 photos

THE MIRACLE BRAVES OF 1914
BOSTON'S ORIGINAL WORST-TO-FIRST CHAMPIONS
Long before the Red Sox "Impossible Dream" season, Boston's now nearly forgotten "other" team, the 1914 Boston Braves, performed a baseball "miracle" that resounds to this very day. The "Miracle Braves" were Boston's first "worst-to-first" winners of the World Series. Refusing to throw in the towel at the midseason mark, George Stallings engineered a remarkable second-half climb in the standings all the way to first place.
Edited by Bill Nowlin
$19.95 paperback (ISBN 978-1-933599-69-4)
$9.99 ebook (ISBN 978-1-933599-70-0)
8.5"X11", 392 PAGES, over 100 photos

THAR'S JOY IN BRAVELAND!
THE 1957 MILWAUKEE BRAVES
Few teams in baseball history have captured the hearts of their fans like the Milwaukee Braves of the 1950s. During the Braves' 13-year tenure in Milwaukee (1953-1965), they had a winning record every season, won two consecutive NL pennants (1957 and 1958), lost two more in the final week of the season (1956 and 1959), and set big-league attendance records along the way.
Edited by Gregory H. Wolf
$19.95 paperback (ISBN 978-1-933599-71-7)
$9.99 ebook (ISBN 978-1-933599-72-4)
8.5"x11", 330 pages, over 60 photos

NEW CENTURY, NEW TEAM:
THE 1901 BOSTON AMERICANS
The team now known as the Boston Red Sox played its first season in 1901. Boston had a well-established National League team, but the American League went head-to-head with the N.L. in Chicago, Philadelphia, and Boston. Chicago won the American League pennant and Boston finished second, only four games behind.
Edited by Bill Nowlin
$19.95 paperback (ISBN 978-1-933599-58-8)
$9.99 ebook (ISBN 978-1-933599-59-5)
8.5"X11", 268 pages, over 125 photos

CAN HE PLAY?
A LOOK AT BASEBALL SCOUTS AND THEIR PROFESSION
They dig through tons of coal to find a single diamond. Here in the world of scouts, we meet the "King of Weeds," a Ph.D. we call "Baseball's Renaissance Man," a husband-and-wife team, pioneering Latin scouts, and a Japanese-American interned during World War II who became a successful scout—and many, many more.
Edited by Jim Sandoval and Bill Nowlin
$19.95 paperback (ISBN 978-1-933599-23-6)
$9.99 ebook (ISBN 978-1-933599-25-0)
8.5"X11", 200 PAGES, over 100 photos

SABR Members can purchase each book at a significant discount (often 50% off) and receive the ebook editions free as a member benefit. Each book is available in a trade paperback edition as well as ebooks suitable for reading on a home computer or Nook, Kindle, or iPad/tablet.
To learn more about becoming a member of SABR, visit the website: sabr.org/join

THE SABR DIGITAL LIBRARY

The Society for American Baseball Research, the top baseball research organization in the world, disseminates some of the best in baseball history, analysis, and biography through our publishing programs. The SABR Digital Library contains a mix of books old and new, and focuses on a tandem program of paperback and ebook publication, making these materials widely available for both on digital devices and as traditional printed books.

CLASSIC REPRINTS

BASE-BALL: HOW TO BECOME A PLAYER
by John Montgomery Ward
John Montgomery Ward (1860-1925) tossed the second perfect game in major league history and later became the game's best shortstop and a great, inventive manager. His classic handbook on baseball skills and strategy was published in 1888. Illustrated with woodcuts, the book is divided into chapters for each position on the field as well as chapters on the origin of the game, theory and strategy, training, base-running, and batting.
$4.99 ebook (ISBN 978-1-933599-47-2)
$9.95 paperback (ISBN 978-0910137539)
156 PAGES, 4.5"X7" replica edition

BATTING by F. C. Lane
First published in 1925, *Batting* collects the wisdom and insights of over 250 hitters and baseball figures. Lane interviewed extensively and compiled tips and advice on everything from batting stances to beanballs. Legendary baseball figures such as Ty Cobb, Casey Stengel, Cy Young, Walter Johnson, Rogers Hornsby, and Babe Ruth reveal the secrets of such integral and interesting parts of the game as how to choose a bat, the ways to beat a slump, and how to outguess the pitcher.
$14.95 paperback (ISBN 978-0-910137-86-7)
$7.99 ebook (ISBN 978-1-933599-46-5)
240 PAGES, 5"X7"

RUN, RABBIT, RUN
by Walter "Rabbit" Maranville
"Rabbit" Maranville was the Joe Garagiola of Grandpa's day, the baseball comedian of the times. In a twenty-four-year career that began in 1912, Rabbit found a lot of funny situations to laugh at, and no wonder: he caused most of them! The book also includes an introduction by the late Harold Seymour and a historical account of Maranville's life and Hall-of-Fame career by Bob Carroll.
$9.95 paperback (ISBN 978-1-933599-26-7)
$5.99 ebook (ISBN 978-1-933599-27-4)
100 PAGES, 5.5"X8.5", 15 rare photos

MEMORIES OF A BALLPLAYER
by Bill Werber and C. Paul Rogers III
Bill Werber's claim to fame is unique: he was the last living person to have a direct connection to the 1927 Yankees, "Murderers' Row," a team hailed by many as the best of all time. Rich in anecdotes and humor, Memories of a Ballplayer is a clear-eyed memoir of the world of big-league baseball in the 1930s. Werber played with or against some of the most productive hitters of all time, including Babe Ruth, Ted Williams, Lou Gehrig, and Joe DiMaggio.
$14.95 paperback (ISNB 978-0-910137-84-3)
$6.99 ebook (ISBN 978-1-933599-47-2)
250 PAGES, 6"X9"

ORIGINAL SABR RESEARCH

INVENTING BASEBALL: THE 100 GREATEST GAMES OF THE NINETEENTH CENTURY
SABR's Nineteenth Century Committee brings to life the greatest games from the game's early years. From the "prisoner of war" game that took place among captive Union soldiers during the Civil War (immortalized in a famous lithograph), to the first intercollegiate game (Amherst versus Williams), to the first professional no-hitter, the games in this volume span 1833–1900 and detail the athletic exploits of such players as Cap Anson, Moses "Fleetwood" Walker, Charlie Comiskey, and Mike "King" Kelly.
Edited by Bill Felber
$19.95 paperback (ISBN 978-1-933599-42-7)
$9.99 ebook (ISBN 978-1-933599-43-4)
302 PAGES, 8"x10", 200 photos

NINETEENTH CENTURY STARS: 2012 EDITION
First published in 1989, *Nineteenth Century Stars* was SABR's initial attempt to capture the stories of baseball players from before 1900. With a collection of 136 fascinating biographies, SABR has re-released *Nineteenth Century Stars* for 2012 with revised statistics and new form. The 2012 version also includes a preface by **John Thorn**.
Edited by Robert L. Tiemann and Mark Rucker
$19.95 paperback (ISBN 978-1-933599-28-1)
$9.99 ebook (ISBN 978-1-933599-29-8)
300 PAGES, 6"X9"

GREAT HITTING PITCHERS
Published in 1979, *Great Hitting Pitchers* was one of SABR's early publications. Edited by SABR founder Bob Davids, the book compiles stories and records about pitchers excelling in the batter's box. Newly updated in 2012 by Mike Cook, *Great Hitting Pitchers* contain tables including data from 1979-2011, corrections to reflect recent records, and a new chapter on recent new members in the club of "great hitting pitchers" like Tom Glavine and Mike Hampton.
Edited by L. Robert Davids
$9.95 paperback (ISBN 978-1-933599-30-4)
$5.99 ebook (ISBN 978-1-933599-31-1)
102 PAGES, 5.5"x8.5"

THE FENWAY PROJECT
Sixty-four SABR members—avid fans, historians, statisticians, and game enthusiasts—recorded their experiences of a single game. Some wrote from inside the Green Monster's manual scoreboard, the Braves clubhouse, or the broadcast booth, while others took in the essence of Fenway from the grandstand or bleachers. The result is a fascinating look at the charms and challenges of Fenway Park, and the allure of being a baseball fan.
Edited by Bill Nowlin and Cecilia Tan
$9.99 ebook (ISBN 978-1-933599-50-2)
175 pages, 100 photos

SABR Members can purchase each book at a significant discount (often 50% off) and receive the ebook editions free as a member benefit. Each book is available in a trade paperback edition as well as ebooks suitable for reading on a home computer or Nook, Kindle, or iPad/tablet.
To learn more about becoming a member of SABR, visit the website: sabr.org/join

Contributors

ROB EDELMAN teaches film history at the University at Albany and offers film commentary on WAMC (Northeast) Public Radio. His books include *Great Baseball Films* and *Baseball on the Web* (which Amazon.com cited as a Top 10 Internet book), and he is a frequent contributor to *Base Ball: A Journal of the Early Game*. His writing also may be found in *NINE: A Journal of Baseball History and Culture*, *Total Baseball*, *The Total Baseball Catalog*, *Baseball and American Culture: Across the Diamond*, and *Baseball in the Classroom: Teaching America's National Pastime*. With Audrey Kupferberg, he has coauthored *Matthau: A Life* and *Meet the Mertzes*, a double biography of *I Love Lucy*'s Vivian Vance and super baseball fan William Frawley.

MICHAEL HAUPERT is Professor of Economics at the University of Wisconsin-La Crosse.

RICHARD HERSHBERGER is a paralegal in Maryland. He has written numerous articles on early baseball, concentrating on its origins and its organizational history. He is a member of the SABR Nineteenth Century and Origins committees. Reach him at rrhersh@yahoo.com.

CHUCK HILDEBRANDT has served as chair of the Baseball and the Media Committee since 2013, and has been a SABR member since 1988. Chuck lives with his lovely wife, Terrie, in Chicago, where he is an exiled Tigers fan who compensates with Cubs season tickets.

GIL IMBER is a baseball rules expert and is a member of SABR's Umpires and Rules Research Committee. He is the founder and chief commissioner of the Umpire Ejection Fantasy League, dedicated to the objective analysis of close and controversial calls in sport with great regard for the rules and spirit of the game. He may be reached via e-mail at gil@closecallsports.com.

TALIN LOUDER is a doctoral student at Utah State University in Logan, Utah. He is studying in the Pathokinesiology specialization of the Disability Disciplines PhD program and works as a Presidential Doctoral Research Fellow in Dr. Eadric Bressel's biomechanics laboratory. His research interests are in sport and clinical biomechanics.

MIKE LYNCH, a SABR member since 2004, is the founder of Seamheads.com and the author of several books about baseball, including *Harry Frazee, Ban Johnson and the Feud That Nearly Destroyed the American League*, nominated as a finalist for the 2009 Larry Ritter Award. Mike is a rabid Red Sox fan thankfully living in Boston.

CHRISTINA KAHRL is an MLB writer and editor for ESPN.com, and was co-founder of *Baseball Prospectus*. She lives in Chicago with her wife, Charley.

ALAN S. KORNSPAN is an Associate Professor in the School of Sport Science and Wellness Education at the University of Akron. Alan received his Ed.D. from West Virginia University in Sport Behavior. His research interests include the history of baseball, the history of the sport sciences, and professional issues in sport psychology.

ANDREW D. KNAPP completed his undergraduate degree in Sport Studies at the University of Akron and his master's degree in Sport Psychology at the University of Tennessee. Currently, Andrew is the Interim Head Cross Country Coach/Interim Co-Head Track and Field Coach at Marietta College.

HERM KRABBENHOFT, a retired organic chemist, joined SABR in 1981. He has done extensive research to ascertain accurate statistics for runs batted in, on which he became hooked in 1961 when he picked up that year's edition of *The Little Red Book of Baseball*. Herm proudly dedicates this article to Seymour Siwoff, the editor, since 1953 of *The Little Red Book of Baseball* and, since 1972 its renamed successor, *The (Elias) Book of Baseball Records*. Thanks, Seymour!

BARRY KRISSOFF is an Adjunct Assistant Professor of Economics at the University of Maryland University College and retired senior economist at Economic Research Service, US Department of Agriculture. His research interest is on the business of baseball, with a current focus on the role of sports' agents in the industry. His first article in the *Baseball Research Journal*, "Society and Baseball Face Rising Income Inequality," was a finalist for the 2014 SABR Analytics Conference Research Awards in the category of Historical Analysis/Commentary. He continues to look forward to a World Series in Washington DC—maybe this is the year!

ANDY McCUE has been a SABR member since 1982, winning the Bob Davids Award in 2007. He served on SABR's board for nine years, finishing with a term as president in 2009–11. He won the SABR-Macmillan Award for *Baseball by the Books: A History and Bibliography of Baseball Fiction* and the Doug Pappas Award for a presentation on Dodgers ownership. His biography of Walter O'Malley, *Mover and Shaker*, is being published by the University of Nebraska Press in 2014.

ROB NEYER is the Senior Baseball Editor at FoxSports.com, and has been a SABR member for longer than he can remember. Rob lives in Portland, Oregon, with his wife and daughter, and hopes to write a book someday.

DENNIS PAJOT is retired and lives in Milwaukee. He was honored to be awarded the 2009 Sporting News-SABR Baseball Research award for his book *The Rise of Milwaukee Baseball*. His recent research interests have been the dead-ball era seasons of the Milwaukee Brewers of the American Association.

BOB RIVES is retired from business and from Wichita State University where he was an adjunct instructor. He lives in Wichita and is Tim's father.

TIM RIVES has written extensively about baseball history. He is the supervisory archivist and deputy director of the Eisenhower Presidential Library and Museum in Abilene, Kansas.

BRYAN SODERHOLM-DIFATTE is a frequent contributor to the *Baseball Research Journal* and presenter at SABR conferences. He also writes the blog Baseball Historical Insight.

LYLE SPATZ is the author of several baseball books, most recently, *Willie Keeler: From the Playgrounds of Brooklyn to the Hall of Fame*, and *The Colonel and Hug: The Partnership that Transformed the New York Yankees* (co-authored with Steve Steinberg). He has been the chairman of SABR's Baseball Records Committee since 1991, and served as the chairman of the committee that chose this year's Henry Chadwick Award winners.

JOHN THORN, the Official Historian for Major League Baseball, is a Chadwick Award recipient.